THE CHINESE ON
THE ART OF PAINTING

TRANSLATIONS AND COMMENTS

BY

OSVALD SIRÉN

SCHOCKEN BOOKS · NEW YORK
HONG KONG UNIVERSITY PRESS · HONG KONG

The text of this book is reprinted by arrangement with the author and the publisher of the original edition, Henri Vetch, Peiping 1936. The Hong Kong University Press, managed by Henri Vetch, has exclusive distribution rights for the Far East.

CONTENTS

ILLUSTRATIONS

INTRODUCTION

MANY students and collectors of Chinese painting have no doubt, like myself, been brought
to a realization of the fact, that a real acquaintance
with the history and significance of this art, as far as it
nowadays can be reached, must be based to a larger
extent on historical records and writings by Chinese
critics of the last thousand years than on the scanty products of ancient painting that still may be seen. However
valuable the latter may be, they are far from sufficient as
a basis for a comprehension of the historical evolution
and still less so for an appreciation of the æsthetic ideals,
which served as guidance and inspiration for the great
painters of various periods. This applies of course
pre-eminently to painting of the earliest periods, but even
the remains of the Sung period (10th-12th century), when
high-class painting was produced in greater abundance
than ever, are mostly only fragments blurred by age, or
copies after famous masterpieces. Their documentary
value is very limited and unequal, and they are altogether
too few and scattered to convey an idea about all the leading
masters and schools of painting. If we want to know
something of these, we must turn to the written documents
left by the painters themselves or by contemporary critics,
who have discussed the practice and theory of the painter's
art. They have been more fully preserved, and they
convey the information in a form which, in spite of a
certain vagueness, and sometimes strange terminology, is
more accessible than the æsthetic symbology of many of
the old paintings.

In view of this it seemed to me of great importance to
translate and co-ordinate from the art-historian's point of
view a certain number of the early Chinese writings on
painting, of which hitherto only minor fragments have
been made accessible to Western students. Completeness

in this field is practically impossible, because the Chinese literature on painting is so vast that it would take more than a lifetime to translate it all, but I trust that the materials that I, with the aid of some Chinese assistants, am able to place before the students will serve to convey a better knowledge of the aims and ideals of Chinese painting during the successive periods. A larger selection would no doubt have greater documentary importance, but it would hardly add very much to the comprehension of the main principles of artistic creation and appreciation in ancient China, since so much of what the Chinese critics and painters of the various dynasties have to say about painting is a repetition of the thoughts of their predecessors. They never tired of discussing certain fundamental ideas, which remained practically the same during more than fifteen hundred years, even though the mode of presentation underwent many characteristic changes. Nor does it seem that the purely technical treatises which are made up of practical rules for students of painting, have much interest for Western art-historians. My main interest was centered on the theoretical rather than on the practical side of the problems.

It may seem surprising to modern students that Chinese critics of the 18th and 19th centuries apply the same principles of appreciation as do their predecessors of the 4th and 5th centuries, but this is only a consequence of the continuity of Chinese pictorial art which followed the same general course of unbroken traditionalism as did Chinese civilization as a whole. At least, so it seems when we look at it from a distance of various centuries ; the continuity is more impressive than many of the brilliant individual departures or fresh side currents. The flow was by no means always the same, smooth and unruffled ; it received from time to time tributaries which modified its course, yet it always drew some water from the original sources, which are as old as the beginnings of Chinese civilization.

The painting and art-criticism of the Chinese were always very closely bound up with their philosophy of life. They reflected the same ideals as those which inspired the philosophic and religious thought. They cannot be fully understood without some knowledge of the latter, even though the artistic creations appeal to us through symbols and means which have a value of their own quite distinct from philosophical definitions or literature. This interdependence is, indeed, most evident in schools of painting which expressed a definite religious attitude, such as the landscape painting of the Ch'an monks, but even when the painters were not adherents of any particular sect or school of philosophy, in the stricter sense of the word, their works were inspired, to no small extent, by similar ideas and experiences as those which found expression in contemporary religion, philosophy or poetry. A natural consequence of this was also that criticism and appreciation of painting never became simply problems of formal analysis but rather ways of approaching the psychological secrets of the artists and of interpreting the spiritual or emotional impetus behind the visual work. According to the æsthetic attitude of most of the Chinese critics, the formal features of design, colouring and outward resemblance will take their place quite naturally and serve their purpose when the essential significance or inner life of a motif has been grasped.

It is evidently not possible fully to understand Chinese painting or art-criticism without some knowledge of the undercurrents of philosophic and religious thought, but a comprehensive presentation of these would easily have transformed this book into a history of Chinese culture and philosophy. I have felt no ambition to write anything like that. In my discussion of the æsthetic treatises I have simply tried to give an account of the leading ideas and to indicate, whenever possible, their origin or their connection with certain schools of religion or philosophy without entering into any detailed discussions of the latter. Only in the case of Ch'an Buddhism has the philosophical side of the problem received a somewhat fuller presentation, because here we find the very essence of the ideas which penetrate Chinese æsthetics and the clearest philosophical reflection of the Chinese attitude towards painting, an attitude which, broadly speaking, existed as an undercurrent since earliest times, though it was most definitely exposed by the Ch'an philosophers.

Otherwise I have left the Chinese, as far as possible, to speak for themselves. Their manner of expression may often seem vague and strange to Westerners, their lack of intellectual analysis and systematic presentation is sometimes disconcerting, but on the other hand, we often meet in their writings a very remarkable intuitive grasp of the essential elements in art and a suggestive mode of revealing them, be it in poetry or in prose. I have tried to respect these peculiarities as far as possible and not to strain the Chinese mode of presentation into more definite intellectual formulas. Certain passages in my translations may thus appear somewhat vague or indefinite, but they are hardly more so than the original texts which often leave room for various interpretations. In rendering them into English I have sought to retain their tone and terminology rather than to sacrifice anything to an easy literary form.

For the arrangement of the materials I have followed the usual historical sequence of dynasties. It seemed the most natural arrangement in a publication which also should have a value as a collection of documents on the history of Chinese painting, but within the respective periods materials of a similar nature have been grouped together in order to illustrate certain leading ideas or currents of style. The general evolution within Chinese æsthetics may not be particularly brilliant, yet every epoch is characterized by certain prevailing ideals, which are brought out in the writings of the time. They gain from this a considerable historical importance beside their general æsthetic interest.

In making my selection of these writings I have naturally been guided by what the Chinese themselves have considered of greatest importance and transmitted in their historical collections of writings on painting and calligraphy, such as *Chin Tai Pi Shu*, *Wang Shih Hua Yüan*, *P'ei Wên Chai Shu Hua P'u*, *Hua Hsüeh Hsin Yin*, *Mei Shu Ts'ung Shu* and others, but in some instances I have also consulted separate editions of the writers' works. It

would have been easy to include more, but for reasons already indicated it seemed hardly necessary for the present purpose. It would have involved more repetitions than novelties. The shorter quotations and all those writings which are of primary importance for understanding the evolution of the Chinese attitude in regard to painting have been included in the running text and co-ordinated with similar writings, but beside these I have included certain documents of a more historical character in the Appendix and also full reprints of longer treatises which are only in part reported in the text. This was done for the benefit of those who might wish to use this publication for other purposes than a study of æsthetics. At the same time it must be pointed out that it is practically impossible to draw a definite line between the æsthetic and the historical elements in the Chinese writings; the Chinese themselves in their discussions of painting never made a definite distinction between these two aspects, and as it has been my endeavour to let the Chinese speak for themselves, the limits for the selection and division of the materials had to be kept quite elastic.

* * *

This publication may in some respects be considered a complement to my *History of Early Chinese Painting* (vols. I-II), which has not as yet been continued beyond the Yüan period. The painters and writers previous to the Ming period who are mentioned in the texts published below are with few exceptions more fully characterized in the *History*. For those of later times I have added brief notes or references to such well-known books as Waley's *Index of Chinese Artists* or Giles' *Biographical Dictionary*. In the *History* I quoted more or less extensively from some of the texts published below, but in the meantime the translations of practically all such texts have been considerably improved and completed, because, to quote from the *Analects* (Book VIII): "A man to whom three years of learning have borne no fruit would be hard to find."

In preparing the translations, which are collected in this volume, I had the support of two different Chinese assistants who in 1933 and 1934 spent a few months with me in Stockholm, but as neither of them was familiar with the English language, the responsibility for the renderings rests with the author.   These would however have shown more shortcomings and inequalities, if it had not been for the kind assistance of Mrs Florence Ayscough who during my stay in Shanghai, in February 1935, read through the whole manuscript and introduced a number of valuable suggestions and corrections.   Her deep interest in Chinese thought and her experience as a translator became to me a support and an encouragement, for which I rest under deep obligation.   Further assistance in completing the Chinese index and in reading the proofs has been extended to me by Mr. Yang Chou-han, Mr. J. Hope-Johnstone and Mr. H. Vetch, who has spared no efforts in trying to make this publication attractive to the author as well as to the public.   My sincere thanks are due to them all.

Peking, June, 1935.   O. S.

The publisher gratefully acknowledges the advice and aid given by Dr. James F. Cahill, curator of Chinese Art at the Freer Gallery, in the selection of illustrations for this edition.

FROM THE HAN TO THE
T'ANG DYNASTY

NO doubt, painting existed in China as an independent art long before the Han period, but our knowledge about this early pictorial art is hardly sufficient to allow definite conclusions as to its artistic significance or its æsthetic background. From the way it is mentioned by poets and writers, it may be concluded that it was done for definite moral, ceremonial or political purposes, but very little is said as to its stylistic character and appearance. Certain traditional views of the earliest forms of painting are indicated by historians of T'ang and pre-T'ang times, most completely perhaps by Chang Yen-yüan who, although he is not the earliest writer on painting, gives the most interesting account of its development and of its methods and aims. In the first chapter of his *Li Tai Ming Hua Chi* (concluded 845), called " The Origin of Painting " he writes as follows :

" Painting promotes culture and strengthens the principles of right conduct. It penetrates completely all the aspects of the universal spirit. It fathoms the subtle and the abstruse, serving thus the same purpose as the Six Classics, and it revolves with the four seasons. It originated from Nature and not from any decrees or works of men."

According to this old writer, painting like the art of writing, with which it was most closely associated, had a divine origin ; it was taught or revealed to men by spiritual beings of mythical periods who gradually made out pictorial signs and images as symbols of thought. Chang Yen-yüan's exposition of how this was done may be read in our translation of his chapter on the " Origin of Painting " ; * it seems superfluous to repeat it here, it may simply be pointed out, that painting was to the Chinese from the very beginning a means of symbolic expression. Gradually

---

* Cf. Appendix III.

it came to serve ceremonial, religious and political purposes and became also a method of recording historical events. At the same time it gained of course in decorative beauty and importance, but this side of its function is not particularly brought out by the old writers.

The latter part of Chang Yen-yüan's exposition refers to painting of the Han period by quotations from two or three writers of the second and third centuries who express rather diverging opinions about the importance of Han painting. From these and other writers it becomes evident, that most of the famous paintings of this period were executed on the walls of the palaces and sanctuaries and represented prominent characters of ancient times or mythological subjects of the kind that we know from the engraved stone slabs of many burial chambers. Beside these there were, no doubt, minor paintings on paper or silk representing legendary or historical motives, but most of the historical pronouncements seem to refer to the monumental wall paintings. To quote from the first chapter of *Li Tai Ming Hua Chi*:

" The written records tell about the acts of men, but they cannot convey their appearances. The poems and ballads sing about their virtues, but they cannot represent their images. By the art of painting the two sides may be combined. Therefore Lu Chi (261-303) said: ' The exercise of painting may be compared to the recitation of ballads and songs extolling the beauty of great actions. Nothing is better than words for praising things and nothing is better than pictures for recording shapes.' These words are quite correct.

" Ts'ao Chih (192-232) says: ' When one sees pictures of the Three Kings and of the Five Emperors, one cannot but look at them with respect and veneration, and when one sees pictures of the San Chi (the last debased rulers of the Hsia, Shan and Chou dynasties), one cannot but feel sad. When one sees pictures of rebels and unfilial sons, one cannot but grind the teeth. When one sees pictures representing men of high principles and great sages, one cannot but forget one's meals. When one sees pictures of faithful subjects who died at the call of duty, one cannot but feel exalted. When one sees pictures of exiled citizens and expelled sons, one cannot help sighing. When one sees pictures of vicious men and jealous women, one cannot but look askance. When one sees pictures of obedient empresses and good secondary consorts, one cannot but feel deepest admiration. By this we may realize that paintings serve as moral examples or as mirrors of conduct.' "

These early representations of famous characters may have been of a more typical kind than the portraits of later dynasties, yet they served to evoke or suggest in a symbolical way the presence of the great men of ancient times, and were, indeed, a kind of substitutes for the departed or, as the Chinese say, " transmitters of their spirit." They became thus more or less imaginative works of art whose importance depended on their power to evoke certain characters, actions or events. Chang Yen-yüan is no doubt in deepest earnest when he extolls these paintings as more important from a historical point of view than any written records or biographies and opposes the famous philosopher Wang Ch'ung (A.D. 27-97), who had expressed an opposite point of view in the following way : ' Looking at such paintings is like contemplating dead people ; one sees their faces, but this does not equal perceiving their words and actions.' To which Chang Yen-yüan makes the following remark : " It seems to me that such talk is like throwing ridicule on Tao and abusing the Confucian scholars, or like putting food into the ear, or playing the reed-organ to an ox ! "

Although Chang Yen-yüan's general attitude was based on paintings of a more developed kind than the works of the Han period (as will be shown in the following), he was certainly not lacking in admiration for the great art of the early masters. Its moral purpose or power to inculcate high ideals was to him a classic feature, a sign of greatness and strength. The same attitude is no less characteristic of the earlier critics such as Hsieh Ho (circ. 500) and Yao Tsui (circ. 550) who, however, offer very little information about the painting of the Han period. Yao Tsui, who wrote his *Hsü Hua P'in* about the middle of the 6th century, gives a more vague account of the common origin of writing and painting and refers quite briefly to the works executed under the Han emperors :

" The greatest marvels of painting are not easily explained in words. Its primary elements have been transmitted from antiquity, but the style has changed in accordance with the circumstances of modern times. The numberless images conceived in the minds of the painters are transmitted to future ages at the point of the brush. Fairies and spiritual beings were made manifest on high towers, sages and Immortals were represented in great compositions on the walls of the schools. In the Yün Ko (the ' Cloud Pavilion' of Han Wu Ti) there were paintings which inspired reverence, and in the courts of the palaces there were paintings of tribute-bearers from far-off lands. But all these ancient records of painting can hardly be discussed. However, there are still pictures in existence by men who are gone and dead long ago, but only those who have acquired great learning are able to distinguish the coarse from the fine, avoid the traps and grasp the meaning. Things grow worse and then mend, men pass through periods of flourishing and decay, some reach great fame at an early age, some at the beginning of their manhood, and it would be a mistake to compare the genius of the former with the gifts of the latter."

The above is composed as an introduction to Yao Tsui's notes on some painters (in completion of Hsieh Ho's *Ku Hua P'in*) which furthermore contains an enthusiastic appreciation of Ku K'ai-chih's art and certain remarks on the legendary origin of painting with somewhat obscure references to Taoist writers, as may be found in our attempt at a translation of the whole introduction. (See Appendix II.)

It may be added here that some of the early Taoist philosophers like Chuang-tzŭ, Han Fei (died 233 B.C.), Huai Nan-tzŭ (died 122 B.C.) and Chang Hêng (A.D. 78-139) also are quoted in *P'ei Wên Chai Shu Hua P'u* among the writers on painting, but their short pronouncements can hardly be said to contain anything of æsthetic significance. The first and foremost exposition of the Chinese attitude towards painting was, indeed, Hsieh Ho's famous treatise, but before we enter on a discussion of this important work, it may be well to recall that there were some other painters, shortly before Hsieh Ho, who expressed themselves on the practice and theory of their art.

Most famous among them is Ku K'ai-chih (circ. 344-406) who is said to have written certain essays, the one about the methods of making copies by tracing, the other dealing with certain elements of landscape painting, but they have not been preserved except in corrupt fragments which are reported by Chang Yen-yüan (*Li Tai Ming Hua Chi*, chap. v.)* The contents of the former are highly technical and interest us only in so far as they show that copying and tracing were far developed methods already in the 4th century. It contains however also some remarks about portrait painting which are furthermore illustrated by certain traditions in regard to Ku K'ai-chih's way of doing his portraits. The other essay is a rather detailed description of a Taoist picture called *Yün T'ai Shan* (the Cloud Terrace Mountain), in which the " Heavenly Master," Chang Tao-ling, is represented among awe-inspiring peaks and bottomless ravines adored by two disciples. It reflects a highly imaginative interpretation of certain elements of landscape painting, but it can hardly be taken as a proof for Ku K'ai-chih's importance as a landscape painter. He may indeed have had a keen eye for certain effects of nature, but we have no reason to suppose that he used them otherwise than as accessory motifs in the background of his figure compositions. As a figure painter he was, relatively speaking, further developed, and if we may believe the stories about his portraits, he must have possessed in an eminent degree the power of " transmitting the soul " or the inner life of the models. His portraits are sometimes praised in conformity with the old tradition

---

* Waley in his *Introduction to the Study of Chinese Painting*, pp. 47-49, has extracted the main points from the writings attributed to Ku K'ai-chih and also communicated the traditions and stories related to the painter.

as substitutes for the depicted as for instance the picture which he made of a neighbour's girl. When he had drawn the portrait, he placed a pin in the heart of it (because the girl had resisted him), whereupon the girl fell ill. But as Ku removed the pin, the girl became well again.

The appreciation of portraits as "doubles" remained of fundamental importance all through the classic ages, even though the artistic transformations endowed the later portraits with a rather different æsthetic significance. It is reported that Ku sometimes did not put in the pupils in the eyes of the figures for a long time, and when asked about the reason for this, he answered : " The limbs may be beautiful or ugly, they are really of little importance in comparison with those mysterious parts, the eyes"—a saying which is in full accord with the preceding story. His way of emphasizing some special feature in order to bring out the character of the model is often quoted by later writers : " Once he made a portrait of P'ei K'ai and added three hairs on his chin, which made the beholder feel very keenly the sagacious character of the man." He also made a portrait of Hsieh K'un (a musician) placing him among rocks and peaks and said : " This man must be represented among hills and valleys."

Beside portraits Ku K'ai-chih painted all sorts of fantastic subjects, illustrations to legends and poems, etc., which kindled his imagination and gave him an issue for his " madness." Painting was to him pre-eminently a symbolic means of expression, and the symbols to which he gave the closest attention were the human figures, because they required, according to his own saying, the deepest thought.

Hsieh Ho who wrote his *Ku Hua P'in Lu* about a century later placed Ku K'ai-chih in the third class of the old painters with the verdict that " his style was fine and subtle, his brush without a flaw, yet his workmanship was inferior to his ideas, and his fame surpassed his real merit." This somewhat deprecatory classification provoked a strong protest from Yao Tsui who wrote about half a century later : " Hsieh Ho's words, that his fame surpassed his merit, are really depressing ; it is most regrettable that he placed Ku in an inferior class. It was caused by (Hsieh Ho's) erratic feelings rather than by the qualities and faults (of Ku K'ai-chih). The saying : ' he who sings well will have few in harmony with himself ' is true not only in reference to ballad singers, and one may weep blood over false reports not only concerning the uncut gem. It seems to me that Hsieh Ho by his endeavour at classification has destroyed all reason and ruined it for ever." *

This same opposition against Hsieh Ho's classification of Ku K'ai-chih among relatively inferior painters is again repeated in the preface to the *Hsü Hua P'in Lu* (the continuation of Hsieh Ho's treatise) which is ascribed to a writer of the T'ang period called Li Ssŭ-chên (circ. 689). Whether this attribution of the *Hsü Hua P'in Lu* is correct or not, it is quite evident that the preface is copied from Yao Tsui's treatise including the ' Ehrenrettung ' of Ku K'ai-chih. But when Chang Yen-yüan in the 9th century once more reconsiders the question of Ku's artistic standing, he takes a different view, which he expresses as follows : " In examining carefully Hsieh Ho's criticism I find it absolutely just and correct, and I cannot agree with Yao Tsui's and Li Ssŭ-chên's deviating classifications. Li opposes Hsieh Ho by saying that Wei Hsieh should not be placed above Ku ; this is entirely without foundation, and really quite saddening." But it may be questioned whether any of these writers formed his opinion on an actual study of the old masters' works. Chang Yen-yüan seems to have drawn his conclusion mainly from the report that Ku K'ai-chih had a great admiration for Wei Hsieh ; and as to Yao Tsui, he refers to " historical records " but to no existing paintings. All this early history of painting in China is a web of more or less corrupt records and traditions handed over from generation to generation and written down by men who did not hesitate to repeat what they had heard or read. It is a literary record rather than a critical art-history ; it transmits the traditional opinions about the relative merits of the

---

* The full text of Yao Tsui's criticism with his references to stories, etc., is reported in Appendix II.

painters but very little in regard to their actual works or æsthetic ideals.

A contemporary of Ku K'ai-chih, Tsung Ping (375-443), *tzŭ* Shao-wên, is mentioned as a prominent painter of landscapes and a great *ch'in* player. He loved to stroll about among the mountains and rivers in Wu and Ch'u and lived for some time in a hut on Hêng Shan (in Hunan), but when he grew old and weak he returned to Chiangling (in Hupeh) where he spent the rest of his life. He said : " Now I am ill, and I can only meditate on Tao and travel in my dreams." The impressions which he had gathered during his earlier years he translated into pictures which covered the walls of his house, and to these he wrote a " preface " or rather a kind of explanatory text, which, in spite of its somewhat abstract character, is of considerable interest, because it contains the same fundamental viewpoint for the appreciation of landscape painting as we will find further developed by the critics of later times.

His text is reported as follows in *Li Tai Ming Hua Chi*, second part, chapter VI :

" The wise ones cherish Tao and harmonize (conform) with the objects ; the virtuous men conceive in their pure minds the beauty of the forms. As to landscapes, they have a material side but also a spiritual influence. Therefore Hsüan Yüan, Yao K'ung, Kuang Ch'êng, Ta K'uai, Hsü Yu, Ku Chu and other (Taoists) travelled among the mountains of K'ung-t'ung, Chü-ts'ŭ, Miao-ku, Chi-shou and Ta-mêng. This has also been called to find pleasure (in mountains and water).* The wise men follow Tao in their souls, and the virtuous men captivate Tao by the forms of the landscapes, but is the pleasure of the virtuous as great as that of the wise ?

" I am longing for the Lu and the Hêng mountains and to the countries of Ch'u and Wu from which I am cut off. Who does not perceive old age coming on ? † I feel ashamed of myself, because I cannot concentrate my

---

* Cf. *Analects*. Book VI, chap. 21 : " The wise find pleasure in water, the virtuous find pleasure in hills."

† *Analects*. Book VII, chap. 18.

spirit and adjust my body ; I am distressed to be one of the *Shih-mên* class (retired from active life).* I can only do my pictures and spread my colours over the cloud covered mountains. The reason for doing it has always been to transmit for future ages the hidden meaning which lies beyond all descriptions in words. The mind (heart) can grasp the contents of books, but that is not like strolling about and enjoying nature with the eyes. The forms must be rendered by forms and the colours must be imitated with colours. Furthermore as the K'un-lun mountain is very large and the pupils of my eyes are small, I cannot discern its full shape if it is very close to my eyes, but if the distance is several miles, it may be completely contained in the pupils of the eyes. Only by receding a little (from the mountain) can one see something more of it.

" Now as I do my painting (spread the silk), the forms of the K'un and the Lang mountains shine far away and are enclosed within a square inch. A vertical stroke of three inches equals a height of 8,000 feet, and a horizontal stroke of a few feet equals a distance of hundred miles. Therefore, in contemplating paintings, one may regret those which show lack of skill but not the small pictures which render the likeness perfectly in a natural way.

" In this way one may represent in a picture the beauty of the Sung or the Hua mountain and their mysterious spirit.† Such paintings satisfy the eyes and the mind (heart) by their good reason. If they are done with great skill they harmonize with the eyes, move the heart very deeply and excite the soul, and the soul is satisfied as it grasps their fitness. What need is there then to return to the dark and dangerous cliffs. The divine soul has no limits ; it inhabits the forms and stimulates everything.

" One may observe the character (reason) of things in their shadows, and if one is able to draw these in a wonderful fashion, one will indeed accomplish (the paintings).

---

* *Analects.* Book XIV. chap. 41.

† The expression is : *hsüan p'in* 玄牝, which is used in *Tao Tê Ching* for the mysterious female spirit of the Universe.

" Thus by living leisurely, by controlling the vital breath, by wiping the goblet, by playing the *ch'in*, by contemplating pictures in silence, by meditating on the four quarters of space, by never resisting the influence of Heaven and by responding to the call of the wilderness, where the cliffs and peaks rise to dazzling heights and the cloudy forests are dense and vast, the wise and virtuous men of ancient times found innumerable pleasures which they assimilated by their souls and minds. What more should I desire ? If I too can find this happiness in my soul ; is it not better than everything else ? "

Tsung Ping's method of satisfying his longing for the woods and hills seems rather akin to the attitude of the learned painters of the Ming period (the representatives of *wên jên hua*), who also practised their art as a substitute for ramblings in nature, as a means of enjoying in imagination the classical pleasures of mountains and water. Tsung Ping did it because he was ill and unable to move, while his late followers did it on principle. The life of the imagination seemed to them more real than the life of the objective world. We have no means of deciding how far Tsung Ping was able to suggest the effects of nature, how far he grasped the relative relation of objects, the light and the atmosphere, but to judge by his words, he must have had a notion of these things and have known how to suggest distance by decreasing size. And the love of nature, the feeling of unity with the mountains and vales was no less profound and inspiring with him than with the painters of later periods.

Another landscape painter of the same period, i.e. the Sung dynasty (420-478), who also has left some notes on his art, was Wang Wei, *tzŭ* Ching-hsien. He is said to have been a learned man and such a great lover of antiquities, that he remained in his house for ten years occupied with such studies, but he had also a deep feeling for the moods and motifs of nature which he expressed in painting. In a letter to a friend he said : " I understand painting by my natural disposition as well as the crying crane knows his way through the night. I take note of the things in my mind and my eyes ; my love of landscapes (nature) has led me on and made me try to represent it in painting." He wrote some ' Notes on Painting ' of which a portion is communicated in chapter VI of *Li Tai Ming Hua Chi*, though probably in a somewhat free transcription, which contains the following :

"Yen Kuang-lu said that pictures are not simply produced by the practice of artistic skill, they must also correspond to the *I Ching* (Book of Changes). Men who are able to write *chuan* and *li* characters claim that this is the very height of skill, but I wish to make them understand the art of painting and thus to overthrow their opinion. In discussing painting people usually pay attention only to formal aspects and effects, but the ancients did not make their paintings simply as records of the sites of cities and country districts or to mark out the limits of towns, villages and watercourses. They had their origin in forms, but these were made to blend with the spirit and to excite the heart (mind). If the spirit has no perception of them, they exercise no influence ; the eyes can see only the limits, but not the whole thing. Yet, with a stroke of the brush one may suggest the whole sky, one may give the full shape of a body or the brightness of the eyes. With some curving lines one can represent the Sung Mountain and obtain its effect within a ten feet square, and with a running (swift) brush one can do the T'ai-hua Mountain. With some irregular dots one can represent the dragon-face (the imperial countenance), its eyebrows, its forehead and chin in perfect ease. One can represent high peaks with thick growth like covering clouds and suggest with some horizontal and vertical strokes the transformations (effects) of life and movement. If one works with compasses and squares one can represent the forms of every kind, be it palaces, sanctuaries, boats, carriages and utensils, or dogs, horses, birds, fishes and the like. Such is the effect of painting.

To look at the autumn clouds makes the soul soar as a bird, to feel the wind of spring makes the thoughts go far and wide. Even if one has the pleasure of antiquities in metal and stone or of precious jades and trinkets, it does not equal such delights. To open the picture and prepare the board, to exert oneself with strange mountains and seas, with green forests and the soaring wind, with the foaming waters and the rushing cascades—how wonderful! It needs only the turning of the hand to bring down the brightness of the spirit into the picture! Such is the lust (joy) of painting."

Wang Wei's remarks on the importance of landscape painting as a means of reawakening in the mind the moods and motifs of nature are essentially of the same kind as the observations of Tsung Ping, though his manner of expression has a more literary or poetic tone. Both these men stand out in their writings as romantic landscape painters of a remarkably advanced type. Their point of approach is practically the same as Ching Hao's or Kuo Hsi's, though as yet not so fully expressed or applied. If their paintings were preserved, they would probably impress us as more primitive or old-fashioned than their words, because these were men striving to open new roads for painting, they were the precursors of the great school of landscape painting which reached its full development in the 10th century. The things which then were done completely, with full mastery of the technical means, are foreshadowed in the observations of these men of the 5th century.

*   *   *

Hsieh Ho who wrote his *Ku Hua P'in Lu* at the end of the 5th century mentions briefly not only Ku K'ai-chih but also Tsung Ping and Wang Wei; the importance of his work is, however, not to be sought in the somewhat scanty historical information that it contains but in the general principles which he formulates as a basis for the appreciation of painting. They can hardly be said to represent any new or original ideas, but they contain the essentials of the traditional attitude, and they were never entirely discarded or replaced by any other principles of corresponding importance. Hsieh Ho says himself, that he simply transmits certain ideas which always have existed as the warp and woof of Chinese painting, but his great merit is to have expressed them in terms which were acceptable not only to his own time but also to subsequent generations of painters and critics. We shall have occasion to return to them over and over again, as we pass through the theoretical discussions of the various ages, and we shall then note that, though the interpretation of certain principles may vary, they are nevertheless accepted as the general foundation for Chinese art-criticism.

Hsieh Ho introduces his principles with the following words :

" All pictures should be classified according to their merits and faults. There are no pictures which do not exercise some influence, be it of an elevating or debasing kind. The silent records of ancient times are unrolled before us when we open a picture. Although the Six Principles existed (since early times), there were few who could master them all, yet from ancient to modern times there have been painters skilled in one (or the other).

" Which are these Six Principles ?

" The first is : Spirit Resonance (or, Vibration of Vitality) and Life Movement. The second is : Bone Manner (i.e. Structural) Use of the Brush. The third is : Conform with the Objects to Give Likeness. The fourth is : Apply the Colours according to the Characteristics. The fifth is : Plan and Design, Place and Position (i.e. Composition). The sixth is : To Transmit Models by Drawing.

" Only Lu T'an-wei and Wei Hsieh applied completely all these principles. There have always been good and bad paintings ; art as such is art, whether old or modern. I have now carefully arranged some painters of old and modern times and classified them according to the above principles, but I have cut out all introductory remarks and entered into no discussion of the origin of painting. According to tradition, it took its origin from divine beings, but these have never been seen or heard."

Then follows the classification ; twenty-seven painters are mentioned, shortly characterized and divided in six classes. The most important of these characterizations may be read in translation in the Appendix 1.

The above-mentioned principles express essentials in Chinese painting, i.e. fundamental features, which must be observed if the painting is to answer its purpose and become a significant work of art. Or, it may be said, that they indicate the path of the painters ; they are sign-posts along the road which must be observed, if he is to arrive at his goal. At the same time they constitute a general basis for appreciation and criticism, they offer certain points of departure for any one who wants to penetrate into the painter's work.

But their inclusiveness and terse formulation have in some cases conduced to a somewhat paradoxical vagueness, which becomes still more apparent when they are translated into a foreign language. The Chinese expressions leave room for different interpretations, though within definite limits, so that the essential meaning of the principles remains unaltered. This difficulty of interpretation applies particularly to the first principle which is the most important of them all ; it is to this that the discussions of the succeeding generations of critics are attached, because here exist possibilities of philosophical or æsthetic interpretations which are practically excluded in reference to the five others. These latter principles do not call for much comment ; they are stated in an unequivocal fashion and are more or less self-evident.

The structural brush-work has always been accepted as an element of primary importance in Chinese painting, forming not only the backbone but the very life-nerve of the painter's art. The prominence of this can neither be exaggerated nor misunderstood. All writers on Chinese painting, whatever school or current of style they belong to, insist upon it. It is the *sine qua non* of the painter's technical accomplishments.

The third point : to conform with the objects in order to give their likeness, is evidently a demand for objective correspondence with nature, though it would certainly not be correct to take it as an exigency of realism. The objects of nature, the figures, flowers, animals or whatever motifs that might be chosen, were never to the Chinese simply decorative forms or appearances, they always carried a meaning, a spirit which had to be expressed through the form. There is a symbolism not of intellectual but of an æsthetic or spiritual kind; its form is never constant.

The fourth, fifth and sixth points relating to colouring, composition and the copying of classical models are all of greatest importance from the professional viewpoint and abundantly discussed by later writers. It may not be necessary to dwell on them here in detail, though it should be pointed out, that colouring does not refer simply to the use of pigments but also to the proper use of ink by which colouristic effects may be suggested, and that composition in Chinese painting is pre-eminently a problem of "spacing," or of placing the objects so, that the intermediate spaces become eloquent and æsthetically significant. The transmission of the old models by copying is the traditional path of learning, but it does not necessarily lead to reproductions of old paintings; it leads to a creative activity in conformity with the ideas and forms of the old masters.

The first principle, *ch'i-yün shêng-tung*, will occupy us in every section of this exposition of the Chinese attitude towards painting; it is unavoidable as the most inclusive formula for the essence of the painter's art. It suggests more than it defines and can consequently hardly be rendered into English by four words. The first character, *ch'i*, signifies the life-breath of everything, be it man, beast, mountain or tree. It may be rendered by the word spirit or spiritual, but also by the word vitality, which is a result of the activity of the spirit. If the former expression is used, it must be understood, that it signifies a cosmic principle and not any kind of individualized spirit. It is akin to Tao as well as to the Confucian "Spirit of Heaven and Earth." Both correspondences have been discussed by various interpreters; the difference may, after all, not have been very essential to Hsieh Ho. *Yün* is the Chinese expression for resonance, consonance, harmonious vibrations, etc., and it is used particularly of poetic compositions in which certain parts correspond. As it is here used in conjunction with *ch'i*, the meaning seems to be, that the vitalizing spirit or power should reverberate or resound harmoniously through the paintings imparting expression or spiritual significance.

The two words *shêng tung* are more definite, the first is commonly used for life or birth, the second for movement or motion of a physical kind. The whole formula might thus be rendered in English as " resonance or vibration of the vitalizing spirit and movement of life." If it be objected that the meaning of these words is very vague, particularly when applied to painting, it may be replied, that this is in full conformity with the Chinese mode of expressing such ideas. It was left to the intuition of the individual interpreters to develop it further and to give it the meaning that was closest to their respective manner of painting or trend of thought. How this was done in the various ages will be gradually shown in the succeeding chapters. At this place we will only note the earliest interpretation which is offered by Chang Yen-yüan, who devotes a special chapter to the " Discussion of the Six Principles of Painting." A few extracts from it may here be quoted : *

" Few painters of old have combined all the Six Principles, but I shall here discuss them further. Some of the ancient painters knew how to transmit the likeness of shapes without regard to structure and vitality (spirit), but the art of painting should be sought for beyond outward likeness. This is however difficult to explain to common people. Paintings of the present time may possess outward likeness, but the resonance of the spirit does not become manifest in them. If the spirit-resonance is sought for, the outward likeness will be obtained at the same time.

" The representation of natural objects requires likeness of the shapes, but the shapes must all have structure (bone) and life (spirit). Structure, vitality (spirit) and shapes originate in the directing idea and are expressed by the brush-work. Therefore, those who are skilled in painting are also good in calligraphy.

" Ghosts and human beings possessing life and movement must show the operation of the spirit to be perfect.

---

* A full translation of the chapter is included in Appendix III, pp. 227-229.

If they do not have this spirit-resonance, it is in vain that they exhibit fine shapes, and if the brush-work is not vigorous, their fine colours are useless. Such pictures cannot be called wonderful.

" As for planning and design, and right positions, it is the most common thing in painting."

The only painter who, according to Chang Yen-yüan, possessed a complete mastery of all the Six Principles was Wu Tao-tzŭ : " He exhausted completely the creative power of nature (he was creative to the utmost), and the resonance of the spirit was so overwhelmingly strong (in his works), that it hardly could be confined to the silk." His pictures " were divine things " or, as said by another critic : " a divine power worked through him," which is simply another way of emphasizing his extraordinary spiritual vitality.

It may be said, that in Chang Yen-yüan's descriptions the *ch'i yün* becomes a more individualized quality than appears in the very vague expressions of Hsieh Ho, yet to him too it is a spiritual force imparting life, character and significance to material forms, something that links the works of the individual artist with a cosmic principle. But this is active in the artist before it becomes manifest in his works ; it is like as echo from the divine part of his creative genius reverberating in the lines and shapes which he draws with his hand. To call it rhythm (as sometimes was done) is evidently not correct, because it is not intellectually measured or controlled, quite the contrary, it manifests unconsciously and spreads like a flash over the picture or over some part of it. This is further developed in another chapter of the *Li Tai Ming Hua Chi*, which is called " Discussion of the Brush-work of Ku K'ai-chih, Lu T'an-wei, Chang Sêng-yu and Wu Tao-tzŭ." * Here the old historian gives one of the closest definitions ever attempted by the Chinese critics of the painter's attitude to his work and his means of expression. The artistic significance of the brush-work in painting as well as in calligraphy is brought out in terms full of meaning ; old masters like Ku and Lu are

* For a full translation of this chapter, see Appendix III, pp. 229-231.

extolled and their styles briefly characterized, but however wonderful they may have been, none of them reached that inexhaustible source of inspiration from which the divine Wu drew his creative impetus.

" He concentrated his spirit and harmonized it with the working of Nature (or, the Creator), rendering the things through the power of his brush. His ideas were, as has been said, fixed before he took up the brush ; when the picture was finished, it expressed them all."

To illustrate this the writer refers to Chuang-tzŭ's well-known stories about the cook of Prince Hui and the stone-mason from Ying, who performed the most difficult things apparently without effort, because they had grasped the secret of Tao, the " Way of Heaven, which is not to strive, and yet to know how to overcome." In this same way really great works of art must be done ; as explained by Chang Yen-yüan : " He who deliberates and moves the brush intent upon making a picture, misses to a still greater extent the art of painting, while he who cogitates and moves the brush without such intentions, reaches the art of painting. His hands will not get stiff ; his heart will not grow cold ; without knowing how, he accomplishes it."

Chang Yen-yüan expresses here the same essential truth that over and over again was asserted by the ancient philosophers of China, be they Confucian, Taoist or Buddhist : To understand the meaning or significance of a thing, one must become the thing, harmonize one's consciousness with it and reach the mental attitude which brings knowledge without intellectual deliberation. Or, in the words of Confucius : " He who is in harmony with Nature hits the mark without effort and apprehends the truth without thinking." The attitude is exactly the same as the Taoist idea of the identity of the subjective and the objective. " Only the truly intelligent understand this principle of identity. They do not view things as apprehended by themselves subjectively, but transfer themselves into the position of the things viewed. And viewing them thus they are able to comprehend them, nay, to master them ; and he who can master them is near. So it is, that to place oneself in subjective relation with externals, without consciousness of their objectivity, this is Tao." *

" Tao that is displayed is not Tao. Speech which argues falls short of its aim. Charity which has fixed points loses its scope. Honesty which is absolute is wanting in credit. Courage that is purposely violent must itself fail. These five are, as it were, round, yet they tend to become square. Therefore that knowledge which stops at what it does not know, is the highest knowledge." †

These quotations from the second chapter of Chuang-tzŭ, " The Identity of Contraries," could easily be continued with a number of similar pronouncements by the same philosopher or by other Taoist writers, but they may suffice to show how the Taoist philosophy served as a main basis for Chang Yen-yüan's æsthetic attitude. The Taoist conception of real knowledge or insight, as an identity between the knower and the known, is applied by Chang Yen-yüan on the painter and his work, and also on the beholder and the painting, and in applying this mode of perception on the artistic activity he lays one of the corner-stones of Chinese æsthetics. It became accepted by most of the subsequent writers on painting as something almost self-evident. They never take the trouble of systematically defining or discussing this attitude but make us nevertheless realize, by the way they describe the artist's psychology and his creative activity, its fundamental importance.

Highly interesting in this respect are certain passages in Chang Yen-yüan's " Discussion of the Painter's Use of Facsimiles," a chapter made up of philosophical speculations, æsthetic opinions, and technical information.‡ It opens with some vague remarks on the cosmic processes, regulated by Yin and Yang, etc., by which forms are fashioned and colours produced. In the following paragraph the author sounds a warning against striving

---

* Giles' translation ; *Chuang Tzŭ*, p. 20.

† Translation by Yu-lan Fung ; *Chŭang Tzŭ*, p. 57.

‡ For a full translation of this chapter, see Appendix III, pp. 231-233.

for " completeness " in representation ; he seems to think that formal completeness is not desirable, if the painter has succeeded in conveying an impression of something true and convincing by a rendering which is formally incomplete. " But if one has no knowledge of completeness, then the thing will certainly be incomplete " ; or in other words, the thing must be complete in the mind, even though the manner of the pictorial rendering does not seem to be complete, otherwise no work of art will result. More original are the following remarks :

" If one misses the self-existent, the picture falls into the divine class ; if one misses the divine, the picture falls into the wonderful class ; if one misses the wonderful, the picture falls into the class of finely executed things, which have the weakness of being too cautious and minute."

These five classes contain all the pictures worth discussing, but only people who have a surpassing spirit, great knowledge, contentment and a pure mind will be able to understand and discuss painting. " The workman who wishes to do his work well must first sharpen his tools."

The intermediate portion of the chapter is devoted to rather specific questions of different kinds of silk, colours, glue and varnish, which may be of a historical interest but have no immediate æsthetic importance, and the same is true of the information regarding the habit of making copies or facsimiles which could serve as duplicates of the old pictures. But at the end of the chapter he tells about his admiration for Ku K'ai-chih's picture of Wei Mo Ch'i (Vimalakirti), and here he speaks of the " mysterious fitness," which is a criterion of the highest class of pictures, those which are " self-existent " or self-evident, i.e. beyond all intellectual definition. " One does not get tired by looking at it a whole day. By concentrating the spirit and far-reaching meditation one realizes the self-existent ; both the (painted) thing and oneself are forgotten ; the realization is separated from the form. ' The body becomes like dry wood, and the mind becomes like dead ashes.' He reached the

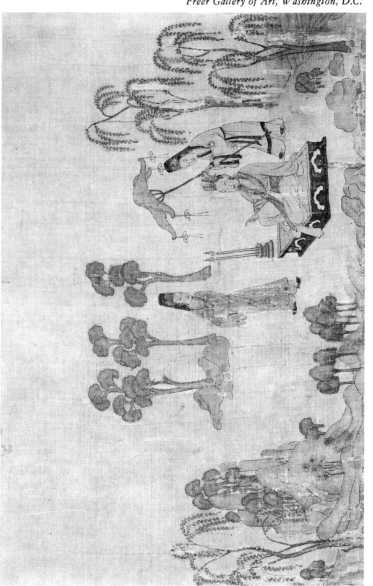

NYMPH OF LO RIVER

After Ku K'ai-chih (Born ca.345; 12th or 13th cent. copy)

PLATE III

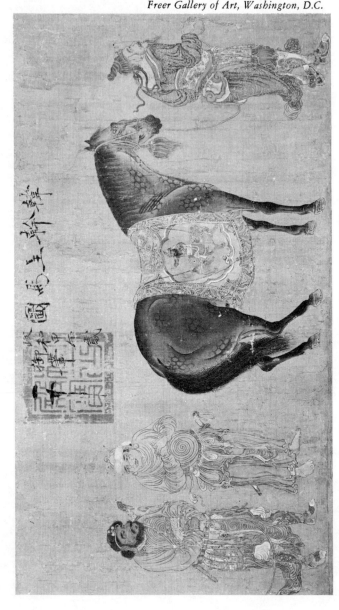

TARTARS BRINGING A TRIBUTE OF HORSES
After Han Kan (T'ang dynasty, 8th cent.; 14th or 15th cent. copy)

mysterious fitness (*miao li*), which may be called the Tao of painting."

Indeed ; this mysterious fitness was the very secret of Tao. It is illustrated over and over again by Chuang-tzǔ and his followers : It was the secret of Prince Hui's cook who could cut whole bullocks without the least forcing or scratching of the chopper, because he knew how to follow the natural veins and cavities. It was likewise the secret of the wheelwright, who knew how to co-ordinate mind and hand and mastered an art, which could not be transmitted by words or mechanical skill. It is the thing that cannot be reached by any conspicuous efforts, intellectual deliberations or arguments. " When there is argument, there is something the argument does not reach. The sages embrace all things, while men in general argue about them in order to convince each other. Great Tao does not admit of being spoken."

It can only be indicated by symbols such as the great emptiness, the root, the unity or essential of all that is. " The function of the ear ends with hearing, that of the mind with symbols or ideas, but the spirit is an emptiness ready to receive all things. Tao abides in the emptiness "— a condition which however does not signify vacuity or the absence of life and consciousness but rather the contrary, as it is the very source out of which all forms of conscious life emerge. A conception which also is abundantly illustrated in Chinese painting where the forms often seem to issue from some illimitable fluid or space represented by the bare silk. Chang Yen-yüan realized this just as well as most of the later critics, and in defining his attitude he made free use of the Taoist philosophy. It would be tempting to quote several passages from Chuang-tzǔ which offer close parallels to Chang Yen-yüan's æsthetic pronouncements, but one or two more must here suffice :

" That which can be seen with the eye is form and colour ; that which can be heard with the ear is sound and noise. But alas ! The people of this generation think that form and colour and sound and noise are means by which they can come to understand the essence of Tao.

This is not so. And as those who know do not speak, while those who speak do not know, whence should the world derive its knowledge ? "

" Painting must be sought for beyond the shapes," was the declaration of Chang Yen-yüan, to which he added : " but this is difficult to explain to common people." The mysterious resonance of the spirit (*ch'i yün*) was to him essentially a manifestation of Tao, a breath or pulse-beat of the undefinable spirit of life.

" Only the truly intelligent know the unity of things. They therefore do not make distinctions, but follow the common and the ordinary. The common and the ordinary are the natural functions of all things which express the common nature of the whole."

Here again Chuang-tzŭ offers a more philosophical exposition of an idea which Chang Yen-yüan also is aiming at when he indicates the highest or most essential quality in painting. To him it was the " self-evident " or rather, self-existing, something superior to all conscious efforts, a reflection of the eternal fitness of things, which indeed is an expression for their spiritual unity. It is from the Taoist point of view the highest criterion of proper action and of perfect art. The characterizations which Chuang-tzŭ gives of the wise ruler or perfect man may also be applied to the great painters :

" The mind of the perfect man is like a mirror. It does not move with things nor does it anticipate them. It responds to things, but does not retain them. Therefore he is able to deal successfully with things but is not affected." *

* * *

The Taoist attitude so clearly exemplified in the æsthetic passages in *Li Tai Ming Hua Chi* is also expressed by other writers of the T'ang period, though none of them equals Chang Yen-yüan as a critic of art. Their pronouncements are more fragmentary but some of them express quite characteristic ideas which are well worth

---

* Giles' translation.

recording (They are quoted here as reprinted in *Shu Hua P'u*, vol. 15).

The poet and official Fu Tsai, *tzǔ* Hou-chih, wrote the following remarks on a painting representing a pine-tree and some stones by his friend the ex-official Mr. Chang :

" When I am viewing the work of Mr. Chang, I find that it is not a picture, but really Tao. Whenever he goes to work he leaves behind all cunning skill ; his thoughts are penetrating into the mysterious (transformations). The things are in his spirit and not in his eyes. Thus, what is conceived in the mind is carried out by the hand. The aspect of loneliness is brought out in the representation of the tree, which is quite majestic. The spirit of it blends with the boundless and approaches the divine.

" If one measures things with too narrow standards and calculates their beautiful or ugly features with vile eyes ; if the goblet (ink-pot ?) is dried up and one licks the brush hesitating a long time, the whole painting becomes like a tumor or an excrescence. Why should one talk about such things ? "

A somewhat different point of view is expressed by the well-known poet Po Chü-i, who insists upon the correspondence between the painter's work and the models of nature, but at the same time makes it clear that there must be a complete union between the artist and his motif if the picture shall acquire æsthetic significance :

" Painting is not only skill, though likeness cannot be rendered without skill. Study should not be pursued only by following a teacher ; reality (objective nature) should be taken as master. Therefore, to express an idea or to represent an object properly, it must be turned over and over again in the mind, until it unites with the soul, as in the case of Ou-ho who employed the spirits as his servants."

Akin to the above statement are the remarks by Ou-yang Chiung, a writer of the posterior Shu dynasty (10th century), who points out that " among the six principles of painting the formal likeness (*hsing ssǔ*) and spirit-resonance (*ch'i yün*) are the two foremost. When there is spirit-resonance but no formal likeness, the 'solid qualities are in excess of accomplishments,' * but when there is formal likeness and no spirit-resonance, the thing has flower (ornamental beauty) but no fruit (inner reality)."

The *ch'i yün* becomes here again the criterion of a superior reality, the spiritual seed or fruit of the work which is more permanent than all its flowery beauty.

A famous essay on painting sometimes included among the T'ang writings is also the *Hua Hsüeh Pi Chüeh*, said to contain Wang Wei's (*tzü* Mo-ch'i) (699-759) thoughts on " The Secret of Landscape Painting." If this supposition involves some truth, it can only be of a relative or indirect kind. The essay in its present form was hardly written until three or four hundred years after Wang Wei, and even though it may contain certain traditional elements of method or composition ultimately derived from the art of Wang Wei, it seems more closely related to landscape painting of the Northern Sung than of the T'ang period. To take it as a proof of the high development of landscape painting in the 8th century would hardly be correct, but it has had a certain importance for landscape painters of later times.†

Chang Yen-yüan devotes also a special chapter of his *Li Tai Ming Hua Chi* (part I, chapter v) to landscape painting ; it is not theoretical or technical in the same sense as the above-named treatises, but mainly historical and quite fragmentary. The first part of it may however be of some interest in this connection as it contains a characterization of landscape painting of the pre-T'ang and early T'ang period. It runs as follows :

" There are still some famous pictures handed down from the Wei and Chin dynasties, and I have had occasion to see them. The landscapes are filled with crowded peaks, their effect is like that of filigree ornaments or horn combs. Sometimes the water does not seem to flow, sometimes the figures are larger than the mountains. The views are generally enclosed by trees and stones which

---

* *Analects*. Book VI, chap. 16.

† A full translation of this treatise is included in my *History of Early Chinese Painting*, Vol. I. and it seems superfluous to repeat it here.

stand in a circle on the ground. They look like rows of lifted arms with outspread fingers.

" If one carefully examines the ideas of the old masters and particularly their strong points, one finds that they do not keep to the common effects (transformation). At the beginning of the present dynasty there were the two Yen* who relied on their own skill and learning (not on their predecessors), and also Yang Ch'i-tan and Chan Tzǔ-ch'ien, † who specialized in painting palatial buildings and temples.—Gradually the old manner changed, but the painters still shaped the stones like dripping ice crystals with sharp edges, and in representing trees they drew every fibre and carved every leaf. The more they exerted themselves in the painting of orchards and willow groves the poorer these became. They did not as yet master the colouring. Only Wu Tao-hsüan, whose superior brush-work was inspired by heaven, was since his youth conscious of a mysterious spiritual power. He often painted on the temple walls strange rocks and broken river-banks in such a way that one could feel them with the hand. When he went to Shu he painted there some landscapes and these caused a transformation in landscape painting. It was started by Wu and accomplished by the two Li.

Then followed Wei Yen‡ who painted wonderfully the trees and stones and Chang Tsao§ who reached the very limit. He used a rabbit hairs brush with a blunt point and rubbed the ink with the hand, and such was his skill that the result looked quite natural and complete. There were furthermore Wang Wei whose pictures were very deep (full of meaning), Yang P'u-yeh, whose pictures were strange and spirited, Chu Shên who did rich and luxuriant things, Wang Tsai, who possessed the secret of skill, Liu Shang who grasped the likeness of things, and still others. No later painters have surpassed them."

---

* Yen Li-pên and Yen Li-tê, latter half of 7th century.

† Yang Ch'i-tan and Chan Tzǔ-ch'ien, both still active at the beginning of the 7th century.

‡ Wei Yen, early 8th century. Cf. Giles, *Introduction* p. 65.

§ Chang Tsao is usually classified as the most prominent follower of Wang Wei ; Yang P'u-yeh, Chu Shên and Wang Tsai were minor landscape painters of the 8th century.

It may be particularly observed that Chang Yen-yüan attributes the fundamental transformation of landscape painting, which was accomplished in the 8th century, to Wu Tao-tzŭ and Li Ssŭ-hsün and not to Wang Wei, who in the Sung and Ming periods was extolled as the greatest of all the landscapists, the one who first expressed in painting the poetic import or spiritual significance of natural scenery. We shall in the following have many occasions to quote enthusiastic interpretations of Wang Wei's divine art, composed by the poet-painters of Sung as well as by later representatives of the " Southern School," but none of these seem to have realized as well as Chang Yen-yüan, that it was Wu Tao-tzŭ rather than Wang Wei who first liberated landscape painting from the close and finicky method of the pre-T'ang masters and gave it a wider and deeper range of expression. He evidently painted things with a hitherto unknown effect of reality and with an overwhelming resonance of the vitalizing spirit.

In view of the many classifications and historical divisions of ancient painting which are offered by later critics, particularly in the Ming dynasty, it may also be of interest to note that Chang Yen-yüan divides the evolution of painting into four periods, i.e., 1. the most ancient, from Han to the Three Kingdoms, 2. the middle ancient, comprising the Chin and Sung dynasties (circ. 265-478), and 3. the least ancient, which corresponds to the so-called Six Dynasties (circ. 479-581). These three periods represent to him archaic or primitive art, while the 4th period, which includes the Sui and most of the T'ang dynasty (covering about two and a half centuries), represents to him " modern art." The division is evidently quite schematic, but it seems to imply that the most important step in the evolution of painting was accomplished during the Sui and early T'ang period. The pictures of the most ancient period were, according to Chang Yen-yüan, all lost; those of the middle ancient period extremely rare, while those of the least ancient period still existed in sufficient number to allow a critical study and estimate of the painters. The price of the pictures should be fixed not only according to their age but also with regard to the importance of the masters. Thus, works by Tung Pei-jên, Chan Tzŭ-ch'ien, Chêng Fa-shih, Yen Li-pên, Wu Tao-tzŭ and a few others may be estimated as highly as the very exceptional works by Ku and Lu, worth up to 20,000 taels. But the estimates are seldom just, they are usually done in a too narrow and prejudiced fashion, says the author : " These things must be discussed in a broad and comprehensive way and not hurriedly if one wants to reach a complete understanding of them... If one likes a picture, then it must be valued like gold and jade, but if one does not like it, then it is worth no more than broken tiles. It all depends on the man. How could then definite prices be fixed ? " — A wise remark indeed, which shows that the value of painting in China some 1200 years ago just as well as in our days was a question subject to changing modes and prejudices.

The chapter in *Li Tai Ming Hua Chi* from which the above passages are quoted opens with a reference to Chang Huai-kuan's classification of calligraphic writings. It was done in a book called *Shu Tuan*, written 724-27, which evidently enjoyed great popularity among the scholars of the period. The author had here introduced three classes, *shên* (divine), *miao* (wonderful) and *nêng* (able or skilful), in which the calligraphists were placed according to their relative merit, and he had furthermore defined ten different styles of writing. This grading of the scale of merit into three different steps or classes was taken over by the critics of painting and became from this time onward a standard element in the writings on the history of painting. The names of the two upper classes, *shên* and *miao*, are accepted by all subsequent writers, but the third class is called variously, sometimes *nêng*, sometimes *ch'iao* (skilful) or *ching* (refined or skilful). The last name is employed by Chang Yen-yüan in his previously quoted chapter on "The Importance of making Facsimiles." He divides the three chapters in upper and lower degrees and places above them all the pictures which he calls *tzŭ-jan* — " self-existent." He felt, as already pointed out, that there were certain exceptional pictures, in which the knowledge of Tao had been evidenced and which consequently stood above all intellectual definitions.

When these classes are introduced by subsequent writers, they are often completed by a fourth one, called *i* and intended for the most spontaneous or impetuous painters, who did not seem to fit into any of the other classes. But there is no definite rule or consensus of opinion as to the order of the *i* class in relation to the others. We will find it variously placed on the scale. The first writer who introduces it is Chu Ching-hsüan in *T'ang Ch'ao Ming Hua Lu* (published at the very end of the T'ang dynasty). In the preface to this work, which consists of biographical notes on some leading painters of T'ang, he says : " I make records only of the things I have seen, but when I know a thing I do not hesitate to express my stupid opinion about it. According to Chang Huai-kuan, calligraphy* should be classified in three categories, i.e. *shên*, *miao* and *nêng*, and in each of these he distinguishes a superior, a middle and an inferior degree. Those outside the three categories have no method at all. But there is also the *i* class (or category) which may be characterized either as excellent or as vile (high or low)." The author himself places it as a kind of appendix after the three general classes and includes in it only three men.

In the continuation of the preface Chu Ching-hsüan repeats the traditional estimate of human figures as the foremost motif, while birds and animals are placed as the next highest ; landscapes as the third and buildings as the fourth. Wu Tao-tzŭ, the heavenly genius, is the only master in later times who equalled Ku and Lu, and next to him stood Chou Fang. All the rest of the 124 painters are placed in inferior classes. Then he gives the following eloquent characterization of the great painters : " The ancients called the painters Sages, because they reached by their creative activity the very limits of heaven and earth and made manifest the brightness of the sun and the

---

* The reprint of the text in *Wang Shih Hua Yüan* has at this place *hua* and not *shu*, but it may be a mistake, because Chang Huai-kuan discussed calligraphy and not painting.

moon. By moving the brush (made of finest hair) they could represent all the innumerable things, which take their origin in the mind (heart), and unroll within some square inches thousands of *li* so that they may be held in the palm of the hand. Both the shifting (stirring) spirit and immovable matter may be rendered by some light touches of ink on the silk either through forms or by suggestion without forms. That is the beauty."

Such was indeed the power of the best painting in China ; it conveyed by inference more than it defined in shapes, it used both the forms and the absence of forms to transmit the resonance of the stirring spirit and to open up vistas into the realms of a world beyond intellectual definition.

*　　*　　*

In addition to the discussions of the four classes, which have been quoted above, may still be mentioned the rather original definitions offered by a somewhat later writer. Huang Hsiu-fu was no longer of the T'ang period, his main activity seems to have belonged to the latter half of the 10th century. It was then that he wrote down his records about the painters of Shu, which were published in 1005 under the title *I Chou Ming Hua Lu*, with a preface by Li Tien. This friend of Huang introduces him as one of the great " sages of painting " who should be deeply honoured, " because they have the thoughts of the Great Creator, which is something unfathomable." For them " it is of little importance if the pictures are minutely executed, nor do they call them beautiful, because of their rich colouring. They look at the forms but forget them and hold that the ideas should precede the brush-work."

Huang Hsiu-fu, who is said to have been one of these highly illuminated critics, bases his records of the painters from Shu on the division into the four classes, the first being *i*, spontaneous, the second *shên*, divine, the third *miao*, wonderful, and the fourth *nêng*, skilful, and he introduces each class with a short characterization. These highly condensed introductory remarks make it evident that the author was familiar with Chu Ching-hsüan's above-mentioned discussion of the same subject and most closely connected with the T'ang tradition of criticism, even though he composed his work after the close of the period :

1. "The spontaneous (*i*) style of painting is the most difficult. Those who follow it are unskilled in the use of compasses and squares for drawing circles and squares. They scorn refinement and minuteness in the colouring and make the forms in an abridged manner. They grasp the self-existent, which cannot be imitated, and give the unexpected. Therefore this is called the spontaneous manner" (Only Sun Wei is placed in this class).

2. "Generally the art of painting represents things according to their forms. But when the inspiration of heaven is very high, when the thoughts harmonize with the spirit, when the ideas are conceived and the style is established in conformity with the creative power of Nature, then it may be said, that the painted things disappear as the cupboards are opened or, that they fly away from walls which are breaking down.* Therefore this is called the spiritual manner."

3. "Painting is done by men, and every man has his own natural disposition. The brush-work may be fine and the ink wonderful, but one does not know why it is so. It is like (the cook) opening up the ox with the edge of the blade or like (the stone-mason) chipping off (the scab) with the hatchet without hurting the nose.† This manner is transmitted from the mind to the hand and exhausts the subtlest mysteries. Therefore it is called the mysterious manner" (This class is divided into a higher, a middle and a lower degree, comprising together 28 men).

4. "Painting which represents animals and plants with all their characteristics just as they are made by Heaven, and which combines the great mountains and streams with the fishes diving in the water and the birds

---

* References to current stories of wonderful paintings.

† References to Chuang-tzŭ's expositions of the working of Tao.

soaring in the air giving everything its proper form, is called the skilful manner " (This class is also divided in a higher, a middle and a lower degree which together comprises 27 men).

The question of the order and the characteristics of the four classes is taken up again by several of the successive writers who will be quoted in the following chapters, but none of them gives more suggestive definitions than those offered by Huang Hsiu-fu. What they have to add or to modify does not change the essential points of his estimate of the merits of the various classes which evidently was based on a very intimate knowledge of painting previous to the Sung dynasty.

THE SUNG PERIOD

LANDSCAPISTS AND POET-PAINTERS

THE great development of monochrome ink painting during the Five Dynasties and the Northern Sung period gave rise to a rapidly increasing discussion about the aims and methods of such artistic expression ; in fact, most of the great painters at the beginning of the Sung dynasty devoted themselves to monochrome landscape or bamboo painting, and several of them have written about their art or discussed it in words reported by their friends and followers. If the theoretical discussions of the T'ang period and earlier times had been largely based on figure painting, the situation was now modified in favour of landscape painting, particularly of the monochrome type ; and beside this there grew up some still more specialized forms of naturalistic painting as for instance of flowers, birds and animals. Thus, it may be recalled, that the members of the Emperor Hui Tsung's Academy were particularly trained in highly naturalistic modes of flower-and-bird painting, whereas the scholars and poets, who formed a more or less opposite movement, devoted themselves with the greatest keenness to the painting of bamboo and plum-blossoms in Indian ink. Bamboo painting, more than anything else, became the speciality of those highly cultured men, for whom painting was very closely associated with calligraphy and poetry, and a whole literature grew up around it.

It seems hardly necessary to dwell here on the most specialized treatises devoted to bamboo or plum-blossom painting, but two of the essays on landscape painting from the beginning of the Sung dynasty call for our attention, because they contain elements of general æsthetic interest.

Foremost among them should be mentioned the essay attributed to Ching Hao, active as a landscape painter during the latter part of the 10th century. This is known as *Pi Fa Chi* (Records of Brush-work)* or *Hua Shan Shui Lu* (Essay on Landscape Painting). It consists partly of descriptions of certain grand mountain sceneries and old pine-trees of the kind that the painters loved to represent, and partly of a dialogue between an old sage and a young painter who takes the rôle of the writer of the essay. Whether this writer actually was Ching Hao is very uncertain, yet it seems beyond doubt, that the treatise reflects the attitude which was most characteristic of the great landscape painters of the 10th century, and it contains certain general ideas about the study and scope of painting which are of great interest. The theoretical passages are reported below and a full translation of the essay (with the exclusion of a lengthy poem) is included in the Appendix.

When the old sage meets the young painter in the forest he asks : " Do you know the method of painting ? " To which he (I) answered : " You seem to be an old uncouth rustic ; how could you know anything about brush-work." But the old man said : " How can you know what I carry in my bosom ? " Then I listened and felt ashamed and astonished ; he spoke to me as follows : " Young people like to study in order to accomplish something ; they should know that there are six essentials in painting. The first is called *ch'i* (spirit or vitality), the second is called *yün* (resonance or harmony), the third is called *ssŭ* (thought or plan), the fourth is called *ching* (effect of scenery or motif), the fifth is called *pi* (brush), and the sixth is called *mo* (ink)."—I remarked : " Painting is to make beautiful things ; and the important point is to obtain their true likeness ; is it not ? " He answered : " It is not. Painting is to paint, to estimate the shapes of things, to really obtain them ; to estimate the beauty of things, to reach it ; to estimate the reality (significance) of things and to grasp it. One should not take outward beauty for reality. He who does not understand this mystery will not obtain truth, even though his pictures may contain likeness." I asked : " What is likeness and what is truth ? " The old man said : " Likeness can be

---

* Cf. Appendix IV, pp. 234-238.

obtained by shapes without spirit, but when truth is reached, both spirit and substance are fully expressed. He who tries to express spirit through ornamental beauty will make dead things." I thanked him and said : "From this I realize that the study of calligraphy and painting is an occupation for virtuous men."

The old man said : "Lusts and passions are the thieves of life. Virtuous men occupy themselves with music, calligraphy and painting, they do not indulge in inordinate lusts. Since you have virtue, I hope you will continue your studies without hesitation ; I will explain to you the essentials in painting :

" Spirit makes the heart (mind) follow the movements of the brush and seize without hesitation shapes of things. Harmony (resonance) consists in establishing correct and perfect forms which are not conventional. Thought causes you to deduct and detach essentials and concentrate on the forms of things. Scenery is (established by) observing laws of seasons, by looking for the wonderful (or mysterious) and finding the true. Brush-work means to follow the rules, but to be at the same time free and flexible in movement, so that everything seems to fly and move. Ink tones should be high and low, thick and diluted, according to the depth and shallowness of various things ; the colouring (suggested by these) so natural that it does not seem to be laid on with the brush."

The six essential points in painting mentioned by the old hermit may be considered as modifications of Hsieh Ho's six principles ; they express practically the same standards of appreciation, though in a less general manner. Thus points one and two correspond to Hsieh Ho's first principle split in two, point three corresponds to Hsieh Ho's fifth principle (composition), point four, relating to scenery or atmospheric effect, corresponds in a more limited sense to Hsieh Ho's third and fourth principles (likeness and colouring), while the fifth and sixth points, relating to the brush-and-ink work, correspond to Hsieh Ho's second principle. Ching Hao's points are evidently formulated exclusively for monochrome landscape painting and are consequently more specific than Hsieh Ho's

PLATE IV

LANDSCAPE
Attributed to Ching Hao (10th cent., Five Dynasties period.)

PLATE V

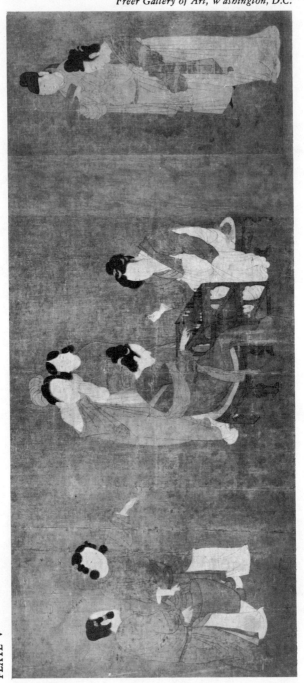

LADIES PLAYING DOUBLE SIXES
Attributed to Chou Fang (T'ang dynasty, 8th cent.)

principles, which were meant for every kind of painting, but the foundation is the same in both cases, i.e. the *ch'i yün*, the resonance of the vitalizing spirit, which remains the fundamental element to all great painters and critics. The subsequent remarks of the old man serve mainly to develop further the importance of the spiritual energy or vitality which cannot be conveyed through ornamental beauty or outward likeness, but must be the result of a communion with the inner reality of the objects.

In continuing the dialogue the old sage offers the following classification of painters which is slightly different from the classification discussed in the preceding chapter : " There are divine (*shên*), wonderful (*miao*—profoundly mysterious), clever (*ch'i*) and skilful (*ch'iao*) painters. The divine painter makes no effort but achieves the forms spontaneously by following the transformations of Nature. The wonderful (or profound) painter penetrates with his thoughts the nature of everything in heaven and earth, and thus the things flow out of his brush in accordance with the truth of the motif. The clever (or astounding) painter draws vast outlines, which are not in accordance with the truth of the motif ; the things he makes are strange, queer and have neither reason nor resemblance. This is the result of brush-work without thought. The skilful painter carves out and pieces together scraps of beauty which but seem in accordance with the great principles ; he forces the drawing and works in a highly exaggerated fashion. It may be said that reality is not enough for him, as he makes such display of floridity."

Ching Hao characterizes the divine (who achieves things without effort), the wonderful (who works in the most perfect intellectual fashion) and the skilful (who is able, but not original) in the same way as do earlier writers, but to these three categories he adds the clever (who is a technical virtuoso without the guidance of reason) instead of the spontaneous or impetuous (*i*). This modification of the scheme proposed by Chu Ching-hsüan and Huang Hsiu-fu may, indeed, be said to have good reason, because the spontaneously impetuous painters are more difficult to distinguish from the divine than are the clever from the

skilful.   But we will find in what follows that the classification, accepted as a classical standard in the Sung period
and quoted for instance in the *Hsüan Ho Hua P'u*, was
not the one proposed by Ching Hao but rather the one
established at the end of the T'ang period.

The observations on the brush-work, which the old
sage then offers to the young painter, are interesting from
a technical point of view, as may be seen in our Appendix,
but more significant for the general appreciation of painting
is his definition of the two kinds of faults :

" The faults in painting are of two kinds : those dependent on shapes and those independent of shapes.
Flowers and trees which do not conform in season, figures
which are larger than the buildings, trees which are higher
than the mountains, bridges which do not rest on their
banks, are measurable faults of form.   Such faults do not
alter the picture.   Faults which are independent of form
are caused by absence of spirit and harmony (resonance),
which makes the forms quite queer.   Then, in spite of all
efforts with brush and ink, everything in the picture is dead.
Such stupid pictures cannot be corrected."

It is not the apparent naturalness or conformity with
common ideas of form or appearance which make a painting a work of art.   Things may be out of reason or out
of proportion and yet serve the purpose of the artist, if
only they are permeated by the æsthetic vitality which
is the secret of the artist's creative mind.   This is the
logical complement to the classification of pictures according to their merits, the best being those which are done
by an irresistible impetus, in which logical reasoning has
no place, and the poorest those which are the result of
laborious skill.   We shall find the same standpoint
defined over and over again by subsequent writers on
painting, though seldom with more clearness and concentration than in the dialogue between the old sage and
the young painter.   The pronouncements on the relative
merits and the classification of painters by Liu Tao-ch'un,
Kuo Jo-hsü and Han Cho offer close parallels to the ideas
expressed in the *Pi Fa Chi*, and it may well be, that they
are partly derived from the same source, but before we

enter into a discussion of these theoretical treatises, we must leave the word to some of the painters of the 11th century who also applied in practice their theoretical speculations.*

Most important is the famous treatise *Lin Ch'üan Kao Chih* (The Great Message of Forests and Streams) which is based, at least in part, on sayings by Kuo Hsi (circ. 1020-90), though composed in its present form by his son Kuo Ssŭ. It contains passages of great interest which throw a vivid light on the painter's activity, his ideals and psychological attitude, but these are interspersed with observations on motifs, effects of nature and geographic conditions, which have little connection with the æsthetic problems of art. We must here limit our quotations to some of the former passages, borrowed mainly from the two chapters called *Shan Shui Hsün* (Comments on Landscape) and *Hua I* (Ideas for Painting).†

" There are various types of landscape painting; some are spread out into large compositions, in which nothing is left out; others are condensed into quite small views, which, however, are not negligible. There are also different ways of looking at landscapes; if one looks at them with a heart of the woods and the streams, their value becomes great, but if one looks at them with proud and haughty eyes, their value becomes quite low.

" Landscapes are large things; he who contemplates them should be at some distance; only so is it possible for him to behold in one view all shapes and atmospheric effects of mountains and streams. As to figure paintings of men and women, executed with a fine brush, they can be unrolled in the hand or on a small table, and thus completely seen and examined. These are all different manners of painting.

---

* It seems hardly necessary to dwell here on the essay on landscape painting known as *Shan Shui Chüeh* and attributed to the great painter Li Ch'êng, because its rather trite and technical contents have no direct connection with the great artist. The treatise was probably composed at the beginning of the 13th century by a minor painter called Li Ch'êng-sou.

† More extensive extracts from Kuo Hsi's lengthy treatise are given in my *History of Early Chinese Painting*, vol. II; only a few passages are here repeated in somewhat improved translation.

" It has been truly said, that among the landscapes there are those fit to walk through, those fit to contemplate, those fit to ramble in and those fit to live in. All pictures may reach these standards and enter the category of the wonderful; but those fit to walk through or to contemplate are not equal to those fit to ramble in or to live in. Why is it so? Look at the landscapes of to-day. They comprise distances of several hundred *li*, but there is not three or four tenths of space fit to idle or dwell in. Yet, they are accepted as of the class of pictures fit to idle or dwell in. But the wise man's yearning for woods and streams is aroused by the existence of such beautiful places. Therefore painters must keep this idea in mind, and beholders should examine pictures according to the same. This may be called not losing the fundamental idea.

" Painting has also its law of physiognomy. Li Ch'êng's progeny was prosperous and abundant; he made the foot of the mountains and the face of the earth very thick and strong, broad and large, graceful at the top and luxuriant below, which is in agreement with the characteristics of having progeny; but I will not dwell particularly on shapes or characteristics, simply give the reasons why this (law?) should be so.

" There is no difference between the study of painting and the study of calligraphy. Those who nowadays study Chung Yu,* Wang Hsi-chih, Yü Shih-nan† and Liu Kung-ch'üan ‡ will after some time become like them. Great men and learned scholars do not limit themselves to one school. It is necessary to combine (several models), and to study and make observations on a broad basis, so that one may form a personal style and gradually reach perfection. Nowadays students from Ch'i and Lu (Shantung) copy only Ying-ch'iu (Li Ch'êng), while students from Kuan and Shan (Shensi) copy only Fan K'uan; they follow only one road in their study, tramping in the footsteps of predecessors, although their respective provinces comprise many thousand *li* and a great many

---

* Chung Yu, d. 230, famous for his skill in the *li*-style.

† Yü Shih-nan (558-638), a brilliant writer in the time of T'ang T'ai Tsung.

‡ Liu Kung-ch'üan (778-865) one of China's most famous calligraphists.

districts and kinds of people worthy to be represented. To follow a single school in one's study has since olden times been considered a weakness, it is like playing only one chord; those who will not hear, should not blame those who do not hear. From earliest times the new always seemed attractive, and the old seemed boring to the ears and eyes of men. Therefore I think that great men and scholars do not keep to one single style or school.

" Liu Tzŭ-hou* has well discussed literary style, but I think that not only literature but everything has its secret rules; this being so always, how much more for painting. But how can it be told? Whatever motif the painter represents, be it large or small, complicated or simple, he should do it by concentrating on its essential nature. If something of the essential is lacking, the soul is not manifest. He must do his work with his whole soul; if he does not work with his whole soul, the essential will not be clear. He must be severe and respectful in his work, otherwise it will lack depth of thought. He must apply zeal and reverence to complete it, otherwise the picture will not be properly finished.

" Therefore when he is possessed by a spirit of laziness but forces himself (to paint), his brush-work will be soft and weak without decision. This is the fault of not concentrating on the essential. When he feels distracted and throws down something in a disorderly way, the forms become obscure and evasive without vigour. This is the fault of not working with the whole soul. When he is light-hearted and excited, his forms will become unsteady, sketchy, incomplete. This is the fault of lacking severity. If he is sluggish and careless, his style will be lax and coarse and not properly adjusted. This is the fault of working without zeal and reverence. Thus, lack of decision leads to faults of definition, lack of vigour to loss of ease and dignity, lack of completeness to faults of composition, lack of orderly arrangement to faults in the relation between the important and the indifferent. These are the greatest faults of painters. But this may be conveyed only to the intelligent.

---

* Liu Tsung-yüan (773-819), a famous poet and essayist.

" I, Kuo Ssŭ, often saw my father working on one or two pictures. Sometimes he would put them away and pay no attention to them. Ten to twenty days often passed before he turned to them again, and he repeated the method three times, his intention being not to be too impulsive. This kind of disinclination, isn't it the same as what he meant by the spirit of laziness ? When, however, he felt inspired and elated, he worked forgetting everything else ; but if some disturbing thing happened, he would put away (his work) and pay no attention to it. This rejection, is it not what he meant by distracted (confused) spirit ?

" On the days when he was going to paint (he would place himself) at a bright window before a clean table and burned incense right and left. He took a fine brush and the most excellent ink, washed his hands and cleaned the ink stone as if to receive an important guest. He let the thoughts settle in his soul, and then he worked. Isn't this what he meant by not to work in the hurry of excitement ? He planned and penetrated it thoroughly, he added to it and made it richer, not only once or twice but over and over again. Each picture had to be repeated, done over (mentally ?) from the beginning to the end with great care as if guarding against an enemy ; only after that was it finished. Isn't this what he meant by not working in a sluggish and careless way ?

" And it may be said that everything, be it large or small, must be handled in a similar way in order to be well accomplished. My father often explained these things to me in great detail, and I have followed his teachings as my guide during my whole life.

" He who learns to paint flowers takes a stalk of the flower, places it in a deep hole in the ground and examines it from above ; in this way the flower may be completely grasped. He who learns to paint bamboos places a stalk of bamboo in the clear moonlight so that its shadow falls on a white wall ; in this way the real shape of the bamboo comes out. He who learns to paint landscapes should not do it differently. He should go himself to the mountains and streams and contemplate them in order to grasp their aspects and meaning. The effect of real streams and valleys is comprehended only at a distance; when seen close by, only their component elements are grasped.

" Clouds and vapours of real landscapes are not the same at the four seasons. In spring they are light and diffused, in summer rich and dense, in autumn scattered and thin, in winter dark and solitary. When not simply disrupted shapes but such general effects are to be seen in the picture, the clouds and vapours have an air of life.

" Mist around mountains is not the same at the four seasons. Mountains of spring are light and seductive as if smiling; mountains of summer have a blue-green colour which seems to be dropping all over; mountains of autumn are bright and clean as if embellished by rouge (cosmetics); mountains of winter are sad and tranquil as if sleeping. When such general ideas are expressed in pictures and the representation is not finicky, the atmosphere of misty mountains is well rendered.

" Wind and rain of true landscapes can be grasped only at a distance; when examined at close range, one cannot make out the aspects of their complex directions and movements.

" Light and shade of real mountains can be seen in their completeness only from afar; if seen close by, they become small patches, and one does not obtain the effects of light and dark, the visible and the invisible.

" Figures on the mountains mark out the roads; high buildings on the mountains serve to make the scenery more important. The woods of the mountains with their lights and shades divide the far from the near. Streams of the valleys should be sometimes disrupted, sometimes broad thus indicating the depth and shallowness of gullies. Ferries and bridges are indications of human activity. Fishing boats and angling rods serve to indicate human intentions.

" Mist and clouds of spring mountains are downy and diffused; the people are happy. Luxuriant trees of summer mountains are abundant and shady; the people are contented. Autumn mountains are clear and pure, while leaves fall; the people are quiet. Winter mountains are covered by dark storm-clouds; the people are silent and lonely.

"Contemplation of such pictures evokes in men corresponding ideas; it is as if one were among the mountains, and the scenery existed outside the imagination. When one sees the quiet streams and the setting sun, one feels like stopping in contemplation; when one sees the lonely men living in the mountains, one feels like staying there; when one sees the cliffs, the streams and the stones, one feels like rambling among them. The contemplation of such pictures arouse corresponding reactions in the heart. It is as if one really came to these places. The conceptions of such pictures are more than wonderful.

"Wonderfully lofty and divinely beautiful are these mountains. In order to exhaust their marvels and grasp the work of the Creator, one must love their spirit, study their essential features, wander about them widely, satiate the eyes and store up the impressions in the heart. Then, even if the eye does see the silk and one realizes that the hand does not govern brush and ink, marvellous, mysterious, boundless becomes that picture of mine!"

Hua I (Ideas or Motives for Painting).

"Men of the world think that pictures are made simply by moving the brush; they do not understand that painting is no easy matter. Chuang-tzŭ said: 'The painter takes off his clothes and sits cross-legged'—a true statement about the painter's ways. The artist must nourish in his heart gentleness and cheerfulness; his ideas must be quiet and harmonious or, as said (in *Li Chi*), 'the heart should be quiet, honest and sincere to the utmost,'* then the various aspects of man's gladness and sorrow and of every other thing be it pointed, oblique, bent or inclined will appear naturally in his mind and be spontaneously brought out by his brush.

"Ku K'ai-chih of the Chin dynasty constructed for himself a high building as a studio for painting; he was indeed a wise man of ancient times. If one does not act

---

* See, Couvreur, *Dictionnaire classique de la langue chinoise*, Sien-hsien, 1930, p. 510.

in this way (not doing so) the inspiration will soon be restrained, distracted, dulled or obstructed, and how could one then represent in painting the appearance of things and of emotions?

"It is like a workman making a *ch'in* (table-harp or lute). He has found at I-yang a *wu-t'ung* tree ; his hands are skilled, his thoughts mysterious, his mind quite clear on the point, and so while the tree (living material) still stands with branches and leaves untouched, he sees the lute made by master Lei quite clearly before his eyes. But the man whose thoughts are troubled and whose body is worn out looks at the sharp chisels and knives and does not know where to begin. How could he accomplish the *Chiao wei* lute * of the five notes and make its sounds reverberate with clear wind and running water ? Indeed as a man of former times said : 'a poem is a picture without form, a picture a poem in form.' Wise men have often discussed this (saying), and we have made it our teacher.

"I have therefore in my leisure hours looked through some poems of the Chin and T'ang periods and sometimes found among them excellent verses which express the things which are in man's heart or the views which present themselves to his eyes.

"But if I did not live in perfect harmony and ease and were not seated at a bright window before a clean table burning incense to dispel all anxieties, the fine verses and excellent ideas would not take shape ; the inner mood and beauty of their meaning would not be realized in my thoughts. How can it then be said that the principal thing in painting is easily reached ? When circumstances are ripe, heart and hand responsive, and one starts with some horizontals and verticals or some central part, 'taking from right and left and finding a source'—lo, a man of the world steps in, leads the thoughts astray and gives a rude shock to the feelings—then, all is out ! Therefore I (Kuo Ssŭ) have recorded some of the beautiful

---

* *Chiao wei* (scorched tail) alluding to a story of a lute made from a charred log of the *wu t'ung* tree, which an enthusiast rescued for that purpose from the flames. Giles, *Dictionary*: 1317. The man who made this famous lute, which produced sounds of unsurpassed beauty was Ts'ai Yung of the later Han dynasty. Cf. Waley, *Introduction*, p. 192.

verses by ancient poets, which my father used to recite and which contain excellent thoughts for painting."

Hua Chüeh (Secrets or Methods of Painting).

"Whenever you are going to use the brush, you must first correlate sky and earth. This means that on a sheet, which is one and a half feet, the upper part should be left for the sky, the lower part for the earth ; between them one may develop the ideas of scenery. I have seen beginners of the present day hastily grasp the brush, throw down carelessly some ideas, shocking the feelings with their smearing and rubbing. When looking at their overfilled sheets the eyes get stuffed, the effect is very unpleasant. Works which are done in such light-hearted fashion cannot express anything high or great.

"When using the brush one should not be used by it, and in using the ink one should not be used by the ink. The brush and the ink are superficial things, but how could those who do not know how to handle them accomplish anything really wonderful ? The difficulty of handling the brush and the ink is the same as in calligraphy which is of the same order as painting. Thus it has been said that Wang Yu-chün (Wang Hsi-chih) liked geese ; the movement of their turning necks seemed to him to resemble the movement of a man's wrist when he is handling the brush. This applies to the use of the brush in painting just as well as in calligraphy. It is generally said, that he who is good in the one is also good in the other of these two arts, because in both movements of the wrist in using the brush must be easy and unobstructed. Someone may ask : what kind of ink should be used ? To which my answer is : 'Use either burnt ink or ink which has been stored over night, or faded ink, or dust-ink ; if one kind is not satisfying, take another.'"

Kuo Hsi's observations on the elements of landscape painting and on the painter's attitude towards his work are so explicit that they hardly call for much comment. The former are evidently meant for students who are entering on the path of practical training, but are at the

PLATE VI

AUTUMN IN THE RIVER VALLEY
Kuo Hsi (Sung dynasty, 11th cent.)

PLATE VII

BUDDHIST TEMPLE AMID CLEARING MOUNTAIN PEAKS
Attributed to Li Ch'eng (Sung dynasty, 10th century)

same time illuminating for all who try to grasp the secrets of Chinese landscape painting; the latter are of a more general kind and give the background of the artist's creative activity. Most important in this respect is the complete detachment from disturbing outward conditions and a profound tranquillity or emptiness of the mind. He returns to this point several times, insisting on it with almost the same force as do the expounders of Ch'an philosophy. It is a pre-condition for the painter's self-identification with the soul of his motif, his becoming at one with its spiritual import.

The work by which this inner significance of a motif is made visually manifest must be neither forced nor hurried; it must flow easily without interference of speculative thought (as with painters of the " divine class"). It cannot be accomplished when the body is tired or the mind distracted, because then the physical and mental instruments of the painter do not respond instantly and willingly to the creative impetus. The work becomes weak, sketchy or loose. A painter must choose the right moment both from the subjective and the objective point of view and then start with utmost decision and full command of all his powers. He must be vigilant and work as if he was guarding against an enemy who is trying to overpower him. The final picture, which may have the appearance of some light touches thrown down at random, is the result of a severe struggle not only in the technical field but also in regard to character and mode of life. The quotation from Chuang-tzŭ : " The painter takes off his clothes and sits cross-legged," is probably meant as a description of the proper mental condition which should be free from all disturbing influences, be they exterior or interior; then, to use another saying of Chuang-tzŭ, " when the mind is in repose, it becomes the mirror of the universe, the speculum of all creation."

Kuo Hsi's remarks about the appearance of mountains and streams, clouds and mist and other natural phenomena are, in part, highly imaginative and suggestive. He seems to consider all these phenomena as more or less individualized manifestations of an all-pervading spiritual life ; hence their expressiveness, their active parts in the great drama of nature, which he unrolls in his painting. From a formal point of view they serve pre-eminently to create space : it is brought out by their relative proportions, by the aerial perspective, by the interplay of clouds and mist into which the forms disappear. The importance of these elements in Chinese landscape painting has often been emphasized, but Kuo Hsi does it in words which reflect the creative imagination of a great artist.

* * *

One of the most characteristic cultural products of the Northern Sung period was the ' gentleman-painter,' the accomplished amateur or dilettante, who was often a real master of ink-painting as well as of calligraphy but shunned the name or position of a professional artist. There were quite a number of highly gifted men, government officials, scholars and philosophers who brought out this ideal by their lives and activities and discussed it in their writings. Artistic occupations, such as painting and calligraphy, were to them recreations to be pursued when they were at leisure from official duties, yet most intimate expressions of their genius, and their writings were poetic translations of their thoughts on nature and art. Their endeavour was to find in life no less than in art that spontaneous ease by which an inspiration of the moment may be fully and naturally expressed when the technical means have been mastered. They speak about it in terms which often have a deep poetic undertone as for instance the following words by Su Tung-p'o :

" My writing is like spring-water in abundance ; it issues everywhere, no matter what the ground may be. Over the level ground it flows quietly murmuring (covering) with ease a thousand *li* in a day. When it comes to mountains and stones, it winds around them and takes on their colour. Really it is not to be defined ; all I know is, that it keeps on moving when it must move and ceases when it must cease."

Su Shih, *tzŭ* Tung-p'o (1036-1101), was one of the most typical representatives of the above-mentioned class of men and the one who has become most widely known and appreciated among his countrymen. Few outstanding personalities in Chinese history have reached a place closer to the heart of the cultured. And the reason for this is not to be sought in what he accomplished as a statesman and official but in his standing as the perfect gentleman-scholar, a poet-painter and an art critic. Here we must mainly confine ourselves to his activity in the last-named direction. To understand this, it may, however, be well to recall in few words Su Shih's methods and ideals as a painter.

He worked exclusively in Indian ink and had two favourite kinds of subject : bamboos and water, motifs which each in their way express a peculiar combination of suppleness and strength. The former in particular were generally interpreted in a symbolic sense : Their energetic growth, their power to remain fresh and green even in the cold season, their habit of yielding and bending before the storm without ever breaking, represented to the Chinese qualities which were traditionally associated with the character of the gentleman-scholar. Su Shih like his friend Wên T'ung painted these elegant and noble plants with a definite emphasis on their symbolic meaning ; he saw in the different kinds of bamboos reflections of various conditions of human life and character, he loved them just as much as the poor painter in whose mouth he puts the words : " I could live without meat but not without bamboos."

Most of his pronouncements on art are given in short poems or colophons on paintings by contemporary artists and friends, among whom Wên T'ung, *tzŭ* Yü-k'o, was the foremost. Yü-k'o, who in ordinary life was a poor magistrate in a small town, stood for Su Tung-p'o as the unattainable master and ideal in the field of bamboo painting. His early death was a bitter bereavement to Su Tung-p'o, who wrote :

" My regretted friend Wên Yü-k'o was a genius in four different ways : 1. in poetry ; 2. in ancient ballads (*ch'u tz'ŭ*) ; 3. in ' grass-writing ' ; 4. in painting. Yü-k'o often said : ' There is nobody in the world who knows me except Su Shih. He recognized at first my best qualities.'—Seven years have passed since Yü-k'o died, but only now I see this work of his and write the following poem :

'The brush and yourself, both are gone. Who can now pour fresh life into poetry ? No one is there to swing the hatchet ; only the materials are left. I mourn the man and break my strings.' "

Yü-k'o's artistic genius and all-absorbing love of bamboos, which was transmitted to Su Shih, are beautifully brought out in several poems some of which, as they reflect the writer's highest ideals of painting, may be quoted :

" When Yü-k'o painted bamboos he was conscious only of the bamboos and not of himself as a man. Not only was he unconscious of his human form, but sick at heart he left his own body, and this was transformed into bamboos of inexhaustible freshness and purity. As there is no more a Chuang-tzǔ in the world, who can understand such a concentration of the spirit ? "

In another poem Su Shih gives the following characterization of Yü-k'o as a friend and of his way of working, which to him was the purest form of artistic activity :

" Wherever Yü-k'o went he sang his poems and painted his bamboos. He had not stayed for a year (as an official) in the capital when he asked leave to return to the country, and as he left, the poems and the bamboo paintings all went with him to the West.

" If he was not seen for a day the people missed him. His mien was stern and cold, but he ' smoothed' the rude and the quick-tempered ; he turned the vile and the mean into kind and generous men. Now he is far away. One may still ask for his poems and beg for his bamboos, but the kind and peaceful man is no longer to be found. In looking at his bamboos I cannot help moaning."

Yü-k'o's own conception of his artistic activity and evolution is reported by Su Shih as follows :

" In his earlier years Yü-k'o painted his bamboos whenever he found some pure white silk or good paper. He grasped the brush quickly, brushing and splashing with it freely. He simply could not help (doing) it. All the people who came to his house grabbed some pictures which they carried away. Yü-k'o did not care about them.

"In later years when he saw people placing brushes and ink-stone on the table he recoiled and went away. And those who came to ask for pictures waited until the end of the year, but did not obtain anything. When someone asked Yü-k'o his reasons for this (change of attitude) he replied: 'In former years I studied Tao but could not reach it; I found no peace of mind and could not accomplish it. Therefore I simply went on painting ink-bamboos expressing through them my restlessness. It was like an illness. Now this illness is cured, nothing more is to be done.'

"As far as I can see, Yü-k'o's illness is not yet cured. Is it not possible that it will develop again? I will wait for its development and take him by surprise—perchance I too may be ill."

When Yü-k'o passed away in 1079 Su Shih expressed his sorrow in several poems and colophons. In one of these he asks: "Who was this man who found happiness in strolling about, chanting poems like a careless Sage, and penetrating the mysteries of the bamboo? From time to time he did a tree or a stone, wild and strange, beyond all rules. The whole world considered them precious, but I am the one who appreciates them most. It has always been difficult for close friends to remain together. Death comes suddenly without waiting . . . ."

In another colophon Su Shih tells us that he had a bamboo painting by Yü-k'o engraved on stone, "so that amateurs who look at it may feel their hearts moved and their eyes startled by the extraordinary sight and also may remember the character of my regretted friend which was bending but never flinching like these two bamboos."

Of greatest interest is, however, Su Shih's description of the manner of bamboo painting which he learned from Yü-k'o. It contains in a nutshell the essentials of Chinese ink-painting as it was understood and practised by these poet-painters, who wrote down their bamboo sketches with the same ease as they wrote the 'running' characters.

" Painters of to-day draw joint after joint and pile up leaf on leaf. How can that become a bamboo ? When you are going to paint a bamboo, you must first realize the thing completely in your mind. Then grasp the brush, fix you attention, so that you see clearly what you wish to paint ; start quickly, move the brush, follow straight what you see before you, as the buzzard swoops when the hare jumps out. If you hesitate one moment, it is gone.

" Yü-k'o taught me thus ; but I could not do it, though I knew it should be so. I knew it in my heart but could not do it. The inner and the outer (faculty) were not as one, the heart and the hand did not co-operate. That is the fault of insufficient study. Those who perceive things within themselves but do not grasp them completely may understand in a general way but when the matter is at hand, they lose the whole thing. And this does not apply only to bamboo painting."

The same thought was expressed by Su Shih more definitely in a colophon on a picture by Li Lung-mien when he wrote :

" There are men who possess Tao and possess art ; others who possess Tao but have not art, although the things take form in their hearts, they do not take form under their hands."

The spiritual inspiration alone, however pure and deep it may be, is not enough to transform a man into an artist ; he must also know how to work, how to make the hand co-operate with the mind, he must possess the power of visualizing his pictures mentally, nay, of becoming the very motifs that he paints. Yü-k'o was, according to Su Shih's poetical expression, transformed into the bamboos that he painted, and " when Han Kan painted horses, he truly was a horse." Also other great masters like Wang Wei, Wu Tao-tzŭ and Li Lung-mien are praised for their complete self-identification with the things that they did with their brush. " When Li Po-shih stayed in the mountains he did not pay attention to one thing only but his spirit joined in with ten thousand things and his mind penetrated every kind of workmanship."

This same preparatory process for creative work is also described by Su Shih as grasping the essential points of the inner character of the motive : " Looking at pictures by scholars is like examining horses ; one finds that they manifest the points which carry expression and life, whereas ordinary painters often grasp only the riding-whip, the hairy skin, the stable-manager, the fodder and grain but nothing of the beauty. After having seen a few feet of such pictures one feels tired."

And these points which carry expression and life constitute what Su Shih sometimes called " the constant principle " or " the inherent reason of things," as for instance in the following quotation : " Among the painters of the world some know how to represent form, but the inherent reason of things can only be grasped by superior scholars (or gentlemen.) In Yü-k'o's paintings of bamboos, of stones and decaying trees this reason is certainly to be found. Some of them seem as if they were alive, some as if they were dead, some are warped like barren and contracted fists, some are tall and slender, vigorous and luxuriant. The roots, the branches, the joints, the leaves, the pointed shoots, the thread-like veins, all exhibit innumerable transformations and are quite alike. But each thing is at its proper place in accordance with nature's creations and satisfies the ideas of men, because it contains the gentleman's spirit."

The fitness of things is, indeed, an essential condition for their artistic significance. As everything has its proper place in Nature's great organism and thereby receives its particular expressiveness or significance, so should it also be represented by the painter, who, if he is a superior man, co-operates with nature and thereby makes manifest the inherent characteristics of whatever he paints. He is then no longer bound by any imposed rules or conventions, because he carries all in his heart.

In a poem written on a picture by Secretary Wang from Yen-ling, representing some broken branches, Su Shih says :

" Those who criticize pictures as forms are like children, and those who compose poetry according to formal rules are no real poets. Poetry and painting follow the same laws ; it is by divine inspiration that they become pure and original.

"Pien Luan painted birds as if alive, Chao Ch'ang gave the spirit of flowers. These two branches are perfectly spaced, they contain all essence and rhythm. Who says that a dot of red does not bring out the spring that never changes ? "

The second poem written on the same picture is too beautiful not to be quoted :

"The thin bamboos are like hermits, the lonely flowers like pure virgins. The birds are fluttering among the branches moving the flowers, which are moist with rain. A pair of birds on the point of soaring, a rustle among the thicket of leaves. Look how the bee is sucking the flowers, filling its loins with their honey—the painter possessed the skill of heaven ; he rendered the air of spring with his brush. I think he was truly a poet ; he has given the harmony, and asks for a poem."

The most striking description of Su Shih's own way of working is given in his letter to Ku Hsiang-chêng, in whose house he had been entertained and where he had painted some bamboos on the wall :

"When my dry bowels are refreshed with wine, the rapid strokes begin to flow and from the flushed liver and lungs bamboos and stones are born. They grow in abundance and cannot be suppressed. I painted them on the snow-white walls of your house. All my life I loved poetry as well as painting ; I scribbled my poems and defiled the walls, and was often cursed in return. But you are not angry, nor do you curse me, for which I am more than glad."

Su Shih may have allowed himself a certain amount of poetic exaggeration in his self-characterization ; yet there can be little doubt, that he felt the need of wine to kindle the flash on inspiration and improve the speed of the brush. His friend Mi Fei confirms this in one of his notes about Su Shih's bamboo paintings. He says in part :

"Su Shih painted his bamboos in one stroke from the ground to the top. I asked him why he did not paint them by joints? To which he answered: 'Do the bamboos ever grow in joints?' He prepared them clearly and beautifully in his mind, as he had learned to do from Wên T'ung. He said himself: 'I picked some fragrant petals with Wên. . . . '

"When I came back from Hunan and passed Huang-chou, I saw the gentleman for the first time; he was jolly with wine and said: 'Paste this paper on the wall, it is Kuanyin paper.' Then he rose and painted two branches of bamboo, a dry tree and a strange rock."

No wonder that Su Shih approvingly quotes some words by Chu Hsiang-hsien, a contemporary landscape painter, also known as 'the Hermit of the West Lake', a genius who "never passed any examinations and never sold his pictures," he said: "I write in order to express my heart, I paint in order to satisfy my mind; that is all"—just like Yü-k'o, the unmatched genius and representative of the gentleman spirit in art, or like Su Shih himself who said: "In my poetry I am not aiming at skill, in my writing (or painting) not seeking for the strange. The boundless gift of Heaven is my master."

In spite of Su Shih's highly unconventional attitude and his insistence on painting as an expression of the sudden flash of inspiration, he did not approve of loosely executed or blurred paintings. This becomes evident in some of his classifications of the painters and is also hinted at in the following colophon on a painting by Chao Yün-tzŭ or Chao, the Son of the Clouds, who painted in a very rough manner, because he was unable to use a finished style:

"In Chao Yün-tzŭ's paintings the brush-work was quite sketchy, but the ideas were fully expressed. He was not able to produce finished pictures, though he pretended that he used a rough and vulgar manner in order to startle or to make fun of the people who came to see him. He acted like Liu Hsia-hui, who was lacking in respect, and like Tung-fang Shuo, who amused himself at the expense of the world. He was the foremost among the jokers. Someone said that Yün-tzŭ was saving the world, but in Shu the clouds which are driven by the wind are called 'mad clouds'."—Evidently a play on the painter's name.

Ai Hsüan was a prominent academician, who worked in the highly finished style which was practised under the guidance of the imperial art patron Hui Tsung; yet Su Shih had a great admiration for his work :

Ai Hsüan from Chin-ling painted birds and animals, flowers and bamboos and was the foremost (painter of those things) in recent years. The older he grew, the more wonderful his brush-work became. Although it was no longer clear and even, the spirit of it was most uncommon. . . ."

Still, pictures of this kind were not considered by Su Shih as of the highest class :

"Paintings representing human figures are divine (*shên*); paintings representing flowers, bamboos, birds and fishes are marvellous (*miao*), paintings of palaces and utensils are works of skill (*chiao*). Landscapes belong to a superior class, but it is difficult to make them pure, strong, original and to represent their endless transformations."

A further development of Su Shih's ideas about portrait painting is to be found in the following notes on his own portrait painted by Ch'ên Huai-li. He insists here on the necessity of seizing those particular features or peculiarities which reflect the character of a man, and of representing him freed from all conventional stiffness :

" The difficult point in portrait painting is in the eyes ; Ku K'ai-chih said : ' The expression in portrait painting is all in the eyes ; the second point is in the cheek-bones and the chin. I have often looked in the lamplight at the shadow of my chin on the wall and asked someone to make it into a picture on the wall without putting in eyes or the eyebrows. Nobody who saw the result could help laughing, knowing that it was I. When the eyes as well as cheek-bones and chin give a true likeness, the rest follow suit ; because the eyebrows, nose and mouth may be modified so as to obtain resemblance.

" Portrait painting and physiognomy are the same art. In order to grasp the character of a man one must observe him and his manners secretly in a crowd. But nowadays the painters make (their models) put on official clothes and caps and sit down with their gaze fixed on one object, their faces are mute and their manners restrained. How could such a man's character be seen?

" There is some part in every man where his particular disposition resides. Some have it in the eyebrows, some in the nose or the mouth. Ku K'ai-chih said : ' By adding three hairs on the cheek I brought the portrait to life.' In this case the man's characteristics were in the cheek and the beard.

" Yu Mêng (an actor) imitated Sun Shu-ao by clapping his hands, talking and laughing to such a point that people said : ' The dead have returned to life.' Did he do it by imitating the whole body of the man? No, he did it by grasping the peculiar characteristic of the man. If the painters understood this principle, each one of them could be called a Ku K'ai-chih or a Lu T'an-wei.

" Ch'ên Huai-li from the Southern Capital made my portrait. Everybody thinks that it is perfect. Huai-li's manners are those of a first-class scholar. He is very respectful and his ideas reach beyond the brush-and-ink work. That is why I have made him known by writing the above."

Su Shih was after all, a man of classical taste, and the old masters like Ku K'ai-chih and Lu T'an-wei were to him examples of the highest perfection in figure painting. He evidently found in them, in spite of a certain primitiveness, a convincing rendering of form and character, the two qualities which to him were essential in great art. He calls these qualities " the constant form " and " the constant principle " and points out their decisive importance in painting, but does not give any further explanation as to their range of meaning or application. We are left to draw our own conclusions from the following æsthetic pronouncement :

" Often in talking about painting I have said, that human figures, birds, buildings and utensils all have their constant form, whereas mountains, stones, bamboos, trees, waves, clouds and mist have no constant form but a

constant principle. The loss of constant form is understood by everybody, but when the constant principle is
wanting, there are even among connoisseurs some who do
not understand it. All those painters, who try to deceive
the world and to create fame for themselves lean on (avail
themselves of) things which have no constant form.

"However, the lack of constant form does not get
beyond the formal loss; it does not spoil the whole thing,
but if the constant principle is not right, the whole thing
is ruined. With things which have no constant form, one
must pay special attention to the constant principle.
Among painters there are those who can render the form
in a minute fashion but as to the principle, it can be
rendered only by high characters and men of extraordinary
talent."

The "constant form" is evidently to Su Shih an
objective, formal quality, something which must not be
neglected in figure painting and in the representations of
buildings, etc. It seems closely akin to what we would
call correct proportions. But it is rather surprising that
he does not attribute any importance to it in connection
with such elements of landscape-painting as mountains,
trees and stones; they are simply classified with water,
mist and clouds, possibly because the artistic significance of
the landscapes was pre-eminently a matter of atmosphere,
distance and light. In such means of pictorial expression
it is no longer a question of constant form, but of the
more subtle and less tangible quality which he calls "the
constant principle." This is what gives a spiritual
significance to a work of art and it may thus, as already
pointed out, be identified with the all-important *ch'i yün*,
the resonance of the spirit. Su Shih's standpoint in regard
to the essential qualities in painting and the relative merits
of the old masters is quite in conformity with the classic
tradition, but he has his own way of expressing these
thoughts which gives them a fresh interest and sometimes
a beauty not to be found in the theoretical treatises. It
would be tempting to quote here a few more of his poems
on paintings or painters; because they are often
beautiful and contain vivid descriptions or characterizations

but they hardly contribute any critical ideas of general interest beyond those already discussed.

* * *

Several of the literary men who formed the circle of Su Shih have expressed themselves on painting in terms which are no less explicit than are those of the great poet. They too concentrated their main attention on the relative importance of formal likeness and spiritual value and arrived at conclusions very much like those pointed out above. Their pronouncements serve to give added relief to the ideas of Su Shih.

Shên Kua (1030-93), a close friend of Su Shih, who lived in retirement after he had suffered a disastrous defeat as a general, wrote in his " Dream Book " (*Mêng Ch'i Pi T'an*) :*

" The wonderful parts (or the mystery) of calligraphy and painting must be realized by the soul ; they can hardly be discovered in mere forms. Those who look at pictures are always able to point out faults of form, of likeness, of design and colouring, but I have seldom found people who have penetrated into the mysterious reason and depth of creative activity. Thus, for instance, Chang Yen-yüan criticizes Wang Wei for having painted things without regard to the four seasons, as he represented peach-blossoms, apricots, hibiscus and lotus-flowers in the same picture. I have in my possession a picture by Wang Wei representing Yüan An lying in the snow, and in the snow grows a banana. He had conceived the thing in his mind ; his hand responded, and it was done as conceived. This was because his creative activity and his reason resided in the spiritual part of his nature and because he grasped to a high degree the idea (inspiration of Heaven). But this is difficult to explain to common people."

It may, indeed, be difficult to explain the reason of it all, but the important point is, that the critics of the Sung period considered conformity with the seasons and the like far less significant than the painter's inspiring vision. Only a genius would dare to follow the impulse

* Cf. *Shu Hua P'u* Vol. 15, l. 14.

of his heart in spite of its deviation from the common and the ' natural.'

Tung Yü, *tzŭ* Yen-yüan, another friend of Su Tung-p'o, was prominent as a connoisseur of painting and particularly estimated as a writer of colophons. Some of his writings were collected in the *Kuang Ch'uan Hua Po*, from which a few extracts may be quoted :*

" Those who discuss painting say : ' The most wonderful point is in the birth of the idea (the conception) without loss of truth.'—By this statement they think that they have exposed the whole art of painting. But it has sometimes been asked : ' What is conception ? ' (how does the birth of the idea take place ?) To which may be answered : ' It is almost the same as naturalness ' (to be natural). If it is asked : ' What is naturalness ? ' One may answer : ' Those who do not differ from the truth will obtain it.' Futhermore, looking at the things made by heaven and earth, one may find that one life (or spirit) causes all the transformations. This moving power influences in a mysterious way all objects and gives them their fitness. No one knows what it is, yet it is something natural. The painters of to-day are truly wonderful ; they form the shapes and spread the colours in imitation of the objects trying thus to obtain their likeness. This is from the first to the last done by human power. How could it be harmonized with the working of nature ? "

Tung Yü's words give a more general philosophical explanation of the artist's conception than had been offered by previous critics : It should be, according to him, a sudden realization of the fundamental naturalness or truth of a motif, the inherent vitality which is produced by the all-pervading spirit or life. This pantheistic attitude is essentially the same as may be found in many romantic painters and philosophers of later date in the Western world, and which, *au fond*, even though they may not have expressed it in words, never was quite foreign to the great masters' conceptions. To Tung Yu this moving power is what gives objects their fitness and

---

Reprint in *Wang Shih Hua Yüan.*

causes all the transformations in nature. It cannot be defined; it must be observed and experienced by the artist who otherwise never will be able to render the true nature or significance of shapes and colours. This is further explained by the same writer:

"Likeness is much appreciated in painting, but is that merely a matter of the outer form? The important point is not to look for this quality in that which makes outward likeness (resemblance). The painters of to-day in brushing the ink and arranging the colours are copying the shapes, and when they find that they have obtained resemblance, they are swelling with happiness. The colours, red, white, green, purple, the pistils, stamens and petals of the flowers, their forms and position, etc., are well rendered, so that even ordinary people recognize the sunflower or the peony. All the hundred flowers and the peculiar blossoms are rendered according to their shapes. How could it then be said, that likeness is so precious? From this it may be realized that those who have not their heart in painting (a deep understanding) look first for the created things." The popular tendency was evidently then, just as in later times, to look for objective resemblance with material things rather than for æsthetic significance.

But of the work of real artists he says:

"Out of the forms of nature the images are produced; they are brought out by the conception which seizes the natural. They are first seen in the mind like flowers and leaves detaching themselves and beginning to sprout. Then they are given their outward shapes and colours by the work of the hand. They (such painters) seldom seek for likeness as support for their ideas (conceptions)."

The vision or conception of the mind is the primary thing. It marks the birth of the picture, and may be likened to the first sprouts of the plants. Drawing and colouring are secondary; if the conception is right, they also will fill their proper functions. The work of the hand must be guided by the vision of the mind, not by exterior models. This is a principle of leading importance, emphasized by many critics as for instance by Su Shih in his words quoted above: "You must first realize the whole thing completely in your mind," etc.

Tung Yü returns to the same point more than once, varying his expressions slightly; "When discussing paintings people talk about their likeness, and in talking about the shapes, they often say that the pretentious pictures do not convey an outward (resemblance). But if they say that the soul of things has been grasped and perfectly expressed, then certainly the traces of the brush-work are obliterated. Can that be done simply by matching the red with the green, or by seeking for the resemblance and copying it on a scroll by means of boundary lines? Painters who work in this way do not know how to ' take off the clothes and sit cross-legged '; they should rather give up painting and run into the garden."

In real pictures which render the soul of things, the technical execution should no longer be obvious, the brush-strokes should not attract too much attention, the colouring and decorative effect should be subservient to the truth conceived in the mind—a mystic communion with the all-pervading life or spirit which again is hinted at by the often quoted saying of Chuang-tzŭ: "The painter takes off his clothes and sits cross-legged."

*   *   *

Mi Fei (1051-1107) was, no doubt, one of the finest connoisseurs in the Sung period and his famous collection of paintings consisted of very choice things, but in his pronouncements on art collected under the title *Hua Shih*, he dwells less on general principles than on merits and faults of single specimens.* He is full of spite and satire against the rich people who collect old paintings, but he hardly ever gives a definite conclusive statement as to the quality which should be decisive for artistic appreciation. It is rather implied than defined in his critical words.

" The wealthy people of to-day who have a natural liking for art and want to pose as refined (connoisseurs) borrow the ears and the eyes of others ; such men may be called amateurs. They place their pictures in brocade

---

* Reprint in *Chin Tai Pi Shu.*

PLATE VIII

HILLS IN MIST
Attributed to Mi Fei (1052-1109, Sung dynasty)

PLATE IX

TRAVELING AMONG RIVERS AND MOUNTAINS
Fan K'uan (Sung dynasty, 10th-11th cent.)

bags and provide them with jade rollers and consider them as most precious and secret things, but when one opens them, one cannot help being overcome by laughter. I often pressed my hand on the table and cried out : ' It is enough to make one die of shame.' Wang Hsin often heard me make this exclamation, and he too said it very often. He taught it to Ts'ao Kuan-tao who often repeated it. Every time he saw a laughable thing, he exclaimed : ' Mi Yüan-chang said, it is enough to make one die of shame.'

" Modern painters very seldom represent ancient motifs. Those who do that, do not investigate old costumes and head-gear, so all their work makes one laugh."

Mi Fei expressed himself very contemptuously not only about collectors but also about the contemporary painters ; none of them was, according to his judgment comparable to the masters of T'ang and pre-T'ang times ; most of their works he found " good only for defiling the walls of tea-houses and wine-shops." He says : " They do not belong to the class of men whom I discuss ; even nameless and unclassified old specimens of brush-work may be esteemed as better friends."—It is almost surprising to find that those whom he appreciated most were the classical masters of well established fame ; even Li Lungmien, the greatest of his contemporaries, is not mentioned without criticism and a hint that he was hardly as good as Mi himself. Mi Fei's scornful criticism seems, indeed, to be coloured by exaggerated self-esteem and lack of sympathy, which made him unable to see the merits in men who did not follow the same manner as himself.

The following classification of various kinds of pictures is also characteristic of Mi Fei : " The study of Buddhist pictures implies some moral advice ; they are of a superior kind. Then follow landscapes, which possess inexhaustible delights, particularly when they have haze, clouds and mist effects ; they are beautiful. Then come pictures of flowers and grass. As to pictures of men and women, birds and animals, they are for the amusement of officials and do not belong to the class of pure art treasures."

Here again Mi Fei speaks from a strictly personal point of view. His own activity as a painter was mainly limited to those hazy landscapes executed in Indian ink, while the painters of the official or academic class devoted themselves largely to figures, animals and birds. This may have been a sufficient reason for him to despise such kinds of paintings, yet, in another connection, he presents some general reasons for this classification:

"Generally speaking, figures, bulls and horses may be drawn after models and be made alike; landscapes cannot be made by copying but only by the skill of the heart which is superior in the things that it grasps."

One may, indeed, wonder why no other motifs than landscapes might be grasped by the heart and be utilized as symbols of artistic expression. However this may be, the remark by Mi Fei is another characteristic testimony of the supreme position of monochrome landscape painting among these masters of the Northern Sung period.

Mi Fei's son, Mi Yu-jên, followed very closely in the footsteps of his father as a landscape painter and he was no less convinced of his own artistic excellence, although he devoted much of his time to a very successful official career. The sayings of his which have been reported, are coloured by his self-esteem:

"The people of the world know that I am skilful in painting, and they vie with each other to get hold of my works. But there are very few who know how I do my painting; they have not got the eye of superior (spiritual) perception and are incapable of understanding it. It is not done by glancing at old and modern painters. The merit (conditions) of the old paintings is (to me) like a hair in the big ocean. The things do not touch or excite me when I sit down quietly, cross-legged like a monk, forgetting all the troubles and harmonizing myself with the vast blue emptiness."

Mi Yu-jên evidently sought his inspiration in the state of introspection or meditation which was practised particularly by the painters who stood in touch with the school of Ch'an Buddhism. To them it became a means of developing the intuitive and creative faculties of the mind, and it was practised not only by artists but also by beholders who wanted to penetrate into the real meaning of a work of art. Thus we are informed by the well-known writer and connoisseur Huang T'ing-chien (1050-1110), a close friend of Su Shih and Mi Fei, that he did not understand painting before he learned how to enter into meditation and to realize " the state of no-vexation " ; " then, in looking at pictures, I understood completely the cleverness and stupidity, the skill or vulgarity of the painters down to the smallest detail, and I entered into the mysterious. But how could one speak about this to people who have seen only a few things and heard only a little."

The real understanding and appreciation of painting was to these men something almost as difficult and mysterious as creative activity ; it demanded a power of penetration and communion with the spirit of the work not inferior to the *ch'i yün* of the painters.

*　　*　　*

The activity of the great painters and gentleman-scholars, whose words have been quoted in the preceding pages, was in most cases limited to the latter half of the 11th century ; they passed away at the very beginning of the Emperor Hui Tsung's reign (1101-1126). Consequently they took no part in the efforts to organize the artistic activity and æsthetic interests in an official institution. The *T'u Hua Yüan*, or the Imperial Academy of Painting, was mainly the result of the emperor's personal interest in painting. His ambition was to direct it not only in an administrative sense but also from an æsthetic point of view. He was the highest authority in matters relating to art as well as to religion and he took an active part for instance in selecting subjects for the examinations and in criticizing and correcting the works of the painters.

We are told by Têng Ch'un, the author of *Hua Chi*, a collection of biographies of painters of the Northern Sung period (published 1167), that the emperor used to gather painters in the palace gardens and have them paint various kinds of flowers and birds in order to test their power of observation and their faculty of giving life-like representations of the charming models. On one occasion some of the painters were told to make a picture of a pheasant walking in the garden. They did wonderful things, which seemed strikingly natural, but the emperor said, that they all were wrong. Nobody could see the reason for this condemnation, but some time later on the emperor called them together again and pointed out, that when a pheasant is climbing a rock, it does not lift the right foot first, as represented by the painters, but the left!

This anecdote may serve as an example of several similar ones, reported by Têng Ch'un and other writers, which all tend to show that the imperial art patron was particularly interested in a minutely naturalistic type of painting. To quote the above-mentioned writer: " His expert knowledge was complete and thorough, his brush-work divine; he mastered every kind of subject and combined all the Six Principles of painting but specialized in feathers and furs " (birds and animals). It might seem as if such an attitude would be most closely connected with Confucian conservatism and a rather positive philosophy of life, free from romantic dreams or flights of imagination, but this was by no means the case in regard to Emperor Hui Tsung. He was a most enthusiastic supporter of the Taoists; the longer he lived, the more he became involved in the phantasmal experiments and speculations of the Taoist doctors. To what extent such views inspired his own artistic creations is a question that may here be left open, but it should be observed that they find interesting expression in the famous catalogue of his picture collection, known as *Hsüan Ho Hua P'u*. In this publication the pictures are divided into ten different classes or categories, of which the first is devoted to ' Taoist and Buddhist Painters', and is introduced by the following remarks:

" The aim of the Taoists is to acquire virtue, to rely on kindness and to find recreation in the arts.* That is

---

* This phrase is a free quotation from *Analects*, Book VII. 6. Legge translates it as follows : " Let the will be set on the path of duty. Let every attainment in what is good be firmly grasped. Let perfect virtue be accorded with. Let relaxation and enjoyment be found in polite arts."

their art. He who sets himself on the path cannot forget the fine arts; on the contrary, he finds special enjoyment in them. Painting is also one of the arts. When one approaches the wonderful one knows not whether art is Tao or Tao is art. Thus Tzŭ Ch'in cut the baton (for beating the drum) and Lun Pien made the wheel* (according to Tao); in the same way the ancients painted scholars. They made people look at these with reverence, and as people looked at the images, they realized the virtues of the models. That cannot be called a small advantage."

The manner of expression in the above quotation may seem rather vague, but its general sense seems to be, that cultivation of Tao is a preparation for enjoyment and understanding of art. The standpoint is the same as that already defined by Chang Yen-yüan, though expressed with more emphasis in regard to Taoist virtues and the essential unity between Tao and art.

Another of the short introductions in the *Hsüan Ho Hua P'u*, which is of particular interest in this connection, is the one devoted to landscape painting. It also reflects the Taoist standpoint and gives at the same time some hints about the particularly strong and weak points in the works of the 'gentlemen-painters.' It reads as follows:

"The mountains give protection, the streams give moving energy, the ocean extension, the earth support. The spiritual beauty of Nature (the Creator), the brightness and darkness of *yin* and *yang*, the distances of thousands of miles, all this can be represented within a few feet. But if one does not carry in the heart the hills and valleys, which are to be represented, one cannot do it. From the T'ang to the Sung period the most famous landscapists were not professional painters but mostly high officials (i.e., 'red girdles'), or great scholars (gentlemen). These men grasped the spirit-resonance, even though they sometimes were wanting in brush-work; or, if skilled in brush-work, feeble in composition. Those who combined all the wonderful points were seldom found. The ancients

---

.* Tzŭ Ch'in and Lun Pien are master artisans quoted by Chuang-tzŭ as examples of men who knew how to work in accordance with Tao.

were dangerously in love with springs and stones and had an incurable weakness for mist and clouds. They were hermits and scholars who attracted ridicule : Landscape paintings cannot be sold in the street ; they do not correspond to the taste of common people."

According to this statement, landscape painting was still one of the most exclusive kinds of painting, practised mainly by gentlemen-scholars as a kind of romantic expressionism or visual poetry. It was the art of the most advanced geniuses, who in some instances were no less prominent as writers, poets and critics than as painters. Their words must for us serve as substitutes for much that has been lost with their pictures.

THE SUNG PERIOD

HISTORIANS AND THEORETICIANS

IF we turn from poets and painters to historical writers and critics we shall find that they present the subject from a somewhat different point of view. They do not dwell only on the psychological attitude of painters, the inspiring force and its transmission by brush-strokes, but enter also into definitions of faults and merits and discussions of the traditional four classes and six principles of painting. It may be, that none of these men penetrated as deeply into the mysteries of the artists' creative activity as did Kuo Hsi or Su Shih or gave as striking expression to the essentials in art, but they tell us more about how paintings should be appreciated and classified. Yet, it must be remembered that they are not analytical in a modern sense, they never attempt anything like a comprehensive system of æsthetics, but limit themselves to comparatively brief comments on the traditional principles. It is only towards the end of the Ming dynasty that theoretical discussions swell out into more independent treatises.

The earliest of these historical writers who may be remembered in this connection is Liu Tao-ch'un who was active during the first half of the 11th century. His biographies of painters of the Five Dynasties period, *Wu Tai Ming Hua Pu I*, was published in 1059 (the date of the preface), and this was followed by a similar work on some painters of the Northern Sung period, called *Shêng Ch'ao Ming Hua P'ing*.* The preface to this book is not dated, but it contains some interesting remarks on what the author calls the " six qualities " and the " six important points " in painting, beside some advices as to the critical study and classification of pictures, and may consequently be quoted in its entirety :

" The secret of understanding painting consists in knowledge of the six important points and discrimination

---
* Both works are reprinted in *Wang Shih Hua Yüan*.

of the six qualities (or merits). Which are the six important points ? Spirit-resonance combined with strength is the first ; skill in all manners and rules, the second ; strange effects combined with reason, the third ; rich and variegated colouring, the fourth ; natural movement, the fifth ; to learn from the masters and avoid their faults is the sixth.

" Which are the six qualities ? To be coarse and vulgar, yet strive for brush-work, is the first ; to be hard and rude, yet strive for refinement, the second ; to be delicate and skilful, yet strive for strength, the third ; to be violent and eccentric, yet strive for reason, the fourth ; to be without ink (to work in a dry fashion), yet strive for tone, the fifth ; to paint in an ordinary fashion, yet strive for quality, is the sixth.

" When one knows the six important points and one is able to discriminate the six qualities, one can quite naturally make distinctions, even though the pictures (are so numerous that they) fill up boxes and cover walls.

" Generally speaking, one should avoid looking at pictures when the weather is covered and dark, when there is a strong wind whirling about, in a room which is facing North (dark) or at night in the light of a candle. Under such conditions one should not look at pictures, because it is quite impossible to grasp their rare and wonderful aspects and very difficult to estimate the six important points and the six qualities. One must do it on a bright day when the clouds have cleared away and the sky is pure, in an empty room facing South, using the principal wall for spreading the pictures. The spirit should be perfectly calm, all anxieties brushed away and the eyes unobstructed. The proper method of looking is, first to observe the general appearance, then to decide what is to be retained and what rejected, to grasp the fundamental idea, and finally to search out its reason. This method is the very key to the estimation of pictures. If one observes some faults in a picture one should not criticize them but rather look for the skilful parts, and if one observes some merits in a picture, one should not extoll them but rather search for its stupid parts. Experienced beholders grasp out of all the merits and faults the six important points and rely on the six qualities. And they know how to qualify their estimation by applying the three classes.

" The three classes are called divine, wonderful and skilful. If one understands to which class the picture belongs, there will be no talk of qualities and faults, no criticism or praise, nothing about skill or lack of skill; the estimation will be self-evident. It may be said, that looking at pictures of Sakyamuni Buddha makes one esteem grandeur and mercy, looking at pictures of Lohans makes one wish to be like them (?), looking at pictures of Taoists makes one wish to be lonely, leisurely and pure, looking at figure paintings makes one esteem the mien and manner of refined spirits, looking at pictures of animals makes one esteem tameness and domestication as well as unrestrained wildness, looking at flowers and bamboo makes one esteem graceful beauty and quiet charm, looking at birds makes one wish for wings to soar about, looking at landscapes makes one esteem far expanses and vast and desolate places, looking at demons and spirits makes one esteem muscular strength and strange transformations, looking at wooden buildings makes one esteem constructive beauty and receding depth. Modern painters sometimes neglect the six important points and sometimes leave out the six qualities, but think that they are nevertheless able to reach the goal. It is just as strange as a man climbing up a tree to catch fish, or some one drawing water to obtain fire. Such things are impossible."

Liu Tao-ch'un's six important points are evidently formed after the model of Hsieh Ho's Six Principles, though he has tried to make them rather more specific in relation to painting. He has combined the two first principles into one point, instead of conformity with the objects he emphasizes movement and instead of composition he demands original (strange) effects combined with reason, and in addition to all the others he brings in (as the second point) " skill in all manners and rules," which also may apply to the brush-work. Whether his modifications mark a progress in the definition of the fundamentals of painting may be questioned, but they show at least a new attempt, a fresh intellectual approach to the traditional problems.

The " qualities," which are defined by opposition of terms, are of a more general nature and can evidently not all be combined in one picture ; they are virtues or merits depending on the painter's character as much as on his training and mastery of the means. We will find that later critics often used similar antithetical terms, and it may well be that Liu Tao-ch'un was the first who introduced them.

The rest of his preface reflects a most conscientious manner of approach. Pictures should be studied only under proper conditions and in a methodical fashion which makes it possible to grasp their merits, even if they are not entirely good. Every picture should be judged according to the " important points " and placed in its proper class, then all quarrels about merits and faults would cease. When they are rightly understood, they all have a message to convey and exercise an influence according to their motifs and the way in which these are rendered. The fundamental importance of the art of painting is still, according to Liu Tao-ch'un as it is to his predecessors of earlier periods, to make the beholder experience the same identification with the thing depicted as the artist felt at the moment of creation. Otherwise there will be no enjoyment, no realization of the meaning of art.

*   *   *

Slightly younger and better known than Liu Tao-ch'un was Kuo Jo-hsü whose treatise *T'u Hua Chien Wên Chih* became one of the most appreciated writings on painting of the Sung period. It forms a kind of continuation to Chang Yen-yüan's famous work and is mainly filled with biographical records about painters from the end of T'ang down to the year 1074. As an introduction to the historical notes he has written some short chapters on theoretical topics such as " *Ch'i yün* which cannot be learned," and " Merits and Faults in the Use of the Brush." Kuo Jo-hsü's work was, according to the preface, composed in the Yüan Fêng era (1078-1085) and has passed through several editions. It is often quoted by the leading critics and serves, also in its theoretical sections, as a guide for later writers on similar subjects.

The first named chapter, which is devoted to a discussion of *ch'i yün*, opens with an enumeration of Hsieh Ho's Six Principles* and is continued as follows : " The definition of the essentials of the Six Principles has not changed since ancient times. The structural use of the brush and the four following principles may be acquired by study, but the spirit-resonance (*ch'i yün*) must be inborn in the painter. It can certainly not be acquired by skill or dexterity, nor can one arrive at it through months and years (of study). It is secretly blended with the soul ; one does not know how, yet it is there.

" I have often tried to explain it and to observe it in the extraordinary works of ancient times made by high officials, great sages, hermits and superior scholars. They exercised their art in accordance with virtue, penetrated into the hidden mysteries and expressed their noble sentiments in painting. When men are of a high class, the spirit-resonance must also become high, and when the *ch'i yün* is high, it is inevitably followed by *shêng tung* (the life-movement). Then it may be said, that their works contain the very spirit of the spirit and the essence of ability. A picture which is permeated by *ch'i yün* is considered a precious thing by the whole world, but if this quality is lacking, neither skill nor thought can prevent it from becoming artisan's work. Although it is called a picture, it isn't really painting.

" Master Yang did not receive it (the *ch'i yün*) from his teacher, nor did Lun Pien transmit it to his son. It is obtained by the individual through the inspiration of Heaven, and it issues from the recesses of the soul. It may also be perceived in the styles of people's signatures,†

---

* In Kuo Jo-hsü's transcription of Hsieh Ho's Third Principle the word *Shên*, spirit, has been substituted for the word *Wu*, objects ; it reads thus in translation : " Conform with the spirit to give likeness " : a rendering which evidently contains a very arbitrary transposition of Hsieh Ho's ideas, if it is not a slip.

† *Ya tzŭ* is an expression used for the more or less illegible signs or identity marks, written in grass characters, which commonly ser*r*e as signatures.

which may be called the seals of their hearts (minds), because they originate in the heart and are shaped by thought (mind). All the vestiges which unite (blend) in the heart may be called seals. They are innumerable as they include all the affections, anxieties and experiences which influence the heart, and when they blend with it, they become seals. What then about calligraphy and painting, which are done by transferring thoughts and sentiments to silk or paper? Are not these also seals? The signatures (*ya tzŭ*) preserve the nobility and meanness, the adversities and successes (of the writer). How could calligraphy and painting fail to reflect the high or the low *ch'i yün*? Painting is (in this respect) quite the same as calligraphy. Master Yang said: 'Words are sounds of the heart (mind), calligraphy is painting of the heart; both reveal whether the man is a superior character or of a low kind.'"

Kuo Jo-hsü's exposition of *ch'i yün* contains no fundamentally new ideas, but it throws more light on the subject than do any of the earlier discussions. He represents this mysterious quality as a vitalizing force issuing from the innermost recesses of the painter's consciousness; "it belongs to the individual who gives it out from the recesses of his soul." It is inborn in the painter as a gift of Heaven and grows in silence like a flower, which cannot be forced or constrained by outward means. All the emotions and experiences through which the painter may pass leave impressions on his heart, they become like seals or marks on his heart and contribute to mould his character. And when he expresses himself in writing, the written signs or characters will inevitably reflect his inner disposition, a fact which forms the base of " divination " by graphology. The same holds true of painting which, like calligraphy, serves to transfer—by means of brush-strokes—"thoughts and sentiments on silk." The two arts reveal in a similar way " the seals of the heart," in other words, they reflect the character of the man, which is simply an outward clothing or practical manifestation of *ch'i yün*, the source of art. Consequently only noble souls and high characters can produce really fine paintings.

The conclusion is inevitable and has been repeated over and over again by Chinese critics, but the estimate of a man's character may, of course, vary to some extent, according to the standards applied. Mi Yu-jên who quotes the theory about the written characters as " the seals of the heart," makes the following remark :

" According to this statement, paintings must also be the seals of the heart, but since ancient times nobody who was not a genius could understand it. Indeed, how could it be understood by the simple workmen of the market-places ? "

The problem of art-appreciation had evidently also its ethical side, or it may rather be said, that the ethical standards of these men also found an æsthetic expression. The two sides of the question were so closely interlinked, that it seemed unnatural to draw any dividing lines ; all the forces of the artist's personality had to be harmoniously blended and tuned in order to serve the creative activity. This was the precondition ; then followed the actual artistic work, the visualizing of the inspiring ideas and their transmission by brush and ink to the paper or silk. This side of the problem is to some extent discussed by Kuo Jo-hsü in the chapter dealing with " Merits and Faults in the Use of the Brush " :

" In painting, *ch'i yün* grows out of the wanderings of the heart. The spiritual beauty is produced by the use of the brush ; from this one may realize how difficult it is to use the brush properly. Thus Ai-pin said : ' Only Wang Hsien-chih could do the one-stroke writing, and only Lu T'an-wei could do the one-stroke painting.' One manner of writing does not suit every kind of composition ; nor does the shape of one object correspond to all ; yet one can do them completely from beginning to end with one stroke of the brush. The brush must be nimble, move swiftly in a continuous and connecting manner, so that the flow (arteries) of life is not interrupted as the thoughts precede the brush. But the brush is also in the thoughts, and when the picture is finished, all the thoughts are there, and the image corresponds completely to the spirit. When the painter is inwardly serene, when his spirit is at ease and his thoughts calm, the mind is not exhausted and the brush not restrained.

" Formerly when Prince Yüan of Sung desired to have some pictures executed, all the painters arrived promptly, saluted him reverently and stood upright with their brushes and papers. But one of them arrived late ; he came in very quietly and made no fuss about presenting compliments. Nor did he remain standing, but slipped into a side-room. As the master sent somebody to look after him, he was found seated cross-legged, partly undressed. The prince said : ' That is good, he is a real painter.'*

" In painting there are three kinds of faults, all connected with the use of the brush, i.e. 1. Stiffness, 2. Carving, 3. Tying (or Knotting). Stiffness depends on a weak wrist and a too dense brush, which does not move (give and take) freely ; the shapes of the objects become flat and thin ; the strokes have no rounding sweep. Carving is caused by hesitation in the turning of the brush ; the heart and the hand do not correspond, and the outlines of the pictures are drawn in sharp angles. Tying results if the brush does not move when one wants it to move and does not spread (or scatter), when it should do so ; the work becomes like a thing congealed and obstructed which cannot flow freely :—By this I have not exhausted the three faults, only raised one corner (of the question). The painters seldom pay attention to all these faults, and the beholders are obliged to wash them out."

The secret of the brush-work, according to Kuo Jo-hsü, is its uninterrupted flow, the spontaneity and agility with which it transfers the thoughts and sentiments of the painter. The greatest calligraphist and the greatest painter of antiquity reached the very acme of this art by writing whole pages or doing complete pictures with one continuous stroke. But this is possible only when mind and heart are in harmonious co-operation with the hand, and the whole nature of man is in equipose as indicated in

---

* The anecdote is borrowed from Chuang-tzŭ. It is included in Giles' translation, p. 270, where it is told in slightly different words, ending : " He will do it," cried the prince, " he is a true artist." It has been damned as a forgery considering the anachronism of brushes and ink, which, however, does not lessen its value as an illustration.

the previous chapter. Then nothing prevents the flow of *ch'i yün*; the mind reflects the inspiring flame and the brush transfers it freely to the silk.

The three faults which Kuo Jo-hsü describes as the results of weakness, hesitation and inability to move the brush with sufficient ease at will are the common obstructions to a free and uninterrupted flow of the brush. They became, as said above, accepted by later critics, who sometimes completed them by definitions of other faults. It is possible that Kuo Jo-hsü took them over from some earlier writer, but it was in his words that the ideas survived. His position as a critic and historian of painting became gradually almost as well established as that of Hsieh Ho or Chang Yen-yüan, even though his contributions to the history of Chinese æsthetics were more limited than were those of his predecessors.

*　　*　　*

Closely connected with Kuo Jo-hsü's treatise are some of the critical observations by Han Cho, a little known painter and military official in the reign of the Emperor Hui Tsung. His essay which is called *Shan Shui Ch'un Ch'üan Chi* and preceded by a preface, dated 1121,* is largely devoted to landscape painting and contains very detailed observations about the proper way of painting mountains, water, trees, stones, clouds and mist, rain and snow, figures and buildings, etc., but it includes also notes on brush-work and on *ch'i yün*, and a final chapter on " How to Observe and Discriminate Pictures." Some of his observations are of particular interest to us, because they contain more explicit descriptions of the painter's work than do most other writings of the same period. The author was evidently familiar with Kuo Jo-hsü's treatise, but he enlarges upon it and adds some further comments by which the intimate relation between the technical execution and the inspiring impulse is well brought out. The main part of the chapter on brush-work is worth quoting in this connection :

" Painting is brush-work in accordance with the revolutions of the mind (or heart). It must be conceived

---

* Reprint in *Wang Shih Hua Yüan.*

before it takes shape. It is reached only after the rules have been mastered. It is secretly united with the Creator and with the power of Tao. When the brush is grasped, it scatters numberless images, and one may with a tuft of hair sweep over a thousand *li*. Thus the brush serves to establish shape and substance and the ink to divide the light from the dark. Complete landscapes are made with brush and ink. In Wu Tao-tzǔ's pictures the brush was overwhelmingly strong; he brought matter into subjection with his painting. It has often been said, that Wu Tao-tzǔ's landscapes show brush but no ink, and that Hsiang Jung's landscapes have ink but no brush. These two masters were not completely good, only Ching Hao grasped the merits of the two sages and formed a style which was entirely good.

" If the ink is used too abundantly, the proper style is lost, the brush-work is spoilt and becomes muddy. If the ink is too sparse, the breath of life becomes timid and weak. Too much and too little are both faults.

" The most important point is to follow the rules and the style in a natural way; the *ch'i yün* will be complete and the living thoughts will be perfectly expressed. If this is lost sight of, the work will be defective. But how could one explain this to stupid and vulgar people?

" Do not grasp the brush before the spirit and the thoughts are concentrated. The ideas must all be in the eye before they are carried out with the brush; afterwards they may be developed in accordance with the style (rules); and then it may be said, that what is grasped by the mind is expressed by the hand.

" There is a kind of free and simple brush-work by which the thoughts may be completely expressed, and there is a very elaborate manner which yet is fine and delicate. Some painters give the living spirit with bold and strong brush-strokes, some work swiftly, and their brush-strokes flow easily. The whole warp and woof of the picture is in the brush-stroke.

" Yet, the faults in painting are quite numerous, and the greatest among them is the fault of vulgarity. It arises from superficiality, from attachment to the low (or commonplace), from neglecting the rules and from working without a plan. The brush is moved about in a confused way, and the forcible attempt to make things look pure and old-fashioned give them an appearance of being parched and dry. It is also foolish to work in such an elaborate and tight manner that one becomes entangled and tied up, or to make display of a brush-work which is not natural to oneself. These are faults in the use of brush and ink, against the rules and against *ch'i yün*.

" It has been said of old, that there are three faults in the use of the brush. The first is called stiffness, the second is called carving, the third is called tying (knotting). The fault of stiffness is caused by a weak wrist and a tight brush ; the movements (taking and giving) of the brush are quite defective, the forms of the objects are flat and one-sided ; there is no rounding sweep. The fault of carving results when the brush-strokes are emphasized, the movements of the brush are congealed, and the outlines are drawn arbitrarily in sharp angles. The fault of tying results when the brush does not move as one wants it to move and does not spread out when one wants it to spread ; the strokes become congealed and obstructed and do not flow freely. There is one more fault which may be called the fault of frostiness (?), which arises when the brush-strokes are careful and fine, yet stupid and conventional without suppleness ; although the brush and ink are moved the objects become as if dead, the forms as if carved and the picture quite frosty.

" When one starts to work with the brush one should first seek for *ch'i yün* and then mark the main structure (the bones) of the painting ; the finer points may be worked out afterwards. If the formal aspect is not properly prepared, all skill, elaboration and refinement cannot prevent your losing the *ch'i yün* ; but if you strive for *ch'i yün*, then the formal likeness will also result quite naturally. Furthermore, by thorough study one may also find that the principle of landscape painting is to keep to reality. If reality is not sufficient, one should lay down the brush, otherwise there will be too much ornamental beauty. Reality means substance and body (trunk), ornamental beauty is gracefulness ; substance and body originate from nature, ornamental beauty and gracefulness from the works of man. Reality is the root, ornamental beauty the branches. The style must be natural, but it can be reached only through practice. One must not neglect the root in following the branches, or forget the style in practising skill, as is done by the painters who are occupied only with ornamental beauty and are deficient in style. He who attends only to gracefulness and refinement destroys the spirit of life. It is a common fault. Who knows this principle of keeping to reality and leaving out ornamental beauty ?

" The brush may be used in a rough way or in a delicate fashion, it may be scattering, or it may be equalizing, it may be heavy or it may be light. None of these manners should be used alone, because then the distinction between the near and the far will not be clear, the effect of *ch'i yün* will be weak, and there will be no real picture. If the brush is too coarse, the picture will look empty and streaky, and if the brush is too fine, the *ch'i yün* will be destroyed. Each wrinkle, each dot, each hook, each stroke should reflect a thought and be according to the rule. If one does not follow the rules of the old masters, but draws real mountains, and if one does not divide the near from the far, the shallow from the deep, the picture becomes like a map. How could it then have style and *ch'i yün* ? "

Although very little is known about Han Cho's personal history, it may be supposed, that he was a member of the Emperor Hui Tsung's Academy, or at least, that he was closely associated with the kind of painting particularly cultivated by the academicians. His words reflect their attitude towards art and nature. His primary demands are for naturalness or the kind of reality which originates from nature, and for strict adherence to the rules (or conventions), whereas the greatest fault he can think of is the fault of vulgarity—observations which make us recall the painting competitions in the imperial gardens where the artists vied with each other in giving the most refined and faithful renderings of the trees, flowers and birds. Yet, the demand for spirit-resonance or vitality was no less essential for this highly naturalistic art than in other schools of painting, even though its expressions were subjected to definite rules and a strict adherence to objective nature (reality): " The most important point is to follow the rules and the style in a natural way, then the *ch'i yün* will be complete," and " if the formal aspect is not properly prepared. . . . you will lose the *ch'i yün*." The demand was not for spontaneity and superiority to binding rules, as with Kuo Hsi and Su Shih, but for careful observance of the rules. The manner should be correct, all exaggerations, whether in the direction of looseness or tightness, should be carefully avoided ; they will lead to vulgarity, to confusion or dryness. " If reality (*shih*) is not sufficient, one should lay down the brush." The most perfect style is the one which comes closest to nature ; empty skill and dexterity are destructive, because they lead away from nature. It seems almost as if Han Cho thought that hard and conscientious practice, in accordance with the rules, could turn a practitioner into a great painter ; yet he points out, that the spirit-resonance is of supreme importance and that this quality also may become a support of formal likeness, when properly expressed. His words may be said to reflect a kind of compromise or an attempt to combine, at least theoretically, the different attitudes towards painting which were represented by the various schools or masters.

The faults in brush-work which he enumerates are practically the same as those defined by Kuo Jo-hsü (from whom the definitions may have been copied) ; the additional fourth fault, which arises from a stupid and conventional handling of a pointed brush, is hardly more than a variation on the second or the third. But this may indeed have been the kind which was most common among academic painters.

In the chapter, called " How to Observe and Discriminate Pictures," Han Cho speaks again about the importance of *ch'i yün* and of proper style : " If the idea of life is pure and in accordance with the reason of things, it reveals practice and good style ; such pictures correspond to the rules."

Then he proceeds to enumerate six points or qualities which are of fundamental importance in painting and which consequently should also be looked for by those who "observe and appreciate pictures." They are no inventions of his ; we have met with them in the writings of Liu Tao-ch'un and Ching Hao, who expressed the same ideas in slightly different terms. Han Cho was, no doubt, familiar with the theories of the earlier writers, though he does not mention them except by a very general hint : "People of former times said there are six essentials in painting." His own definitions of the six important points are as follows :

"The first is *ch'i* (spirit or vitality). Those who master *ch'i* move the brush in accordance with the shapes (*hsing*) and obtain their likeness (*hsiang*) without error. The second is *yün*. Those who master *yün* give shape to the invisible (secret) as well as to the visible things in an original manner. The third is called *ssŭ* (thought or reflection). Those who reflect grasp with utmost keenness the important points and that which is appropriate to the objects. The fourth is called *ching* (scenery or atmospheric effects). Those who master *ching*, regulate the scenery in accordance with time and experience ; they grasp the mysterious (wonderful) and invent marvellous things. The fifth is called *pi* (brush). Those who are masters of the brush, rely on the rules but know at the same time how to conform with changing effects making them neither too material nor too ornamental ; their brush seems to be flying and stirring. The sixth is called *mo* (ink). Those who are masters of ink differentiate the high and the low, the vaporous and the flat, the deep and the shallow ; their manner is so natural that it seems as if they did not use the brush. He who commands all the six points is the most divine among the divine. But even if the painter does not master all the six points but possesses only one of them, his work may nevertheless be worth consideration."

What Han Cho has to say about these traditional six essential points does not contribute very much to their æsthetic significance. The expressions which he uses as explanations of the various points do not throw any new light; they explain less than they describe. When considered in connection with the preceding chapter they rather confirm the impression that Han Cho tried to interpret things as comprehensively as possible without pushing any point to great clearness or supreme importance. His treatise is to a large extent a compilation, but quite characteristic of the academic trend in Sung painting and consequently of considerable historical importance.

* * *

Kuo Jo-hsü's famous historical work, which contained information about the painters down to the year 1074, was continued at the beginning of the Southern Sung period by Têng Ch'un who compiled a treatise, *Hua Chi*, in which the painters' biographies were carried on to the year 1167.* In the preface to this book he writes:

" Since olden times there have been many amateurs, who have studied the art of painting very carefully. Consequently the records about it form more than one book. But in the T'ang period Chang Yen-yüan collected all the information about famous painters and classified them. His work reaches from Hsüan Yüan (prehistoric times) until the first year of Hui-ch'ang (841) and is called *Li Tai Ming Hua Chi*. In the present dynasty Kuo Jo-hsü wrote the *T'u Hua Chien Wên Chih*, which reaches from the first year of Hui-ch'ang to the seventh year of Hsi Ning (1074). These two books are the most important; other books are simply repetitions. From the Hsi Ning era until the present day 94 years have passed, and no amateurs have written on the painters of these years; therefore I have made these records.

" Since olden times men who possessed superior intelligence and refined skill like K'ai-chih, T'an-wei, Mo-ch'i, T'ao-tzŭ and others have been admired by the whole world, while ordinary workmen and common servants may be found in great quantities, but they did not dare to look at the blue sky beyond the dust. Someone said that Kuo Jo-hsü went too far, but I do not think so,

---

* Reprint in *Chin Tai Pi Shu.*

therefore I now place the high officials and hermit scholars in two different classes, thus establishing my own humble opinion. Those who are capable of clear criticism must accept my opinion."

More important in this connection are, however, the general notes on painting which Têng Ch'un adds after the historical sections. He calls them "Miscellaneous Sayings" (*Tsa Shuo*) and dwells here particularly on the close connection between painting and literary culture adding some remarks on the traditional principles of classification and the relative merits of earlier critics :

"Painting is the perfection of culture. Consequently many writers both of past and recent times have expressed their ideas about it. Chang Yen-yüan published a treatise on prominent painters of various dynasties, and more than half the number were of the T'ang period. Shao-ling (Tu Fu) composed poems in which he brought out completely the characteristics of things (forms and faces). Ch'ang-li (Han Yü) wrote essays in which not even the smallest detail was omitted. In the present dynasty Wên Chung Kung (Ou-yang Hsiu), the three Su (Su Hsün, Su Shih, Su Ch'ê), the two Ch'ao brothers (Ch'ao Pu-chih and Ch'ao Shuo-chih), Shan-ku (Huang T'ing-chien), Hou-shan (Ch'ên Shih-tao), Wan-ch'iu, Huai-hai (Chin Kuan), Yüeh-yen and the great master Li Lung-mien have either discussed the noble and essential qualities in art or worked with the brush in surpassing fashion. According to this, painting should not be called the only art ; its adversaries think that there have been since olden times, men who possessed literary culture but no skill in painting and no love of it. To them I would say : 'There may have been men of great culture who did not understand painting, but they were very few, and the men without culture who understood painting were also seldom seen.'

"The range of painting is very wide ; it comprises everything between heaven and earth. By revolving their thoughts and preparing the brush (licking the brush) the painters can represent the characteristics of everything, but there is only one method by which it can be done

OLD TREE AND BAMBOO
Wang T'ing-Yün (1151-1202, Chin dynasty)

PLATE X

PLATE XI

SCENERY OF THE HSIAO-HSIANG REGION
Attributed to Tung Yüan (10th cent., Five Dynasties period)

thoroughly and exhaustively. Which is that? It is called
the transmitting of the spirit. People think that men
alone have spirit; they do not realize that everything is
inspirited. Therefore Kuo Jo-hsü despised deeply the
works of common men. He said that though they were
called paintings, they were not painting (as art), because
they transmit only the forms but not the spirit. Consequently the manner of painting which gives the resonance
of the spirit and the movement of life is the foremost.
And Kuo Jo-hsü said that it has been practised only by
high officials and hermit scholars, which is correct.

" Since early times, experts and critics have divided
paintings into three classes: divine (*shên*), wonderful
(*miao*) and skilful (*nêng*). But Chu Ching-chên of T'ang
who wrote the *T'ang Ch'ao Ming Hua Lu*, added to these
three classes one more, which he called the *i* (spontaneous)
class, and after him Huang Hsiu-fu, who wrote the *I Chou
Ming Hua Chi*, placed the *i* class first, above the divine,
the wonderful and the skilful. Chu Ching-chên said,
that paintings of the *i* class are not restrained by ordinary
rules, they may reveal supreme qualities or faults. Why
should then this spontaneous class be placed after the
other three? Hsiu-fu who placed it above the others
was right. Finally the Emperor Hui Tsung, who made a
special study of the rules of painting established the following order: *shên*, *i*, *miao* and *nêng*.*

" I have often taken up the works of prominent scholars of the T'ang and Sung dynasties concerning painting
and thoroughly examined what all these men have to say,
and thus I have acquired some knowledge of their various
criticisms. Only Huang T'ing-chien is really exact and
severe. Mi Fei has a noble mind and wonderful eyes,
but he often makes exaggerated statements. Tu Fu and
Su Shih do not transmit fixed opinions, yet they are great

* In another connection Têng Ch'un offers the following explanatory remarks
on painters of the *i* class:

" Among the painters of the *i* class Sun Wei is the foremost. Later painters
usually did it in a disorderly fashion. Shih K'o and Sun Tai-ku may also be placed
in this class, but they could not avoid the coarse and the vulgar. As to Kuan-
hsiu and Yün-tzŭ and others, they were not afraid of exaggerations. Their
intentions may often have been noble, but they fell into vulgarity. Indeed, such
were these men."

geniuses, and one positive word of theirs may contain something unexpected which gives the self-evident. Tu Fu speaks of ' surpassing wonders which move the palace walls.' From this one may realize that the figures painted on the walls must have movement in order to be right. He also says : ' Please Sir, let go your brush to make the straight trunks.' To give the beauty of the tall forms one must know how to draw the joints which cannot be done without giving free flow to the brush. Su Tung-p'o again extolled the inherent reason in painting and said that the beginning is, to know the truth and to start from the root."

Têng Ch'un is in full accord with all his illustrious predecessors and has really very little of his own to add to their brilliant discussions. His insistence on the close correspondence between painting and literary culture is only a further development of Su Tung-p'o's saying :

" Poetry and painting follow the same laws ; it is by divine inspiration that they become pure and original."

This was the position of the most enlightened critics of the Sung period ; all that they have to say about the ' important points,' the ' qualities,' principles and classes are only explanatory tributes to an art, which to them was the essential, not to say the highest, expression of the creative mind and of an all-inclusive spiritual culture.

CH'AN BUDDHISM

AND ITS RELATION TO PAINTING

A SPECIAL place within the history of Chinese painting in the Sung period is usually accorded the painters who belonged to the Ch'an school of Buddhism. This may, indeed, be justified by the works of men such as Mu-ch'i, Ying-yü-chien and other Ch'an monks, but it should at the same time be observed, that the æsthetic ideals and modes of painting which are reflected in their works do not differ very radically from those of some of the other painters and critics who were active in the same period. The differences are often questions of degree or individual characteristics, rather than the results of opposite attitudes towards art. The aims and methods of the Ch'an masters were not essentially unlike those of the most prominent landscape and bamboo painters, whose ideals have been discussed in the preceding chapters, only they were carried to a still further stage of subjective impressionism. Monochrome ink-painting became in the hands of the Ch'an masters the most subtle and immediate expression for intuitive glimpses or reflections of their creative minds.

None of these pure Ch'an painters has left any writings or critical observations about their artistic activity—something which to them was entirely beyond intellectual definitions—but their general attitude, the psychological principles at the root of their activity, may to some extent be deduced from a study of the Ch'an philosophy.* This

---

* The word *Ch'an* is an abbreviation of *Ch'anna*, the Chinese rendering of dhyana, a Sanscrit term which usually is translated into Western languages as contemplation or meditation, words which, however, do not render the whole significance of Ch'an to the Chinese but only its meditative side.

The completest discussion of Ch'an and its historical development in China is found in Suzuki, *Essays in Zen Buddhism*, First Series, London, 1927, but in order to understand its philosophy it is necessary to be familiar with such Buddhist scriptures as the *Lankavatara Sûtra* and the *Sûtra spoken by the Sixth Patriarch*. The former has been edited in English by Dr. Suzuki (London, 1932), the latter by Dih Ping Tsze (Shanghai, 1930), and important portions of both have been made more easily accessible (in a rather modified form) in the publication by Dwight Goddard, called *A Buddhist Bible*. (Thetford, Vermont. 1932).

philosophy or school of Buddhism, which had been transmitted to China at the beginning of the sixth century by
the Indian patriarch Bodhi Dharma, was at the end of the
seventh moulded into a characteristically Chinese form
particularly through the activity of the Sixth Patriarch,
Hui-nêng (637-713) who also was the founder of the
" Southern School." He possessed to an eminent degree
the faculty of making the profound tenets of Ch'an
Buddhism acceptable to the Chinese; it became from this
time onward one of the most potent influences in the
cultural life of the nation, inspiring time and again not
only philosophers and artists but also rulers and statesmen
with its message of self-confidence and introspective
illumination. In the Southern Sung period (1127-1279)
it grew into a very widespread movement, fecundating
the fields of art and philosophy, an influence which is
evident in the neo-Confucian philosophy of Chu Hsi and
his followers. Among the artists who took it up some
were actually living as monks in the Ch'an temples around
Hang-chou, but to most of them the Ch'an tenets formed
simply a psychological preparation; they worked so to
say from the Ch'an point of view even if they did not
submit to the formal training or the monastic life of the
actual Ch'an disciples.

The reason for this recurrent success and tenacious
perseverance of Ch'an Buddhism in China, where so
many of the other Buddhist schools gradually decayed
and lost their hold over the minds of men, may be sought
not only in the inherent vitality of its message and its
very broad and practical scope, but also in its close correspondence with indigenous currents of thought which
had their source in Chinese Taoism. The Chinese Ch'an
masters were more or less familiar with Taoistic concepts,
and they presented their teachings in a form which was
more easily acceptable to their countrymen than other kinds
of Buddhism in which the metaphysical and dialectical
subtleties of Indian philosophy were more prominent.
Some of these Ch'an masters went, as a matter of fact, so
far in their endeavour to harmonize their teachings with
the ideas of Lao-tzŭ as to accept the term Tao as a synonym

for Buddhahood. One of them declared right out:
" Buddha is Tao, Tao is dhyana (*ch'an*)."

The most concise summing up of the principles of
the Ch'an teaching is found in the following words, traditionally ascribed to Bodhi Dharma:

> " A special transmission outside the scriptures;
> No dependence upon words and letters;
> Pointing directly to the heart (intuitive mind) of man;
> Seeing into one's own nature and attainment of
> Buddhahood."

Whether the stanza was composed by the First
Patriarch or by a later man (as is more probable), it contains
in a nutshell the meaning and method of Ch'an: According to tradition, it had been transmitted from Sage to Sage,
ever since the time of Sakyamuni himself, not by writing
but from mouth to ear, so to say, by life and example, by
action and application, by symbols and suggestions. The
Sixth Patriarch confirmed this in the following words:
" This teaching was handed down from the past patriarchs;
it is not a system of my invention. Those who wish to
hear the teaching should purify their minds first, and after
hearing it, they ought to clear up their own doubts as
the Sages did in the past." And when an inquirer asked
him whether he could impart any secret wisdom beside
that which had been handed down from generation to
generation, he answered: " What I can tell you is not
esoteric; if you turn your light inwardly, you will find
what is esoteric within you."

This is the way in which all mystics have spoken,
whatever age or school they may have belonged to: Look
within yourself; the treasure of wisdom is buried in your
own consciousness; if you wish to find it, you must search
it out, excavate it by your proper efforts. The teacher
can only point out the way, etc.—But in doing this he
may use various means and methods, fitting to the age
and the surroundings in which he lives. The Ch'an
masters were Chinese, imbued with the Chinese mode of
thinking and talking, and this may to some extent account
for their perplexingly abrupt and paradoxical manner of

imparting their instruction. The Chinese language itself and the way in which it is commonly used, whether in writing or speaking, is not analytical like Western languages but suggestive and evocative ; it usually implies more than the logical sequence of certain thoughts, and leaves a large margin for individual interpretation. The words as well as the written characters become symbols appealing to the imaginative faculty of man rather than to his reasoning mind, or blinds hiding the meaning for those who are not attuned to the ideas of the speaker and his point of view. It is altogether of a more symbolic, i.e. artistic, kind than the modern languages of the Western world.

The Ch'an teachers were evidently far advanced in using words as symbols or blinds ; they did it to such an extent that it sometimes is hard to tell whether their intention was to conceal or to communicate their ideas. Their appeal was usually to the student's intuitive faculty rather than to his reasoning mind. A mental shock was considered more valuable than a logical exposition, if it could be administered so that it served to " open the third eye," or to arouse the creative imagination. Naturally such methods appealed in particular to poets and painters to whom the appearances of the objective world were merely symbols of inner realities. As an example of the Ch'an method of interpretation the following stanza may be quoted :

> " Empty handed I go, and yet the spade is in my hands ;
> I walk on foot, and yet on the back of an ox I am riding ;
> When I pass over the bridge,
> Lo, the water floweth not but the bridge doth flow."

The phenomenal world is filled with mirages of the mind ; nothing of it is real ; they change and shift as the mind moves. This point of view is graphically illustrated by the following incident from the life of Hui-nêng. The master once came to a place where some monks were arguing on the fluttering of a pennant. One of them said :

'The pennant is an inanimate object and it is the wind that makes it move.' Another said : 'Both wind and pennant are inanimate things and the flapping is an impossibility.' A third monk protested : 'The flapping is due to a certain combination of cause and condition,' and a fourth one proposed an explanation in the following words : 'After all, there is no flapping pennant but it is the wind that is moving by itself.'—As the monks could not agree, Hui-nêng interrupted them with the remark : 'It is neither wind nor pennant but your own mind which flaps.'

The reply is most characteristic of the Ch'an attitude, according to which nothing really exists except as a reflection of the mind. The forms and phenomena which we perceive through the activity of the senses or by the discriminations of the intellect have no permanence or existence of their own. They form an ever changing stream of transformations and they would disappear altogether if the ceaseless operations of the reasoning mind and the senses could be stopped. If we want to obtain knowledge about the reality behind the appearances, their essence or 'Suchness,' we must raise ourselves to a state beyond intellection or ordinary thinking in terms of opposites. The thinker must be completely identified with the thought, the perceiver with his object of perception, and ordinary distinctions fade away. It is evident that such a state cannot be described in words which are subject to the reasoning mind, nor conditioned by any terms ; it is the state of 'Suchness' which also has been called the 'Great Void.' But it should be distinctly understood that this expression by no means implies nothingness or absence of life. Quite the contrary ; it signifies the highest form of reality, the universal aspect of life, a state of existence which contains everything but which cannot be realized by man before he has become self-conscious in the highest part of his being. "When you hear me talk about the void, do not fall into the idea of vacuity," said the Sixth Patriarch, and continued : "It is of the utmost importance that we should not fall into that idea, because when a man sits quietly and keeps his mind blank, he would be abiding in a state of the 'voidness of indifference.' The illimitable void of the Universe is capable of holding myriads of things. . . .Space takes in all these and so does the voidness of our nature. We say that Essence of Mind is great, because it embraces all things, since all things are within our nature."

The doctrine of the void (*sunyata*) and of mind-only (*cittamatram*) as presented by the Ch'an philosophers was, no doubt, less speculative than the philosophy of Nagarjuna, yet a teaching of deep and decisive importance for the whole Ch'an training. It was based mainly on the *Lankāvatāra sūtra*, where it is presented in words very much like those of the Ch'an masters, as may be seen from the following quotations :

" What appears to be external does not exist in reality ; it is indeed mind that is seen as multiplicity ; the body, property and abode are nothing but mind."

" It is better to cherish the notion of an ego substance than to entertain the notion of emptiness derived from the view of being and non-being ; for those who so believe fail to understand the fundamental fact that the external world is nothing but a manifestation of the mind."

The great fallacy is not simply to cling to the phenomena of the objective world but still more, to believe that such objective forms represent the only kind of existence and that their absence (" non-being ") is the same as nothingness. This is far from true, because reality (existence) is a matter of consciousness.

" When appearances and names are put away and all discrimination ceases, that which remains in the true and essential nature of things and, as nothing can be predicated as to the nature of essence, it is called Suchness of Reality."

This universal, undifferentiated, inscrutable ' Suchness ' is the one Reality but it is variously characterized as Truth, Mind-Essence, Transcendental Intelligence, Noble Wisdom, etc. It is the same ultimate reality which sometimes is characterized as illimitable Space or the all-containing Void, symbols which evidently have a relation also to the painters' conceptions and modes of expression.

We need hardly to dwell on the well-known fact, that the Chinese painters, and particularly those who worked in Indian ink, utilized space as a most important means of artistic expression, but it may be pointed out, that their ideas of space and their methods of rendering it were far from the same as in European art. Space was not to them a cubic volume that could be geometrically constructed, it was something illimitable and incalculable which might be, to some extent, suggested by the relation of forms and tonal values but which always extended beyond every material indication and carried a suggestion of the infinite. To call it atmosphere or something similar would hardly be correct, because it is not necessarily dependent on tones, vapours or washes of ink, it is just as often rendered simply by the bare silk or paper, the empty background from which the forms emerge.

The formal effectiveness of their space compositions is, indeed, closely connected with the position of the objects, usually quite irregular and often surprising, but the underlying concept, or the source from which it springs, is certainly not merely a formal or decorative device. When fully developed as in the compositions of the Ch'an painters, where the forms often are reduced to a minimum in proportion to the surrounding emptiness, the enveloping space becomes like an echo or a reflection of the Great Void, which is the very essence of the painter's intuitive mind. The correspondence may not be demonstrable, it may be a matter of feeling or intuition rather than a conscious calculation, yet it seems quite obvious when we know something about the psychological attitude which was developed by the Ch'an training. The painters who had arrived at an experience of the inner meaning of things or the essence of reality could hardly avoid using symbols of the same kind as the philosophers. As the things which they conceived were parts of their own consciousness, alive with their own vitality, they were given an added significance by their relation to the illimitable space, which is a symbol of ultimate reality.

The infinite source of knowledge which man carries within himself and his potential faculty of identifying himself with whatever he contemplates, is further developed in the *Lankāvatāra sūtra*, where three different aspects of mind or consciousness are distinguished, i.e. the discriminating (personal) mind, the intuitive mind, and the Universal Mind.

" The discriminating mind is the cause of the sense-minds and is their support and with them is kept functioning as it describes and becomes attached to a world of objects and then, by means of its habit-energy, it defiles the face of Universal Mind. Thus Universal Mind becomes the storage and clearing house of all the accumulated products of mentation and action since beginningless time."

" Between Universal Mind and the personal discriminating mind is the intuitive mind (*manas*) which is dependent upon Universal Mind for its cause and support and enters into relations with both. It partakes of the universality of the Universal Mind, shares in its purity and like it is above form and momentariness. . . But the intuitive mind enters (also) into relations with the lower mind-system, shares its experiences and reflects upon its activities."

The intuitive mind, or *manas*, is thus the link between the universal all-compassing mind by which it shares in transcendental intelligence and the differentiating mind-system which is dependent on sensuous perceptions and tied to the phenomenal world. It is further characterized in the *sūtra* as follows : "While it is not an individualized organ like the intellectual mind, it has that which is much better : direct dependence upon Universal Mind. While intuition does not give information that can be analyzed or discriminated, it gives that which is far superior : self-realization through identification."

The word intuition is here evidently used as a designation for man's highest faculty of perception, a kind of spiritual illumination which manifests only when the thoughts and sense-impressions of personal life have been brought into silence. It is the deepest form of meditation, which however, as sometimes pointed out by Ch'an masters, does not necessarily require the sitting in certain postures or strict formal exercises, but which may just as well be attained while a man is walking or working, if his mind is unobstructed and he meets the experience that lights the flame. It is the mysterious event which is called *wu* or *k'ai wu* (to become, to apprehend) in Chinese, and *satori* in Japanese, and which is the very aim of all Ch'an training. According to Suzuki, it means " the unfolding of a new world, hitherto unperceived in the confusion of a dualistically trained mind,"—a personal experience by which the whole outlook of life is changed. Many expressions are used for it ; as for instance : " the opening of the mind-flower," the " removing of the bar," or " the brightening up of the mind-works," and it is illustrated by striking incidents from the lives of the students. The following may serve as an example :

As Nan-yüeh Huai-jang, a master of the T'ang period, saw one of his pupils seated cross-legged all day meditating, he asked : ' What seekest thou here thus sitting cross-legged ? ' The pupil answered : ' My desire is to become a Buddha.' Thereupon the master took up a brick and began to polish it on a stone. ' What workest thou on so hard, my master ? ' asked the pupil. ' I am trying to turn this into a mirror,' came the answer. ' No amount of polishing will make a mirror of the brick, sir.'—' If so, no amount of sitting cross-legged, as thou dost, will make of thee a Buddha.'—' What shall I have to do then ? '— ' It is like driving a cart ; when it moveth not, wilt thou whip the cart or the ox ? '

The pupil made no answer, but the master explained further : " Dhyana does not consist in sitting or lying, the Buddha has no fixed forms. If thou seekest Buddhahood by thus sitting cross-legged, thou murderest him. So long as thou freest thyself not from sitting so, thou never comest to the truth."

The master evidently wanted to break the set moulds of the pupil's mind and make him realize that the quest in which he was engaged, meant something far beyond any formal exercises. The main thing was to make himself interiorly free, to remove the obstacles and open the way for the light, so that it might penetrate his whole conscious-

ness. The light is the same in all, it is the Buddha-nature
by which man is potentially omniscient and through which
he may see and comprehend the truth. " You should
know, that so far as Buddha-nature is concerned, there
is no difference between an enlightened man and an
ignorant one. What makes the difference, is that the one
realizes it, while the other is kept in ignorance of it,"
said the Sixth Patriarch. And he explains further how,
when it is fully active and realized by a man, it becomes
prajna, wisdom :

" The *prajna* immanent in the essence of mind of
everyone may be likened to the rain, the moisture of which
refreshes alike all sentient beings, living creatures as well as
trees and plants.—When rain comes in deluges, plants
which are not deep-rooted are washed away and die.
The same holds true of the slow-witted when they hear
about the teaching of the ' Sudden School.' The *prajna*
immanent in them is exactly the same as that of the very
wise man ; but they fail to enlighten themselves when the
dharma (truth or law) is made known to them, because
they are so thickly veiled by erroneous views and deep-
rooted infections :   The sun is thickly veiled by the clouds
and unable to show its light until the clouds are blown
away."

The efforts of the Ch'an students were to a large
extent directed to the brushing away of these clouds, the
cleaning of the mind by proper work, life and meditation.
But the opening of the intuitive faculty or the ' third eye,'
as it also was called, could not be forced or coerced by
outward means, postures or practices, nor by the accumula-
tion of intellectual knowledge or the repetition of sacred
formulas as in some other schools of Buddhism. It had
to grow naturally as the flower grows and then open
into bloom when the season was ripe. To quote the
Lankāvatāra sūtra : " So long as the mind is distracted
and making conscious efforts, there can be no culmination
as regards the various vehicles ; it is only when the
mind is alone and quiet that it is able to forsake the
discriminations of the external world and seek realization
of an inner realm."

The words remind us of the art-critics' remarks about 'the divine painter,' he who works not by deliberation but from an irresistible creative impulse, something that is stronger than his ordinary personality and which makes him akin to the 'Great Creator,' the Universal Mind of Nature. In order to reach this state man must rise above all the distinctions and divisions of the discriminating mind or clean it so that it becomes like a bright mirror; only the spirit can reflect spiritual truth. Therefore it was said by a Ch'an master: "Ignore the distinction of subject and object; let the essence of mind and all the phenomenal objects be in a state of thusness. Then you will be in a *samadhi* all the time."

Or as said by Hung-jên, the Fifth Patriarch: "The deepest truth lies in the principle of identity. It is due to one's ignorance that the *mani*-jewel is taken for a piece of brick. But lo! when one is suddenly awakened to self-enlightenment, it is realized that one is in possession of the real jewel. . . . . Those who entertain a dualistic view of the world are to be pitied. . . . When we know that between this body and the Buddha there is nothing to separate one from the other, what is the use of seeking after Nirvana (as something external)." It is all to be found in the innermost consciousness of man, the spiritual heart or essence of his being.

Applied in the field of artistic activity this is a definition of the highest form of conception, the purest kind of inspiration: The knower becomes the object of his knowledge, the artist the thing he visualizes or conceives, and if he possesses the proper means of exteriorization, he will transmit in symbols of shapes or signs something which contains a spark of that eternal stream of life or consciousness which abides when forms decay.

When the distinctions fade away into relativity and the significance of things is esteemed not according to intellectual concepts and outward appearances but by their relation to the spiritual consciousness of man, the small and the large, the high and the low may become of equal importance. A single flower may reveal as much as a whole forest, a grain of dust be as wonderful as a mountain. This essential truth which evidently had a direct bearing on the attitude of the painters is illustrated in many sayings by the Ch'an masters as for instance the following by Yüan-wu (1063-1135), a monk of the Sung period:

"One particle of dust is raised and the great earth lies therein; one flower blooms, and the universe rises with it. But where should our eyes be fixed when the dust is not yet stirred and the flower has not yet bloomed? Therefore it is said that it is like cutting a bundle of thread: one cut cleaves all asunder, and in dyeing a bundle of thread one dyeing will dye all in the same colour. Now, yourself get out of all entangling relations and rip them to pieces but do not lose track of your own inner treasure, for it is through this that the high and the low, universally responding, and the advanced and the backward, making no distinction, each manifests itself in full perfection."

The inner treasure is the essence of mind, the Buddha-nature or spiritual consciousness, which sees and grasps things without deliberation or definitions. The principal aim of Ch'an discipline was to awaken this part of the students' inner nature, to make them self-conscious in a spiritual rather than in an intellectual sense.

The methods and examples of Ch'an training quoted above are all characteristic of the ' Sudden or Southern School,' but it may be recalled, that since the eighth century there existed also another kind of Ch'an, known as the ' Gradual or Northern School.' This division of Ch'an Buddhism into two main schools became of particular importance to the art-historians in China; it was taken by them as the model for the presentation of the development of painting. We will find, that the discussions of the Southern and Northern schools of painting became a topic of great interest to the critics of the Ming period, and as they evidently endeavoured to characterize these schools as parallels to, or results of, the Southern and Northern school of Ch'an, it may be well to add a few words about their differences.

The division occurred at the death of the Fifth Patriarch, Hung-jên, in 675; the master conferred the patriarchal robe on Hui-nêng (637-712), a man of little learning but great character and intuition. The most learned and influential student among Hung-jên's pupils, was however Shên-hsiu (d. 706) who did not find it possible to submit to the leadership of the new Sixth Patriarch. He gathered some followers around him and left the old centre of the Ch'an monks in the South establishing a new monastery in one of the northern provinces (Honan ?).

The main point of division between the two schools referred to the human mind and the way of obtaining enlightenment. According to the Southern school, this could be accomplished by an instantaneous flash of intuition, whereas in the Northern school the emphasis was laid on the gradual development of the mind, a slower process involving more methodical study and intellectual advice. Both methods are based on the *Lankāvatāra sūtra*, where two different types of mind are characterized : Some men will obtain enlightenment only after a long practice of meditation pursued perhaps during many lives ; to others it comes all of a sudden, apparently without conscious intellectual effort. A similar difference is supposed to have existed between the creative methods of the painters, belonging respectively to the Southern and the Northern school, but it may, indeed, be questioned whether the difference actually existed in painting or was as marked as in the two schools of Ch'an philosophy. The parallelism between painting and philosophy was a construction made primarily to extoll the painters of the ' Southern School,' which was considered to be the way of the greatest geniuses. In the philosophical field it may be said, that the gradual method was a natural preparation for the intuitive experience, which was the aim of the Sudden School.

When a monk from the North was asked about his master Shên-hsiu's teachings in regard to morality (*sila*), Meditation (*dhyana*) and wisdom (*prajna*), he said that, according to his master, " refraining from all evil is morality, practising good is wisdom, and purifying the mind is meditation," a statement which drew from Hui-nêng a most characteristic explanation of his point of view :

" The teaching of your master is for the guidance of the followers of the Mahayana school, while mine is for those of the Supreme School. Because someone realizes the *dharma* more quickly and deeply than others, this accounts for the difference in interpretation. . . . In expounding the Law I do not deviate from the authority of the Essence of Mind (i.e. I speak what I realize intuitively). To do it otherwise would betray ignorance of the Essence of Mind (or Self-Nature). Morality, meditation and wisdom—all these are forms of Essence of Mind. When it is free from improprieties it is morality ; when free from ignorance it is wisdom ; when it is not disturbed, it is meditation. If you obtain a thorough understanding of it, you will know that nothing dualistic obtains in it. For him who has once had a thorough understanding of his own Nature (Essence of Mind) no special posture as a form of meditation is to be recommended ; everything and anything is good to him, sitting or lying or standing. He enjoys perfect freedom of spirit, he moves along as he feels, and yet he does nothing wrong, he is always acting in accord with his Self-Nature, his work is play. This is what I call ' seeing into one's own Nature ' (or realizing the Essence of the Mind), and this is done instantaneously, not gradually or stage by stage."

This conception of the Self-Nature or Essence of Mind is evidently very closely related to the definitions of Tao offered by Chuang-tzŭ and other Taoists : He who knows Tao accomplishes everything without exertion. Within is the repose, the inaction, the intuition of fitness by which all things may be accomplished. " The divine man fulfills his destiny, he acts in accordance with his Nature " (i.e. his Essence of Mind)—just as does the ' divine painter.' " Cherish that which is within you and shut off that which is without, for much knowledge is a curse,"—another saying by Chuang-tzŭ which, indeed, might have been formulated by a Ch'an philosopher. Nothing would be easier than to quote several sayings of the same import. The general attitude of the Taoist and the Ch'an philosophers towards man's inner nature was essentially the same (which also may be observed in the field of art), but their ways and methods of approaching the ideals were developed in quite different directions. The doctrine of inactivity and non-resistance became to the Taoists an inducement to negative indolence and self-indulgence ; it seems as if they often mistook a sensuous infatuation for a spiritual inspiration.

The Ch'an students were constantly on guard against such mistakes. They were no romantic dreamers or indolent nature-worshippers, but men of action accustomed to hard work. The Ch'an monasteries were places of such neatness and order that " neat as a Ch'an temple " became a common saying. The students were here occupied with regular field-work as well as with mental exercises ; ' no work, no food,' was a well-known dictum by Hui-nêng. Their whole education was directed to the development of will-power and complete self-mastery, though not the rigid outward discipline but rather the self-mastery which results when the higher nature of man is allowed to hold the reins. Consequently the Ch'an training became a preparation for statesmen and rulers just as much as for artists and philosophers ; it fitted them for life by developing their character and self-reliance.

It may well be admitted that these men too were subject to illusions and deceptive impulses, but whatever conclusions they arrived at, they did not hesitate to apply them in their own lives, to transform them into actions and thus to find out their value. Their mistakes became experiences by which they made progress, as they never lost confidence in their interior resources. They knew that life is a movement that never ceases, a stream which flows on, whether we wish it or not. They realized that the only way of converting into full value what life has in store for us, is by living completely in the present moment, by grasping it by the wings as it flies and not after it has flown. For those who know how to do this, time becomes an illusion ; one sudden experience which penetrates deep into the consciousness may become of greater value than years of intellectual study, one apparently trivial incident may open the spring of a hidden source. It all depends on which side man's nature is touched and awakened to full consciousness. The pitfalls are numerous, as there are many veils to be thrown off before we can see into our innermost Nature which, indeed, is the same as the Heart of the Universe.

But how can such things be made intelligible in words or visual shapes ? In poetry, perhaps, when it is no longer descriptive but retains an echo of the thing behind the words ; in painting which is not imitative but a spontaneous expression for the creative vision. In order to be true and alive these things must be done on the spur of the moment, before the light has faded or the ' spirit-resonance ' has died away. It is evident that no kind of painting could be better fitted for such expressions that the Indian ink-work which by its very nature requires the greatest spontaneity in the handling of the means of expression. It must be done quickly and irretrievably, as the paper soaks up the ink ; every stroke of the brush must be definite, no subsequent corrections or alterations are possible. As is well known, this required the most careful and assiduous training, psychological as well as technical, because the brush-strokes became reflections from the mind transmitted by the skill of the hand. Indian ink-painting in its purest form became thus a kind of Ch'an practice, an example of what the ' direct method ' of Ch'an meant when applied to art. The close correspondence, so evident and æsthetically significant, has been pointed out by several authors and most explicitly in the following beautiful words by Suzuki : " Life delineates itself on the canvas called time ; and time never repeats, once gone forever gone ; and so is an act, once done, it is never undone. Life is a *sumiye* (ink) painting, which must be executed once and for all time and without hesitation, without intellection, and no corrections are permissible or possible. Life is not like an oil painting, which can be rubbed out and done over time and again until the artist is satisfied. With the *sumiye* painting any brush-strokes painted over a second time results in a smudge ; the life has left it. All corrections show when the ink dries. So is life. We can never retract what we

have once committed to deeds, nay, what once has passed
through consciousness can never be rubbed out. Zen
therefore ought to be caught while the thing is going on,
neither before nor after. It is an act of one instant. . . .
This fleeting, unrepeatable and ungraspable character of
life is delineated graphically by Zen masters who have
compared it to the lightning or spark produced by the
percussion of stones."

The painting on the scroll is only a projection of the
one which exists in the master's mind, a record of the
thing that flashed across the mirror of his soul. It may
have been provoked by an incident or an object, but it
is no longer the event or the shape that counts, but its
repercussion, the indelible traces that it left on the mind.
The thing itself becomes a vibration of life ; how much it
conveys or expresses will depend on the sensitiveness of
the receiver and the immediate response of the transmitting
instruments. No painter who did not possess a full command of the technical means could ever transmit such
fleeting glimpses or momentary reflections from a realm
beyond sensual perception. The brush had to respond
instantaneously and unremittingly to the pulse-beat of the
creative soul ; the material labour had to be reduced to a
minimum, a few strokes or splashes which could serve to
reawaken the vision in the beholder's mind.

The works of the Ch'an painters might often seem
lightly done, thrown down without the least exertion,
but the suddenness of the execution would certainly not
have been possible if the masters had not passed through
a long and assiduous training. It was like the sudden
enlightenment, the *k'ai wu* or *satori*, which comes on the
spur of the moment, when the mind has been cleansed
of all beclouding thoughts and attuned to the silent music
that accompanies every manifestation of life. The painters
called this *ch'i yün*, the ' spirit-resonance,' or the reverbera-
tion of ' the Universal Mind ' ; they listened to it in the
innermost recesses of their own consciousness as well as
in every phenomenon of nature : Mountains and brooks,
winds and waves, flowers and falling leaves, all revealed
to them a reflection or an echo of the ' Universal Mind.'

We may call this poetry, or pantheistic romanticism, but to these painters it was actual life and reality. The things that they did, grew out of their own souls ; they were part of their own life and character. It was no longer of importance what they represented, whether it was large or small, a whole landscape or only some fruits or flowers, if only it served to transmit some glimpse from a world beyond material limits of time and space like the enlightened mind of the creative master.

THE YÜAN DYNASTY

THERE are no treatises on painting from the Yüan period of equal importance with those of the Sung, though it is evident that discussion of the aims and methods of painting was continued along the same lines as before. Something of this was also put in writing : several of the leading painters such as Chao Mêng-fu, Huang Kung-wang, Ni Tsan and others wrote colophons or short observations about art* which sometimes are not devoid of æsthetic interest, even though their main importance lies in the biographical or historical field. Beside such short notes, which reflect the ideals of some leading masters, there appeared writings of a more theoretical kind devoted particularly to definitions of faults and merits in painting. They are more or less based on the ideas of the Sung critics, though these are presented with less gusto than in the earlier writings. The somewhat dry formalistic spirit which was growing particularly in official circles becomes discernible also in the writings on art. The general tendencies of Yüan painting may be said to have been on the one hand, a rather conservative traditionalism, which now as before was supported by officialdom, and on the other, a subjective romanticism cultivated by the hermit scholars and painters, and based on the ideals of the landscape painters of the Northern Sung period.

The foremost representative of conservative traditionalism was Chao Mêng-fu (1254-1322) whose great fame is due to his skill as a calligraphist as much as to his painted works. He has defined his standpoint in several colophons on paintings by himself and contemporary artists never forgetting to praise ' the spirit of antiquity,

---

* Their writings are to some extent reported in *Shu Hua Pu*, Vol. 16 and in *Mei Shu Ts'ung Shu*.

(*ku i*), which evidently meant something more than simply adherence to classical models. As for instance :

" The most important quality in painting is the spirit of antiquity. If this is not present, the work is not worth much, even though it is skilfully executed. Men of to-day who know how to paint with a fine brush in a delicate manner and to lay on strong and brilliant colours consider themselves able painters. They are extremely ignorant, because if the spirit of antiquity is wanting, their works are faulty all through and not worth looking at. My pictures seem to be quite simple and carelessly done, but true connoisseurs will realize that they are very close to the old models and may therefore be considered good. I record this for the benefit of real connoisseurs and not for the ignorant."

The classic models preferred by Chao Mêng-fu were not those of the Sung painters but rather of the T'ang period ; Han Kan was his ideal as a horse painter, Wang Wei as a landscape painter, his numerous renderings of such motifs were certainly done less from nature than from a desire to convey the spirit of these ancient masters in pictures of individual character.

A standpoint quite opposite to that of Chao Mêng-fu was represented by Ni Tsan (1301-1374), the most sensitive and unconventional of all the landscape painters of this period. He shunned every kind of official protection and spent his time travelling in fishermen's boats and resting in Buddhist temples. His art was an intimate expression of the poetry of loneliness. Those of his colophons which have been reported are mostly in praise of other men, but in one or two he characterizes his own art :

" What I call painting does not exceed the joy of careless sketching with the brush. I do not seek for formal likeness ; I do it simply for my amusement. Recently I was rambling about and came to a town. The people who asked for my pictures wanted them exactly to their desires representing a particular moment. Then they went away insulting, scolding and cursing in every possible way. What a shame ! But can one scold a eunuch for not growing a beard ? "

PLATE XII

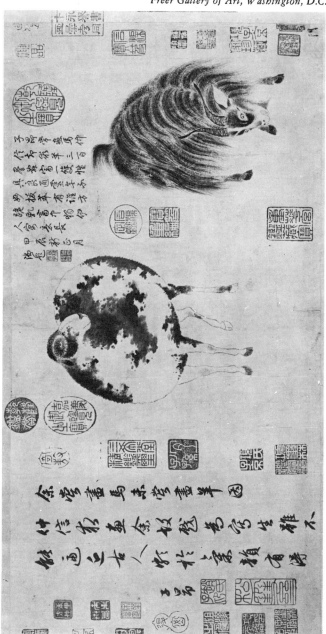

GOAT AND SHEEP

Chao Meng-fu (1254-1322, Yüan dynasty)

PLATE XIII

TREES IN A RIVER VALLEY
Ni Tsan (1301-1374, Yüan dynasty)

When a rich man sent him silk and money requesting a picture in return he refused the gifts and answered: 'I have never during my whole life painted for the vulgar and ostentatious.' But to his intimate friends he gave away his pictures freely, and did not attach any value to them:

"I-chung always liked my bamboo paintings. I did them simply to express my overflowing heart. My endeavour was not to give exact representations of their likeness, the profusion or scantiness of their leaves, the slanting or straight position of their branches, I simply brushed and rubbed for a long time. Ordinary men find them like hemp or rushes; I cannot force such people to see that they are bamboos or to take (any real) interest in them. Nor do I know what I-chung may find in them."

Closely akin to Ni Tsan in his comprehension of painting as a spontaneous recording of fleeting impressions was Wu Chên (1280-1354), the landscape and bamboo painter whom Ni Tsan characterized in the following words: "Mei Tao-jên lived at the Plum-blossom cottage. At his window stood a stone goblet filled with resinous wine. When he got drunk, he swung the brush and painted the air of the mountains, the haze, the mist, and the clouds without a flaw."—Wu Chên considered most of his work as a play with ink (*mo hsi*):

"The work which is called 'ink-play' is the excess (or, very last perfection) of the scholar's poetical and literary writings. It is done according to the inspiration of the moment and is in the opinion of the connoisseurs something completely unrestrained. I have read Ch'ên Chien-chai's poem about ink plum-blossoms which says: 'The thought (or, spirit) is enough, why seek for coloured resemblance?' The painter was in a former life the judge of horses Chiu Fang-kao, thus he also understands painting."

Whatever the last somewhat surprising sentence may allude to, the main point of Wu Chên's epigrammatic saying is to extol the 'ink-play,' the quick and free rendering of the flash of inspiration as the very acme of the painter's art. It seems, indeed, to have made little difference to him whether he wrote it down in the symbols of a few bamboo branches or in the characters of a poem ; the latter have the same suggestive value as the former. There are many such impressionistic sketches by Wu Chên. One may be quoted as an example :

" Branches of Bamboo. The cave is empty without a heart, but THEIR virtue will be known as seasons roll ; they do not change when the sky grows cold and dark, they keep their leaves midst frost and snow."

Another contemporary of these men was Huang Kung-wang (1269-1354) the great landscape painter. He, too, spent much of his time in roaming " as the guest of lakes and mountains " ; but he was perhaps less of a poet and more of a painter in the ordinary sense of the word than Ni Tsan and Wu Chên. According to his advice : " The painter should always carry with him some brushes in a bag, then when he comes across startling trees in a beautiful landscape, he should at once make drawings of them so as to preserve their natural idea (characteristics). He should climb up into high buildings to contemplate the *ch'i yün* of large and open views and to look at clouds. Such views are called mountain-peak landscapes. Li Ch'êng and Kuo Hsi both practised this manner and Kuo Hsi painted stones like clouds."

Huang Kung-wang's notes about landscape painting known as *Nine Principles for Painting Landscapes, Trees and Rocks* seem also to be based on earlier essays on similar subjects : they contain nothing new or original. He speaks about the proper way of drawing the various elements of landscape compositions and of handling brush and ink so as to create atmosphere, mist and cloud effects. All this should be done in close adherence to the great masters of the beginning of the Sung period. " The most important thing in painting is, however, *li* (reason or principle). Wu Yung (a T'ang poet) said : ' A good workman can grasp the *li* of painting in colour but to use the ink properly is very difficult.' Li Ch'êng treasured ink as gold (used it very sparingly). The four things which must be avoided beyond everything else are : slouchiness, sweetness, vulgarity and recklessness."

Huang Kung-wang gives no further indication as to what he meant by this 'reason,' but as he evidently was familiar with the Sung critics, it may be assumed that he used the word in a similar sense as did Su Tung-p'o, who spoke of the inherent reason or principle of things as their essential character or fitness, something not dependent on formal likeness but rather on resonance of spirit. By no other kind of painting could this be rendered as strikingly as by monochrome ink, because here every stroke is definite and reflects the impetus of the creative mind. If there is a flaw, it will show more easily than in a coloured painting. One who could not handle the ink properly was no great master.

The position was no less characteristic of the Yüan painters than of their predecessors. And the faults against which he warns painters are of a moral rather than of a purely professional or technical order: they are flaws in the character of the artist which will be reflected in his work if he cannot rise above them.

More specific observations about the painter's psychological attitude and the proper way of working are to be found in Li K'an's *Essay on Bamboo Painting*, written at the beginning of the 14th century, although the booklet is mainly an account of the writer's development as a bamboo painter and his admiration for the great specialists in this field of earlier times. His ideals were Wên T'ung and Su Tung-p'o and his attitude was altogether determined by the works and writings of these masters. He quotes Su Tung-p'o's word about Wên T'ung's manner of painting (cf. page 56) and adds the following remarks:

" As old Tung-p'o understood the principle but had not enough training to do the thing, how could later men have had it? They only knew that bamboo painting does not consist in making joints and piling up leaves. They have either not conceived the whole thing in their minds, or they aim at the high and far at once, trying to skip the preparatory stages; they give free play to their emotions by rubbing and smearing in every direction. They call that taking a short-cut in the brush-work. Really, one should start by painting joint after joint, leaf after leaf, concentrating the thought on the brush-manner, continuing the training without getting tired. The painter must thus accumulate his power (faculties) until he arrives at the stage when he can rely on himself and possess the bamboo completely in his mind. At this stage he can move the brush and follow the model he sees before him. If not prepared in this way he will grasp the brush in vain and gaze at the thing in front of him without being able to represent it. But if he knows the rules and principles, his work will become faultless and he need have no fear of not succeeding. He may feel bound or restrained for some time, but he will become able to transcend the rules."

The rules for studying bamboo painting which Li K'an develops are practically the same as in the Sung period, but his insistence on the methodical pursuit of the studies is more marked than with any of the earlier writers. It reflects an increasing tendency towards systematization and scholasticism, an attitude which becomes more apparent as the fresh current of creative energy begins to dry away. The æsthetic ideals remained the same as in earlier times, but they became further removed from the actual world of artistic activity and changed into topics of historical study. From this time onward one may observe a growing historical orientation among the painters as well as on the part of the critics.

This is most evident in the writings of Jao Tzŭ-jan and Hsia Wên-yen, which consist mainly of enumerations of faults and merits in painting. In fact these writings are little more than condensations of the principles expressed by Kuo Hsi, Kuo Jo-hsü, Têng Ch'un and others, presented in a rather trite if unusual manner. Jao Tzŭ-jan's essay is not dated, but the author seems to have lived into the Yüan period, although he is commonly included among the Sung critics.* It is called: *Hui Tsung Shih Erh Chi*, "The Twelve Points to be Avoided" or, in other words, the twelve principal faults in painting. We give below

---

* In the *P'ei Wên Chai Shu Hua P'u*, vol. 14, 1.7-9, the author is marked as "Sung," but Giles' *Introduction to the History of Chinese Painting*, pp. 180-ff, places him in the Yüan Period.

the main part of the text leaving out some unessential digressions and repetitions.

The first point to be avoided is : " Over-crowded compositions. Those who paint landscapes should begin by placing the silk in a clear and proper room, and then wait until the spirit is at ease and the thoughts fixed. If the picture exceeds the size of several silk-scrolls, or if the wall is more than 100 feet wide, he should start by drawing with charcoal, fixed on a bamboo stick, the mountains, streams, trees, stones, houses, pavilions and figures, the large and the small, the high and the low, everything in its proper place. Then he should examine this (sketch) carefully at a distance of more than ten steps. If he finds that the drawing will serve, he should take some light ink and fix it approximately. This is called the small (i.e. preliminary) touching with the brush (*hsiao lo pi*). Afterwards he should go on working and brushing without hesitation, and everything will come out right. Furthermore : the picture should be empty at the top and at the bottom and spacious at the side, so that it looks agreeable. If it is filled up like a full stomach, it has no longer any expression."

The second fault is : " Not to divide the things far off from those near by. In painting landscapes one must begin by dividing the far away from the near and by marking in a proper way the high and the low, the large and the small. If the mountain slope is close by, the stones and trees should be large and buildings and figures should correspond, but if the mountain ranges are seen at a distance, the trees must be small, the figures and buildings corresponding. If they are very far away, there would be no figures. The ink should be quite light in the far distance and deep in the foreground : the further away, the lighter the ink, is a principle which holds good."

The third fault is : " Mountains without life-arteries. In representing several mountains in one picture, one should first draw one commanding mountain, and starting from this, other mountains which are rising and falling. The mountains should all be connected by their life-arteries and have a continuous aspect. If the mountains rise in layers, they should have many-doubled feet to support them; it is a great error to represent numerous mountain peaks without feet. Such are the main principles of perfect landscape painting."

The fourth fault is: "Water without a source. The water must come out of a mountain gorge. If there are many mountains beyond, the source must lie high and far off. If the stream is small and tranquil, one must see its source. Flat banks and shallow streams must show playing waves, so that the water seems alive. There are painters who make separate watercourses for each mountain; they are like napkins hanging on frames and look quite ridiculous."

The fifth fault is: "Landscapes without levels and risings (variations in the level of the ground). The ancients did not make their landscapes monotonous; some have sharp peaks and flat extensions, some are winding, some are empty, some rise in layers with trees, groves and buildings, some have many figures, and some have boats. Whenever one makes a picture, one should first have an idea in mind. If it is a large scroll, one should work as stated above."

The sixth fault is: "Paths without beginning or end. The effect of distance (the near and the far) in a landscape depends on the clear division of roads and paths. Some are lost in the woods and come out again at the edge of the water, some are interrupted by rocks being only half visible behind them, some hidden by the slopes are marked out by figures, some lead up to buildings partly hidden among trees and bamboos. All these devices create landscapes without limit."

The seventh fault is: "Stones (rocks) with only one face. Painters of different schools do not make the wrinkles on the stones in the same way; each one must take the manner he has studied as his rule. The stones must have head and feet and their faces must be divided by sharp angles."

The eighth fault is: "Trees which have not branches on all four sides. In paintings of former times the trees are represented according to definite manners: those which stand at precipices are winding and intertwined, those which grow on the slopes are high and straight, they reach with their tops to the clouds; those which grow at the water have an abundance of roots and branches. One should make no division between the right and the left side of the trunks but sometimes represent them from the front sometimes from the back. Some leaves may be painted with single brush-strokes, others with double brush-strokes. The fresh and the faded leaves should be marked according to season."

The ninth fault is: "Hunchbacked and stooping figures. The figures in landscapes are of many different kinds; in the minutely executed pictures one may clearly distinguish their eyes and eyebrows; when a dotting brush is used, it gives strength and an old look. . . . If one makes the figures which are walking, watching, carrying burdens, or riding, hunchbacked or stooping, it is quite wrong. That is a stupid and loose habit which shows carelessness."

The tenth fault is: "Buildings and pavilions in confusion. Although boundary painting (*chieh hua*) is the last speciality, the buildings and pavilions (however small) must be properly joined both in the front and at the back in accordance with the rules of construction. This is most difficult. Some people claim that in painting villages on river banks or huts in the mountains one may draw them and place them quite arbitrarily, yet even if one does not use ruler and foot-measure, they must be made according to the rules of boundary painting."

The eleventh fault is: "To neglect atmospheric effects (mist and clearness). Whether painting is done with water and ink, with colours or with gold and green, the atmosphere must be rendered with ink and have proper lightness and depth. Thus a bright view has an empty and clear sky, a rainy night is dusky and dark, a snow view is somewhat lighter and not like paintings of rain clouds, fogs and mist. The green mountains and white clouds should be used only in summer and autumn landscapes."

The twelfth fault is : " Colouring without proper method. It may be said, that in the use of colours as well as in the use of gold and green there is a heavy and a light method. For mountains one may use the light green of the shells, but trees should be coloured with a composite green ; for figures one should use a preparation with white powder."

The further rules for colouring relate to still more technical details. Jao Tzŭ-jan's treatise might almost be called a grammar of landscape painting ; the various elements of the painter's craft are defined or fixed by rules in accordance with classical tradition. Although formulated from a negative point of view and devoted in particular to the faults in painting, the essay conveys an idea of what was considered of greatest importance in the painter's métier and therefore also necessary for critics to know.

T'u Hui Pao Chien by Hsia Wên-yen is a lengthy work in five volumes published at the very end of the Yüan dynasty, the preface being dated 1365. It has become well known and enjoys perhaps a greater popularity than it merits : the contents are borrowed from earlier publications (particularly Kuo Jo-hsü's and Têng Ch'un's) and arranged without much order or system. The four latter volumes are filled with biographical notes on painters from earliest times to the Yüan dynasty, but the first one is devoted to discussion of theoretical questions. The author enumerates Hsieh Ho's Six Principles in the same way as Kuo Jo-hsü did, emphasizing the all-inclusive importance of *ch'i yün*, which is " secretly blended with the soul, one does not know how, yet it is there." Then he defines the three traditional classes (*shên, miao, nêng*) as follows :

" When the skill of the painter is such that it cannot be found out, he is said to be of the divine class. When the brush and the ink are out of the common, yet appropriate and the expression is overwhelming, the painter is said to be of the wonderful (mysterious) class. When the painter renders the outward formal likeness and does not neglect the rules, he is said to be of the skilful class.

The additional fourth class, be it *i* or *ch'iao*, which was introduced by some of the earlier writers, is not mentioned by Hsia Wên-yen, who in this respect also keeps strictly to the most common ground.

The traditional "three faults" are enumerated exactly as we have found in Kuo Jo-hsü's treatise :

"There are three faults in painting depending on the use of the brush. The first is called stiffnesss, the second is called carving, the third is called knotting. The stiff painter's wrist is weak, his brush is slow (dull) ; he does not know how to take and to give (to move freely). The forms he makes are flat and thin, he does not know how to round them off (to give them roundness). The carving painter moves the brush with hesitation, his heart and his hand do not correspond, and in drawing his outlines he quite arbitrarily makes sharp angles. The knotting painter cannot make the brush move when he wants, nor can he spread out things when they should be spread, his works are like things congealed which cannot move or float."

If the above passages in the *T'u Hui Pao Chien* are copied with very slight modifications from Kuo Jo-hsü's well-known work, the continuation of the theoretical definitions is borrowed from Liu Tao-ch'un. Here Hsia Wên-yen introduces the "six important points" and the "six qualities" in the same terms as those used in the preface to *Shêng Ch'ao Ming Hua P'ing* :

"The Six Important Points :

"*Ch'i yün* united with strength is the first; adherence to the rules and standards is the second; strange transformations (original effects) combined with reason is the third ; rich colouring is the fourth ; free and natural movements make the fifth ; a close study of the great masters and avoidance of the poor ones is the sixth."

"The Six Qualities :

"To be coarse and rough, yet to strive for brushwork, is the first. To be simple and common, yet to strive for refinements, is the second. To be delicate and clever, yet to strive for strength, is the third. To be eccentric and impulsive, yet to strive for reason, is the fourth. To work with spare ink, yet to strive for colour effect, is the fifth. To paint in a common fashion, yet to strive for quality is the sixth."

In the following section the author describes various motifs or models for pictures (*k'ai mo*) i.e. Buddhists and Taoists, emperors and kings, barbarians and conquered tribes, scholars and sages, hermits and recluses, soldiers and noblemen, women and children, who all should be differently represented, and in addition to these he enumerates certain motifs from nature such as trees, stones, mountains, animals, fishes, dragons, etc., though without any remarks of æsthetic significance. More interesting are the few words he adds about sketches for pictures :

" The master of antiquity called their drafts *fên pên* (studies) ; many of them have been preserved by former generations as precious things, because their spontaneous and sketchy character is wonderfully natural. Thus all the *fên pên* of the Hsüan Ho and Shao Hsing periods (1119-1162) belong to the divine or the wonderful class."

T'u Hui Pao Chien is another example of how the fundamental principles of Chinese art-criticism were reiterated quite independently of the stylistic development that painting passed through from one period to another. There is no trace in this work of the new aspects of landscape painting, which became apparent in the Yüan period, no reflection of the ideals expressed in the colophons by Chao Mêng-fu or Ni Tsan. Like so many other Chinese books on painting it is a simple compilation (without any indication of the earlier sources) and quite detached from contemporary art developments. It seems as if Hsia Wên-yen, like some of the professional writers of later times, had had little connection with the actual world of artistic creation ; or if he knew anything about it, he preferred to speak in the accepted terms of his predecessors. The strict adherence to classical models was no less of a guiding principle for the writers than for the painters.

It is thus less in the writings of the historians and critics than in those of the artists and amateurs that we find some fresh impulses or spontaneous expressions for the æsthetic tendencies of their time. The amateur painters and poets of the Sung period were prominent examples of this mode and a few of the artists of the Yüan period were the same, though in a more limited way, as we already have seen. But the most interesting representative of this class of amateur writers of the Yüan period was a doctor of medicine called Wang Li* who also made himself a name as a poet and a painter. He spent some time at the Hua Mountain in Shensi and recorded his journey in forty pictures to which he wrote a kind of preface or introduction,† which reflects better than any other writing known to us the attitude of the romantic landscape painters of the Yüan period. The main part of it may here be quoted :

" Although painting is representation of form, it is dominated by idea. If the idea is insufficiently brought out, it may be said, that the picture has no form either. But as the idea is in the form, it cannot be expressed if the form is neglected. When the form is grasped, the idea will fill it completely ; but when the form is lost, how can there be either form or idea ?

" If one wants to represent in painting the likeness of something, how can one do it if one does not know it by sight ? Did the most famous of the old masters really stumble in the dark ? Those who spend their time copying know nothing beyond the silk and the paper (of their predecessors' pictures), and the further the copies are removed from the originals the poorer they become. The forms are gradually lost and still more so the ideas.

" As long as I did not know the form of the Hua Mountain, how could I make a picture of it ? But even after I had (seen it and) made a picture of it, the idea was still incomplete. Subsequently I brooded upon it in the quietness of my room, when walking about, when in my bed, or at my meals, during daily work, when listening to music, when at leisure or engaged in literary work. One day when I was resting I heard drums and trumpets passing my door ; I jumped to my feet and said : ' I have

---

* Wang Li lived from the Yüan period into that of the Ming, and may thus be classified as belonging to either of these periods.

† Cf. *Shu Hua P'u* vol. 16.

got it !' I rubbed out my old picture and made a new one. At that moment I realized that the way to do it was in the Hua Mountain itself. I thought no more of commonly accepted school manners. These schools and rules have all been established and made famous by men ; am I not a man who can make his own rules ?

. . . .

" The highest spirit and beauty can never be seized with the implements of painting. However, from that moment I advanced very quickly. I now know my own rules and do not trifle or follow in the dust of others. Every time I sit down in the empty hall with a peaceful mind looking in silence at the picture, the idea rises again—but this cannot be explained in words. How do I dare to turn my back on my predecessors ? But how can I help remaining outside the tradition established by them ? It is common to find pleasure in that which is alike to oneself and not to rejoice in that which is different.—I kept the picture in my home, and someone who happened to see it thought that it was contrary to every kind of style. Much surprised he asked me, who my master was ? To which I answered : ' I learned from my heart, my heart learned from my eye, and my eye learned from the Hua Mountain.' "

The attitude of Wang Li is in full accord with that of the great landscape painters of the Yüan period ; his striking remarks express the very spirit of Huang Kung-wang's, Ni Tsan's or Wu Chên's paintings. These masters had little use for established schools and rules. They learned from close observation of nature, they penetrated into the very spirit of the mountains and valleys, and they expressed it in quite unconventional paintings, often sketchy, small and unpretentious but always alive with the very pulse-beat of their own heart.

PLATE XIV

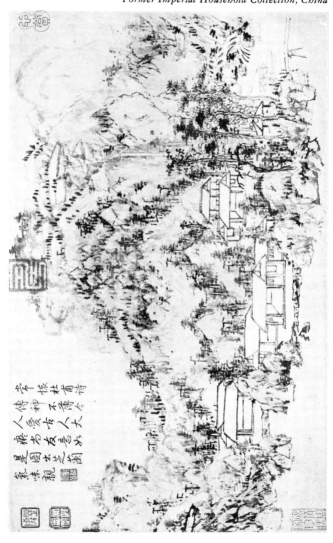

THE ORCHID STUDIO

Huang Kung-wang (1269-1354, Yüan dynasty)

PLATE XV

DWELLING IN THE CH'ING-PIEN MOUNTAINS
Tung Ch'i-ch'ang (1555-1636, Ming dynasty)

THE MING PERIOD

HISTORICAL THEORIES AND NOTES ABOUT
OLD MASTERS

THE Ming period was to a larger extent than any of
the preceding epochs one of historical study and
archæological research. This is reflected in the artistic
activity at the beginning of the period as well as in the
writings on painting. The tendency to forge the link with
the past in the field of art found an official expression in the
re-establishment of an Imperial Academy of Painting which,
like other similar institutions, served as a bulwark for conservative ideas, although it never reached the same importance as did its predecessor in the Sung period. The national
enthusiasm and the Confucian spirit, which had been
reawakened by the Ming restoration, served also to direct
the painters' attention towards earlier epochs, though it
would be wrong to claim that they resuscitated any immediate artistic inspiration. They strengthened the interest in the past, but did not kindle much fresh creative
effort ; this was rather inspired, now as before, by spiritual
currents of Taoist and Buddhist origin. There were still
landscape painters of the same pantheistic attitude as in the
Yüan period and others who followed in the wake of
Ch'an Buddhism.

One of the foremost representatives of the former
was Wang Li, the poet and amateur painter who lived
on from the Yüan into the Ming period and wrote the
very suggestive introduction to the Hua Shan pictures,
quoted at the end of the preceding chapter. His main
point was the complete penetration ('Einlebung') in the
motif, the mental realization of its form and meaning
independently of any established tradition or commonly
accepted school manner. He advocated study of nature
instead of imitation of the old masters and was in this

respect more akin to the Yüan landscapists than to the general run of Ming painters, though it may be admitted that almost every period of Chinese art-history has had some men of this type. Wang Li was, strictly speaking, not advocating any particular school or manner, except that of his own heart, though in his painted work he followed rather closely the stylistic tradition of the Ma-Hsia school.

The foremost historian at the beginning of the Ming period was Sung Lien (1310-1381), best known as editor of the History of the Yüan dynasty. He produced an essay on the *Origin of Painting* of a thoroughly traditional type after the model of Chang Yen-yüan's and other early men's writings.* It is largely devoted to the demonstration of the common origin of painting and calligraphy and of the moral and political importance of painting during the earliest periods. More interesting than these general considerations of primitive painting are the remarks of the author, that " the first great change (in the evolution of painting) dated from Ku K'ai-chih and Lu T'an-wei, the second from Yen Li-pên and Wu Tao-tzǔ and the third from Kuan T'ung, Li Ch'êng and Fan K'uan "—a division of the earliest stages in Chinese art-history, which by this time had become classical, and which also is repeated by most of the later writers. But Sung Lien has nothing to say about the evolution of painting after the Northern Sung dynasty.

The short notes or colophons by some of the well-known painters from the first half of the Ming period reflect the individual attitudes of these men, but contain very little if anything in regard to general æsthetic principles ; they hardly need to detain us in this connection.

The discussions of the general principles of painting did not reach their full development before the later part of the period, and they gradually became closely connected with historical speculations regarding certain schools or currents of style. The Ming critics were, on the whole, more interested in historical questions than were their pre-

---

* Most of Sung Lien's *Hua Yüan* is reprinted in *Shu Hua P'u*, vol. 12.

decessors, though their manner of representing the evolution of painting became constructive rather than analytical; they did it from a theoretical point of view which was applied to ancient as well as to contemporary art. This manner of procedure is most characteristic of Tung Ch'i-ch'ang and his contemporaries (at the beginning of the 17th century) whose theories will be discussed presently, but before we dwell on them, we will communicate some extracts from the writings of Wang Shih-chêng who belonged to an earlier generation.

He was born in 1526 and died 1593, his *tzŭ* was Yüan-mei, but he was often called by one of his *hao*, Yen-chou Shan-jên, because this appellation characterized the man after his retirement from public life when he devoted himself entirely to literary and artistic pursuits. Wang Shih-chêng was one of the best informed art-historians of the Ming period, he possessed an important collection of paintings and a thorough knowledge of the historical sources. He wrote several works of an historical character such as *I Yüan Chih Yen*, from which the following quotation is extracted, and compiled the well-known *ts'ung shu : Wang Shih Hua Yüan* (edited by some friends of his), which contains reprints of most of the standard writings on painting before the Ming period. His services to the history of Chinese painting are generally esteemed very highly.

In the " Discussion of Painting " (*Hua P'ing*) which forms a part of *I Yüan Chih Yen*, he first gives extensive extracts from the writings of certain old critics, such as Hsieh Ho, Li Ssŭ-chên, Chang Huai-kuan and Chang Yen-yüan, in order to illustrate the changing opinions about some of the most prominent old masters, and then he offers a short résumé of the whole evolution of painting according to his own ideas. The first part of the " discussion " may be left out, as the passages which Wang quotes have been communicated in earlier chapters, but Wang Shih-chêng's own views on the evolution of painting have a certain interest as an introduction to the succeeding theories about the Northern and Southern schools. To quote :

"From this (the classifications of the old authors) it may be concluded that Ku K'ai-chih was the first great master but Wu Tao-tzŭ surpassed him in spiritual (mental) energy. Wei Hsieh's style was old-fashioned, Lu T'an-wei was strong and original. These painters may be called the four sacred men, their works are most distant and illustrious. Chang Sêng-yu was almost equally good, he may be compared with So Ching among calligraphists.

"Figure painting passed through a complete change from the time of Ku K'ai-chih, Lu T'an-wei, Chan Tzŭ-ch'ien and Chêng Fa-shih to the time of Chang Sêng-yu and Wu Tao-tzŭ. In landscape painting there was a change at the time of the Great and Little Generals Li, another change was produced by Ching Hao, Kuan T'ung, Tung Yüan and Chü-jan; Li Ch'êng and Fan K'uan also produced a change, Liu Sung-nien, Li Kung-lin, Ma Yüan and Hsia Kuei produced again a change, Huang Kung-wang and Wang Mêng produced another change. Chao Mêng-fu was very close to the Sung masters and particularly strong in figure painting. Shên Chou was very close to the Yüan masters and the very best in land-scape painting. Both followed the old masters, yet it may be said that their manners were only slightly alike (their predecessors'). Mi, father and son, and Kao K'o-kung grasped the resonance (of the spirit) by their sketchy manner, Ni Tsan obtained by his graceful and soft manner the beauty of things. All four belonged to the supremely free (*i*) class, but they were not leading masters.

"Among the painters of flowers and birds Hsü Hsi was divine, Huang Ch'üan was wonderful, Huang Chü-ts'ai was of the second class, and there were still others in the Hsüan-ho era. Shên Chou learned from Hsü Hsi to paint with light colours and watery ink: his pictures were sketchy and light filled with divine beauty and freshness. After him, until the time of Tao-fu,* colour was used less and less.

"Among the schools of (landscape) painting that of the Great and the Little Generals Li (Li Ssŭ-hsün and Li

---
* Tao-fu is the *tzŭ* of Ch'ên Shun (1485-1544) the well-known landscape and flower painter.

Chao-tao) is extolled. The originator of the school was the Great Li, but it is only the Little General Li who is known in the world; I do not know why. I often looked in the home of Hsü Fêng on Little General Li's painting of the 'Sunset over the Sea,' it certainly belongs to the wonderful class. After it had been put to dishonour in the house of the wealthy it came into the Palace Collection but there it was destroyed by fire.

"Generally speaking, the landscape painters before the Five Dynasties were few. The two Li and others worked in an exceedingly fine manner, but it is regrettable that it was so stiff and minute. Wang Wei was the first who was able to express something beyond scenery but he did not do it completely. Kuan T'ung, Tung Yüan, Chü-jan and others gave the real expression, their spirit was altogether bold and free, their vaporous ink quite unequalled. Li Ch'êng carried this to the utmost limit, he was refined but very sparing in his production, so that very few works of his exist. Fan K'uan continued in a very grand manner with great force. Beside these men there were Kao K'o-ming, Kuo Hsi and others, who were excellent painters, but the most esteemed before the South Sung period was Li Kung-lin, Po-shih, who painted in the black and white manner. Ku K'ai-chih and Wu Tao-tzǔ were his distant models in figure painting, while in his paintings of horses and oxen he followed Han Kan and Tai Sung and in his landscapes Wang Wei and Li Ssǔ-hsün. It seems to me that Tung Yüan and Li Ch'êng were not as good as he.

"Wên Yü-K'o painted bamboos, he was the Tso-ch'iu Ming of bamboo painting, while Su Shih was of the same kind as Chuang-tzǔ. Li K'an from Hsi-chai was also a bamboo painter. It has been said: 'Su Shih's brush is wonderful but not true, Li K'an's bamboos are true but not wonderful,' which is quite right. Mei Tao-jên (Wu Chên) was the first who studied thoroughly the transformation (of the bamboos). But among the works handed down as theirs, the true and the false ones are all mixed up. Wang Fu, *tzǔ*

Mêng-tuan,* and Hsia Ch'ang,† *tzŭ* Chung-chao, of the present dynasty may be placed in the class of the skilful, they did not obtain spiritual expression. Among more recent painters there were also some who tried to escape from the stupid and avoid the common.

" Chao Sung-hsüeh, Mêng-fu ; Mei Tao-jên, Wu Chên, *tzŭ* Chung-kuei ; Ta-ch'ih Lao-jên, Huang Kung-wang, *tzŭ* Tzŭ-chiu ; Huang-ho Shan-ch'iao, Wang Mêng, *tzŭ* Shu-ming ; were the four great masters of the Yüan dynasty. Kao Yen-ching (K'o-kung), Ni Yüan-chên (Ni Tsan), Fang Fang-hu (Ts'ung-i) were all of the supreme-ly free (*i*) class. Shêng Mou and Ch'ien Hsüan were of a secondary order. Chao Sung-hsüeh was skilled in painting figures, buildings, flowers and trees, his drawing was most careful and refined. Kao Yen-ching exceeded him only in his sketchy manner of painting, by which he grasped the resonance of the spirit. Nowadays his works are very highly appreciated, they show some difference from the Sung style. Kao Yen-ching followed Mi, father and son, but his resonance (of the spirit) is different. Huang Tzŭ-chiu followed Tung Yüan, but in his old age he changed and became very pure and lofty. Wang Shu-ming followed Wang Wei, his art was luxuriant, deep and rich. Ni Yüan-chên was extremely simple and beautiful ; he was naive, yet mature. It has been said, that it is easy to copy the Sung painters and difficult to copy the Yüan painters, though it is still possible except in the case of Ni Yüan-chên. I do not think that it is so, though I am not able to do it."

Wang Shih-chêng's exposé of the evolution of painting is essentially the same as that which later on was divulged in the writings of Tung Ch'i-ch'ang and his friends, though Wang does not introduce as yet the division into a Northern and a Southern school, nor does he insist upon one type of painting being better than another. He is able to appreciate both Li Ssŭ-hsün and Wang Wei together with their respective followers, and in spite of his ad-

---

* Wang Fu (1362-1415) known as Chiu-lung Shan-jên.

† Hsia Ch'ang (1388-1470), a pupil of Wang Fu, specialized in bamboo painting.

miration for the great landscape painters of the Northern Sung period, he places Li Kung-lin above both Tung Yüan and Li Ch'êng, a verdict which none of the later critics was able to support. Wang's very comprehensive taste was evidently based on a wide knowledge of both the historical and the artistic documents, which, however, did not prevent him from extolling in particular certain masters of the Sung and Yüan periods who also in later times were recognized as the true models.

The writer who more than anybody else decided the drift of art-criticism in the Ming period and whose influence reached furthest was, however, Tung Ch'i-ch'ang (1555-1636), *tzŭ* Hsüan-tsai, *hao* Ssŭ-po, Hsiang-kuang, etc. He occupied successively several high government positions and finally became President of the Board of Rites which, no doubt, added to his social prestige, yet his great renown with posterity is mainly based on his leading position as a calligraphist, painter, writer and connoisseur of art. He was considered not only by his contemporaries but also by the following generation as the greatest authority in questions of art, a distinction evidently based on his wide learning and technical virtuosity rather than on original creative genius.

His writings on art and kindred subjects are more extensive than are those of any other critic in the same period, but this is largely due to the fact that the various publications under Tung Ch'i-ch'ang's name contain essentially the same materials, though in more or less complete form and differently arranged. The shortest one is the *Hua Chih*, somewhat more extensive is the *Hua Yen*, while the so-called *Hua Ch'an Shih Sui Pi* is a still more inclusive work, containing not only notes on painting but also special chapters on calligraphy, on travels, on Ch'an Buddhism and other subjects treated both in prose and poetry. The mutual relation of these different publications and their various editions is a too intricate problem to be discussed here in detail, it should however be remembered that Tung Ch'i-ch'ang himself cannot be made responsible for the somewhat arbitrary and unsystematic character of these books, because they were edited

only after his death and presumably from notes or manuscripts which had not been arranged for print. The men
who were in charge of this editing work seem to have
taken no trouble to sift the manuscripts or to find out to
what extent these contained Tung Ch'i-ch'ang's own
compositions. The closer study of this problem was left
to later students, and it is only in recent years that various
Chinese, Japanese and European critics have ascertained
that important sections of the books on painting published
under Tung Ch'i-ch'ang's name are made up of textual loans
from other writers such as Mo Shih-lung, Chao Hsi-ku
and Chên Chi-ju.* Mo Shih-lung's treatise *Hua Shuo*
is largely incorporated in *Hua Yen* and *Hua Ch'an Shih
Sui Pi*, and the same works contain furthermore extracts
from Chao Hsi-ku's *Tung T'ien Hsin Lu* (of the Sung
Period) and Chên Chi-ju's *Ni Ku Lu* (without any indication of the sources). Tung's own contributions to these
publications are mainly colophons, written in praise
of certain pictures or artists, and technical observations
or professional advice to students of painting. They
are quite unsystematic and full of repetitions and
inconsistencies, but nevertheless interesting and expressive
of the writer's personal attitude towards painting. In
view of the above-mentioned conditions and the large
amount of material, it did not seem to us necessary to give
a full translation of any of the books published under
Tung Ch'i-ch'ang's name, but the extracts offered below
will, no doubt, suffice to convey an idea of the writer's
position as critic and painter. They are mainly taken
from *Hua Yen* (as edited in *Hua Hsüeh Hsin Yin*) but the
same texts are also to be found in *Hua Ch'an Shih Sui Pi*
and, partly, in *Hua Chih*. It is almost immaterial which

---

* The various publications on painting which contain sayings by Tung Ch'i-
ch'ang and their mutual relations are discussed by Yü Shao-sung in his Anno-
tated Bibliography of Books on Calligraphy and Painting (*Shu Hua Shu Lu Chieh
T'i*), Peiping 1931. The same author gives also evidence for Tung's extensive
loans from Mo Shih-lung, Chao Hsi-ku and Chên Chi-ju. The same problem has
been discussed by Omura in his *History of Chinese Art* (in Japanese) and more
exhaustively by Dr. Victoria Contag in two valuable articles in the *Ostasia-
tische Zeitschrift*, 1933.

Mo Shih-lung's *Hua Shuo*, which consists of 16 paragraphs, is included in
Kuang Po Ch'uan Hsüeh Hai and also in *Pao Yen T'ang Pi Chi*, edited by Ch'en
Chi-ju.

of the publications is chosen as a source for Tung Ch'i-ch'ang's main utterances on painting, because the omissions or additions do not alter his essential theories or his position as a critic.

The central topic in Tung Ch'i-ch'ang's writings is the theory about the Southern and the Northern school in landscape painting. It forms the pivot around which his whole critical activity turns. The evolution of painting from the T'ang period down to his own time is considered in relation to this theory ; the painters are arranged in the one or the other of the two camps in such a way that all those who, according to Tung Ch'i-ch'ang, represent superior artistic qualities belong to the Southern, while the painters placed into the Northern school are denied all genius. Tung and his friends were both in theory and practice ardent supporters of the Southern school and felt a deep contempt for painters who followed a different stylistic current. The main centre of the opposite camp was at the time the so-called Chekiang school, and the painters who belonged to it were consequently labelled as of the Northern school. Their models and predecessors were the members of Southern Sung Academy, professional painters who were tied by formal rules and who lacked the ' gentleman spirit,' which expressed itself in a free and unprofessional creative activity. The classification became in many cases very arbitrary which indeed was inevitable, but it served the purpose of extolling the merits of the so-called Southern school.

It may also be questioned whether this theory about the Southern and the Northern school ever could have been established on the basis of actually existing stylistic differences ; they are in some instances hardly discernible. Tung Ch'i-ch'ang and his friends offer very little evidence in this respect ; their main argument is not formed by any kind of stylistic analysis but by philosophical or historical speculations. They were all more or less steeped in Ch'an Buddhism, which still was an important current of spiritual inspiration, and they evidently found it quite natural to seek in the evolution of painting a similar division as that which had taken place in the history of Ch'an in the T'ang period. The characteristics of the Southern and the Northern school of Ch'an were transferred to the Southern and Northern schools of painting, the former representing the free intuitive mode of creation, the latter a more formalistic intellectual approach to the problems of art. This is explained in various theoretical pronouncements as for instance the following, which Tung Ch'i-ch'ang has taken over from Mo Shih-lung :

" In Ch'an Buddhism there is a Southern and a Northern school which first separated in the T'ang period ; in painting a similar division into a Southern and a Northern school was also brought about in the T'ang period. But the men (who represented these schools) did not come from the South or the North. The Northern school took its origin from Li Ssŭ-hsün, father and son, who applied colour to their landscapes : their manner was transmitted in the Sung period by Chao Kan, Chao Po-chü, Chao Po-su down to Ma Yüan, Hsia Kuei and others. The Southern school began with Wang Wei (Mo-ch'i), who used light washes (of ink) instead of a manner with fine outlines, and this was continued by Chang Ts'ao, Ching Hao, Kuang T'ung, Tung Yüan, Chü-jan, Kuo Chung-shu and the Mi, father and son, down to the four great masters of the Yüan period. It was just as in Ch'an Buddhism, after the time of the Sixth Patriarch, the Ma-chü, Yün-mên and Lin-chi (schools) developed as flourishing offshoots (of the Southern school), while the Northern school was fading away. Very important is the saying by Wang Wei, that the clouds, peaks and cliffs should be formed as by the power of Heaven, then, if the brush-work is free and bold, the picture will be penetrated by the creative power of Nature. Tung-p'o praised Wu Tao-tzŭ's and Wang Wei's wall-paintings and said, that as to Wang Wei, there can be no word of dispraise. This is certainly right."

As mentioned above, the significant quotation is taken from Mo Shih-lung, and it may be of interest in this connection to note, that Tung Ch'i-ch'ang himself points out the special importance of Mo in regard to the theory of the Southern and the Northern school. He seems to have had a high regard for Mo Shih-lung as well as for Ku Chêng-i, who both were his somewhat older friends :

"In my home province there were two gentlemen Ku Chêng-i* and Mo Shih-lung, both skilful in landscape painting. Ku Chêng-i was quite famous as he had been active during many years. But when Mo Shih-lung came out (as a painter and writer), the South and the North became gradually separated into two schools. Mo Shih-lung wrote on a small landscape by Ku Chêng-i that he considered it divine and extraordinary, and Ku Chêng-i expressed to me the greatest admiration for Mo Shih-lung's paintings. In this way they praised each other mutually by poems and prose writings : the mutual appreciation and noble spirit of the two gentlemen could make the old people ashamed."

The third critic who dwelt on the separation of the two schools was Ch'ên Chi-ju, he does it in a passage in *Yen Pao T'an Yü* using almost the same vocabulary as do his two prominent friends : †

"The old manner of landscape painting changed in the T'ang period ; from this time onward there were two schools : Li Ssŭ-hsün's and Wang Wei's. The former was continued in the Sung period by Chao Po-chü, Chao Po-su, Li T'ang, Kuo Hsi, Ma Yüan and Hsia Kuei, who all belonged to the school of Li. The latter was continued by Ching Hao, Kuan T'ung, Tung Yüan, Li Ch'êng, Fan Chung-chêng, Mi, father and son, and the four masters of the Yüan period, who all belonged to the school of Wang Wei. The school of Li was coarse and stiff and without any scholarly spirit, whereas the school of Wang Wei was harmoniously pure and detached just as was the Ch'an school of Hui-nêng (the Sixth Patriarch who founded the Southern school). Shên-hsiu (the founder of the Northern Ch'an school) could not attain to it. In addition to these, there were Kuo Chung-shu

---

* Ku Chêng-i, *tzŭ* Chung-fang, painter and author of *T'ing Lin Chi*. Tung Ch'i-ch'ang says in another connection that Ku first worked in the manner of Ma Yüan and Wên Pi but gradually went over to the Yüan masters. Though very different from Mo Shih-lung he was highly esteemed by him.

† The *Yen Pao T'an Yü* is included in the collection of miscellaneous writings known as *Pao Yen T'ang Pi Chi*, which was edited by Ch'ên Chi-ju.

and Ma Ho-chih, who both reached beyond the common world and followed their own paths."

Some uncertainty seems to have prevailed in regard to the position of certain painters ; Ma Ho-chih and Kuo Chung-shu are sometimes placed in the Southern School and so is Hsia Kuei, who in the above quotations is included among the painters of the Northern school. Nor were these critics insensible to the merits of a Ma Yüan and a Li T'ang (Tung mentions them sometimes with approbation), but their natural sympathies, resulting from temperament, philosophical and literary education and from contempt for their rivals of the Chekiang school, were all on the side of the painters of the Southern school and the very famous Ch'an masters who followed and expounded the teaching of the Sixth Patriarch. The general characteristics of Hui-nêng's spiritual message and mode of teaching, his insistence on intuitive comprehension and spontaneous realization of the inspiring flash, have been discussed in a previous chapter, and there is no need here to dwell further on the extraordinary importance of this attitude to the painters and poets. The above-mentioned critics of the Ming period understood it more or less, and accordingly they considered those painters superior who possessed the mysterious power of grasping the soul of things and of rendering it without any intellectual elaboration. They seem to have felt a kind of psychological correspondence between the philosophy of Hui-nêng and the æstheticism of Wang Wei (and his followers), a parallel which may appear strange to us, though it may have been better founded than we are able to ascertain.

When expressed in terms of pictorial execution this æsthetic attitude led to a very spontaneous manner of ink-painting, which finally resulted in the so-called *p'o mo* (splash ink) technique. But whether the painters actually used this or some less splashy way of spreading the ink, they were all trying to use what the Chinese critics call the " short cut " (*hsi ching*) or the art of expressing much by little ; a form of expressionism based on utmost concentration and economy of means. They had no use for descriptive illustrations or faithful reproductions of outer appearances, but avoided them just as much as Hui-nêng and his followers avoided verbose explanations and intellectual discussions. All such methods could only lead away from the essential significance of things.

We know how important this principle had been for the development of Chinese painting during the T'ang and Sung periods, but it was now insisted upon more than ever; in fact, the old painters were classified according to their faculty of applying it. It was the point on which Wang Wei was supposed to have differed essentially from Li Ssŭ-hsün, so that the two masters could be recognized as originators of opposite schools. It was also the favourite manner of the 'gentleman-' or poet-painters of Sung and of the great landscapists of Yüan time. The Ming painters who followed in the footsteps of these predecessors did their best to develop this mode of painting, but the final result, known as *wên jên hua* (literary men's painting), became something highly different from the 'gentleman' painting of the Sung period. Their æsthetic and philosophical culture was no longer of the same quality as in earlier times, the poetic inspiration became intellectualized, the genial ease of the Sung and Yüan masters was transformed into conscious effort, and the 'art of expressing much by little' was more and more lost in the ever increasing compositions of the *wên jên hua*.

Tung Ch'i-ch'ang's critical pronouncements on the two leading currents of style and his characterization of the great landscapists of the Southern school would hardly have exercised such a wide influence had he not at the same time illustrated them in his paintings. His attitude was practically the same as that of Wang Shih-chêng, but more definitely carried out practically (i.e. in painting) as well as theoretically in terms which remained of standard importance during the following generations. We will find them repeated by Shên Hao and the later critics of the Ch'ing dynasty, who take practically the same view of the evolution as does Tung, emphasizing in particular the scholarly (or literary men's) mode of painting and criticizing the 'professional' painters who worked according to definite rules and formulæ. With them as with Tung the æsthetic appreciation consists mainly in the juxtaposition of these two types of painters.

In the following pronouncement Tung Ch'i-ch'ang applies the term *wên jên hua* in a way which makes it practically equivalent to the manner of the Southern school (but like all styles or modes of painting it was subject to gradual changes and decay):

" The literary men's painting started with Wang Wei; then followed Tung Yüan, Chü-jan, Li Ch'êng and Fan K'uan who all learned from him. Li Lung-mien, Wang Chin-ch'ing,* Mi Fei and his son " Hu-erh," all learned from Tung and Chü, and this tradition was continued by the four great masters of the Yüan period, Huang Kung-wang, Wang Mêng, Ni Tsan and Wu Chên in an unbroken line. In our dynasty Wên Pi and Shên Chou were the last representatives of the same tradition. As to Ma Yüan, Hsia Kuei, Li T'ang and Liu Sung-nien they all belonged to the school of General Li (Li Ssŭ-hsün); there is no need of studying them."

A further characterization of the psychological attitude of these painters is contained in a passage by Mo Shih-lung (quoted by Tung Ch'i-ch'ang), which gains a special interest from the way in which the respective styles or æsthetic attitudes of the painters are said to influence the duration of their lives. The importance of a proper style (i.e. of the *wên jên hua*) could hardly be brought out in a more realistic way.

" The Tao of painting is to hold the whole universe in your hand (If you possess the real spirit of art, you can comprehend everything). There will be nothing before your eyes which is not replete with life, and therefore painters (who have attained to this) often become very old. But those who paint in a very fine (or detailed) manner (*k'o hua*) make themselves servants of Nature and impair their longevity, because such a manner adds nothing to the power of life. Huang Kung-wang, Shên Chou and Wên Pi lived to a great age. Ch'iu Ying had a short

---

* Wang Hsin, *tzŭ* Chin-ch'ing, was a prominent collector and calligraphist, also active as a painter, a friend of all the great painters of the Hui Tsung period and a real gentleman.

life; Chao Mêng-fu lived to little over sixty years. Although these two painters did not belong to the same class, they were both men of routine, who did not use painting as a means of expression (of ideas) but for their pleasure. The man who first combined painting as a means of expression with pleasure was Huang Kung-wang who formed a school." In addition to this the following words may be remembered: " Huang Kung-wang became ninety years old and had yet a face as fresh as that of a boy. Mi Yu-jên at the age of eighty showed no fading of his bright soul; he died without illness. They were nourished by the vapours and clouds of their paintings."

This correspondence between the painter's life or conservation of energy and his manner of creation was by no means an invention by Mo or Tung, it has always seemed quite natural to the Chinese that such should be the case. Poor paintings were in their opinion the results of excessive or wrong efforts by which energy was spent contrary to the laws of nature, while good paintings were done with ease in harmony with nature without any excessive display of force. The same idea is also expressed by Wang Shih-chêng in a passage which may be quoted here as a complement to the above.

" When one has mastered the art of calligraphy and one is at the moment of moving the brush and spreading the ink, no more than a fraction of a second is needed to stir the heart. When one has acquired the art of painting and sits down (cross-legged) to work, even the smallest thing is not needed to stir the heart. Poems and literary compositions may both be accomplished, if they, when one is about to write them down, enter into a corner of the heart. From this may be realized why the masters of calligraphy and painting lived to a great age; there was, indeed, a reason for it.

" I have now reached old age; I can devote myself in my solitude to artistic pursuits; I have no need of making a living by it and may follow my own fancies. The things thus done become by themselves most beautiful. Furthermore I understand that Ou-yang Hsiu did not deceive me (in expressing such thoughts). I studied in my early years but did not arrive at perfection, now I am old, and my talents are exhausted, which makes me sigh."

The finest works of calligraphy and painting must be done instantly, not by slow or gradual deliberations, nor by display of energy. The heart may be stirred and the inspiration awakened in an instant of time without any visible signs or means. The exercise of these arts becomes thus a practice in the conservation of energy ; and those who know how to do it properly may indeed live to a great age.

In another connection Tung Ch'i-ch'ang points out that painting has no chance in competition with nature ; the value of the painter's creation depends on the brush-work and on his faculty of transmitting the inner meaning of what he paints.

" When Sung painting had developed as far as Tung Yüan and Chü-jan it freed itself completely from the fine and delicate manner. Only in the paintings of the Chiang-nan mountains did they aim at outward likeness. In pictures of the seashore one should follow the manner of General Li (Li Ssŭ-hsün). For pictures of the Northern mountains, which form like rows of chariots or of mules, one should use the manner of Li T'ang or the manners of Kuo Hsi or Chu Jui.

" If one discusses painting with a view to its faculty to render distance, one must admit that it does not equal real landscape, but if one considers the wonders of brush-work, it becomes evident that real landscapes do not equal paintings. Su Tung-p'o says in a poem: ' Those who consider pictures as representations of outward forms are like children, those who write poetry according to definite rules, are no real poets.' I think that this applies to all Yüan painting. Ch'ao I-tao says in a poem ' The painter gives the outward form of things, these forms must not be altered. The poet gives the thought beyond the painted forms, yet in his works one finds the aspect of a picture.' I think this applies to painting of the Sung period."

Both the above sayings may, in spite of their difference, have been acceptable to Tung Ch'i-ch'ang, because they both point to a creative activity which transcends all formal rules and makes painting akin to poetry, but fundamentally Tung Ch'i-ch'ang stood closer to the Yüan masters. His education as a painter had been based on a study of some of them; he often returns in his notes to Huang Kung-wang, Wang Mêng, Wu Chên and Ni Tsan. He extols their merits but does not as a rule place them on a level with Tung Yüan and Li Ch'êng.

"In my youth I studied the landscapes of Huang Kung-wang. In later years I abandoned him and worked according to the Sung painters. Now again I imitate him occasionally but cannot reach him. Every day I used to copy one or two trees, rocks, mountains or slopes, making the wrinkles (ts'un fa) and applying the tones according to my ideas, but I accomplished it only at the age of fifty. Still, I cannot make figures, boats, carriages and houses, which annoys me. I feel some consolation from the fact that Ni Tsan was a predecessor of mine with the same faults; otherwise I could not defend myself even with a hundred mouths."

"Painting reached its highest development in the Yüan period; only Tung Yüan and Chü-jan (among earlier painters) stood out as exceptions, all the others followed Kuo Hsi. Most famous among them were Ts'ao Chih-po, T'ang Ti, Yao Yen-ching (?), Chu Tê-jun and others, but even ten of them together do not equal one Ni or one Huang; so lofty and refined was the air of these men." In the continuation of the same paragraph he expresses the opinion, that all the great painters of the Yüan period derived their art from Tung Yüan and Chü-jan and this opinion he develops elsewhere as follows:

"At the end of the Yüan period there were two currents of style among the painters, the one based on Tung Yüan, the other on Li Ch'êng. Li Ch'êng's accomplished manner of painting was continued by Kuo Hsi, Tung Yüan's by the monk Chü-jan. The four great schools of Huang Kung-wang, Ni Tsan, Wu Chên and Wang Mêng were all derived from Tung Yüan. They became very famous and were the foremost within the seas. But those who studied Li Ch'êng and Kuo Hsi, like

Chu Tsê-min (Tê-jun), T'ang Ti and Yao Yen-ch'ing, were overshadowed by their predecessors' art of expressing much by little, and they could not establish their own halls of fame. It was just as among the five schools of Ch'an only the Lin-chi school flourished, because it transmitted the principles of the ancestors and was supported by men of high genius."

The parallel drawn between the evolution of Ch'an Buddhism and the development of painting shows how closely Tung Ch'i-ch'ang adheres to this constructive theory which he took over from Mo Shih-lung. He then quotes a passage from Mo Shih-lung, which illustrates what these men meant by following a certain school or current of style; it was the transmitting of the vital spirit rather than of the formal manner:

"I have once said that through the writing of Wang Hsi-chih and his son the style of the Ch'i and Liang dynasties disappeared completely. Since the beginning of the T'ang period their manner was changed by men like Yü Shih-nan and Ch'u Sui-liang; they are quite different (from the Wangs) and yet alike. Wang Hsi-chih and his son seem to be reborn in them. These works may be difficult to understand, because close copying is quite easy but to transmit the spirit and the meaning is difficult. Chü-jan studied Tung Yüan, Huang Kung-wang studied Tung Yüan, Ni Tsan studied Tung Yüan and Mi Fei studied Tung Yüan, and yet they are quite different between themselves. When ordinary people try to imitate an original, how can they transmit its spirit to posterity?"

Although no painters have been more enthusiastic advocates of the study of the old masters than Tung and Mo, they were not blind to the importance of direct observations from nature, and it may be particularly noticed, that Tung emphasizes the connection between the landscape painters and their respective home-provinces; it was natural to him that their art should reflect something of the spirit or character of the nature in which it had grown up:

"Of the four masters of the Yüan dynasty three came from Chekiang, i.e. Wang Mêng from Hu-chou, Huang

Kung-wang from Ch'ü-chou and Wu Chên from Wu-t'ang, only Ni Tsan was born in Wusih (Kiangsu). Their pictures contained the spirit (atmosphere) of the rivers and mountains, which changes according to season. In the present dynasty the only famous man from Chekiang was Tai Chin from Wu-lin; he was the chief of Chê school (I do not know whether Chao Mêng-fu was a Chekiang man). If the Chê school decayed, it was not because it became addicted to sweetness, awkwardness or vulgarity, but because there was no longer any relationship between it and its native province."

A more explicit warning against one-sided study of the old masters and neglect of nature is voiced by Mo Shih-lung and transmitted by Tung:

" Painters of the past usually took the old masters as their models, but it is preferable to take Heaven and Earth as teachers. One should observe every morning the changing effects of the clouds, break off the practising after painted mountains and go out for a stroll among the real mountains. When one sees strange trees, one should grasp them from the four sides. The trees have a left side, which does not enter in the picture, and a right side which does enter; and it is the same way with the front and back. One should observe them thoroughly and transmit the spirit naturally, and for this purpose the form is necessary. The form, the heart and the hand must correspond mutually, and one must forget all about the imagination (what the spirit offers). Then there will, indeed, be trees in the picture, which have life also on the silk; they will be luxuriant without being crowded, vigorous and elegant without blocking the view, all fitting together like members of one family."

It would take us too far to quote here the special instructions that Tung Ch'i-ch'ang offers for painting trees of various kinds, such as pines and willows, or stones, mountains and slopes, open views and sea shores, etc. For each speciality there is some old master who may serve as a model. The general principles are the same as those recommended by the critics of the Sung and Yüan periods:

" The outlines of the mountains must first be fixed and then the wrinkles should be put in. Modern painters pile up small bits to make a big mountain, which is a great mistake. When the old masters composed large pictures, they made only three or four sweeping divisions and accomplished thus the whole composition. It contained many fine parts, but these were subject to the general effect which was the main point. I possess an essay by a man of the Yüan period who discusses Kao K'o-kung's and Mi Fei's manners of painting mountains and expresses exactly the same ideas."

The importance of proper spacing is brought out still more definitely in one of Tung Ch'i-ch'ang's most striking remarks :

" Whenever one paints landscapes, one must pay attention to proper dividing and combining ; the spacing (distribution of the parts) is the main principle. There is the spacing of the whole composition and the spacing of the parts of the picture. If one understands this, one has grasped more than half of the principles of painting." True indeed !

The following observations (borrowed from Mo Shih-lung) are of a more technical order but serve to illustrate some essential features of monochrome landscape painting :

" Men of former times said : ' One must have brush and have ink.' Many people do not understand the significance of these two words, brush and ink. But how could there be pictures without brush and ink ? Still, there are pictures executed simply with outlines and no wrinkles, they are said to be made without brush, and there are other pictures which have wrinkles (*ts'un fa*) but no distinction of the more and the less important parts, of foreground and background, the clear and the dark ; they are said to be without ink. Men of old said : ' One should distinguish three sides on the stones ; that involves brush as well as ink, and one may well agree with it.' "

But it is not only the mountains and stones which occupy Tung Ch'i-ch'ang ; he offers also advice in regard to figures, flowers and birds : " The painted figures must be looking about and speaking. The flowers and fruits must move in the wind and be sprinkled with dew ; the birds should flutter and the animals run. The spirit must be taken from the real things. Mountains and waters, woods and springs must be pure, quiet, solitary and vast. Houses and cottages must have depth and be receding (into the picture). Bridges and ferries must be represented with people who are coming and going. The foot of the mountain should be clearly reflected in the water. The source of the water-course should be clearly marked. Such qualities distinguish the works of a real painter, even though he be not famous."

Tung Ch'i-ch'ang remained, however, as a painter, essentially an eclectic traditionalist. His knowledge was greater than his creative genius. He knew exactly how every kind of stone or tree was painted by the old masters, how they did their wrinkles (*ts'un fa*), their lines and dots, and he was convinced that if the best examples of each kind were intelligently combined, perfect pictures could be produced.

"Someone has said that each one must form his own school, but that is not right. Thus for example, the willow trees should be made after Chao Po-chü, the pine-trees after Ma Ho-chih and the old trees after Li Ch'êng. These are traditional and cannot be altered, and even if they are modified, they will not be very far removed from the original sources. Who can abandon the old methods and create new ones quite independently ? Even Ni Tsan came out of Kuo Hsi and Li Ch'êng, though he added softness and refinement (to their styles). Chao Mêng-fu understood this idea perfectly (he kept close to the ' spirit of antiquity '). Thus, if one combines in the drawing of the trees the most beautiful points of the old masters and does not waste one's force on stones, the trees will become quite naturally beautiful and moist. Those who nowadays wish to follow the old masters, prepare a volume of copies after their trees to serve as a bag of supplies."

Tung Ch'i-ch'ang's opinions about the old masters form the most valuable parts of his notes on art. They are not copied from others, but are generally written down quite spontaneously as a result of his own observations. They contain repetitions and also contradictions; his opinions are not always the same; sometimes he estimates Tung Yüan higher than Mi Fei and places Kao K'o-kung above Ni Tsan, but at other times the order is reversed. And the list of the painters whom he places in the Southern school is not always the same, but he seldom fails to give some reason for his opinion. If we may believe his own words as expressed in the following paragraph, he never discussed painters, whose works he did not know in the original:

"The masters of antiquity are far from us. Ts'ao Pu-hsing and Wu Tao-tzŭ are of a period that is closer to us, but nevertheless one never sees a picture by either of them. How would it then be possible to see something by men like Ku K'ai-chih or Lu T'an-wei? Those who discuss painting should take as their standard things that they have actually seen. People who point to certain old masters and say: 'This is Ku, and this is Lu,' are not only fooling others but are also deceiving themselves. When discussing landscape painting one should take Li Ch'êng and Fan K'uan as standards; for painting of flowers and fruits Chao Ch'ang and Wang Yu should be taken as standards; for plants, bamboo, birds and animals Hsü Hsi, Huang Ch'üan and Ts'ui Po are the standard masters; for horses Han Kan and Li Kung-lin; for oxen the two Taoists Li and Fan (?), for fairies and Buddhas Sun T'ai-ku, for spirits and monsters Shih K'o, for cats and dogs Ho Tsun-shih* and Chou Chao. If one can grasp the manners of these painters, one has reached the extraordinary and wonderful. Some of their wonderful works may still be seen in the possession of great scholars and officials; they are worth thousands of taels. Why should one go back to such a remote antiquity where neither eyes nor ears can penetrate?"

It seems surprising that Wang Wei is left out in the above list of standard or model painters in view of the fact that Tung Ch'i-ch'ang felt an admiration for him that

---

* Ho Tsun-shih is the appellation for a painter who called himself Ho-ho. He is recorded for instance in *T'u Hui Pao Chien* but without dates.

approached religious veneration. In his notes he gives us some idea of the incessant efforts that he pursued during several years to see or obtain an original painting by Wang Wei and how, when he finally succeeded in borrowing such a picture from an official, he fasted three days before he opened it. The experience was to him like an initiation into the mysteries of a truly spiritual art. It was poetry and painting combined into the purest harmony expressed by a man who had reached beyond the limitations of ordinary minds and touched the fringe of spiritual realities.

"Wang Wei was among painters the same as Wang Hsi-chih among calligraphists"—i.e. the man who reformed the whole art—"such men are seldom seen."

"Wang Wei's landscapes are of the divine class. Men of former times who discussed them said, that his cloudy peaks and beautiful rocks were superior to those of nature, and that he by his free manner of painting became as one with the creative power of Nature (the Creator). He was the only man in the T'ang period. Mi Fei, father and son, of the Sung period, were not so far removed from him in time; thus the older Mi could still see the *Wan Ch'uan Hsüeh Chi t'u*. There were several such scrolls but only one which was right, the others were all copies and almost like carved (minutely drawn) paintings." Tung then describes how he came to see an original work by Wang Wei, how he unrolled it after fasting and "got from it something never experienced before." He consented to the owner's wish that he should write a colophon on it and expressed himself as follows :

"The painters before Wang Wei were not lacking in skill only they could not transmit the spiritual quality of a landscape, they were still separated from this by a particle of dust (worldly thoughts). After Wang Wei the painters began using wrinkles (*ts'un fa*) and the soak-ink (*hsüan jan*) method. It was just as when Wang Hsi-chih changed the method of Chung-yu by writing characters which were like the lifting *fêng* bird and the flying *huan* bird (i.e. the male and female of this celestial messenger). They seemed strange, but they are really quite correct. The painters who followed after Wang Wei all expressed some ideas of their own as for instance Wang Hsia and Li Ssŭ-hsün ; the former used the splash-ink (*p'o mo*) method, the latter painted gracefully in colours. As the art of expressing much by little had already been established, it was not difficult to follow suit, just as Ou-yang Hsün, Yü Shih-nan, Ch'u Sui-liang and Hsüeh Sang-kung continued Wang Hsi-chih's style, each in his own way."

Wang Wei's renown as the founder of the Southern school and the *wên iên hua* was closely connected with the theory that he was the first to paint landscapes in the floating ink manner thereby suggesting atmospheric effects. But the full development of this technique was accomplished only by Wang Hsia, who lived nearly a hundred years later and specialized in the *p'o mo* technique, which later on was further developed by Mi Fei, Kao K'o-kung and their followers.

" The painting of cloudy mountains did not begin with Mi Fei : such things were done already in the T'ang period by Wang Hsia who used the *p'o mo* manner. Tung Yüan loved to paint landscapes enveloped by mist, but Mi painted the changing effects of dissolving clouds and mist. It was only through Mi's picture ' White Clouds over Hsiao and Hsiang ' that I learned the secrets of ink-play (*mo hsi*). I painted in his manner my picture of Ch'u Shan."

" Mi Fei established a standard of correctness among the arbitrary customs of the painters. He considered himself of very high standing and said that he had not a single point in common with the manners of the Wu Tao-tzŭ school. He said furthermore that Wang Wei's works were almost like ' carved ' paintings. It is truly ridiculous, because the style of the T'ang masters flourished in the Sung period until it was changed by the Mi. I will not follow the Mi's manner of painting, because I fear to fall into superficiality. Now I simply amuse myself in imitating it, yet I dare not leave out the ideas of Tung Yüan and Chü-jan."

Tung Ch'i-ch'ang was well aware of the dangers involved in this method :

" In recent times when an ordinary man paints in spots, he calls it to make mountains in the Mi style, which

is quite ridiculous. Mi Fei looked down on all his predecessors and considered himself equal to Wang Wei.
It is quite easy to follow such a method and thereby open
a road for later men who want to conceal their faults."

"Only after one has been like Wang Wei may one
use the *p'o mo* manner of Wang Hsia, and after one has
been like Li Ch'êng may one make clouds and mountains
like the two Mi. This should be enough to close the
mouth of those who are mastering painting; then one
can satisfy the ears and the eyes of the connoisseurs."

Wang Wei was the origin, he was the great reformer
like Wang Hsi-chih, but Mi Fei marked the highest perfection in the use of ink as a means of artistic expression and,
therefore, also the danger point which could be followed
only by a decline. Very few later painters could keep
on his level:

"When in poetry one arrives at Tu Fu, in calligraphy
at Yen Chên-ching, and in painting at the two Mi, all the
transformations and possibilities have been exhausted.
Only Kao K'o-kung combined the qualities of them all
and expressed new ideas within the old rules. He was
strange and wonderful and reached the limit of freedom
and boldness, yet with reason. He was the only one among
old and modern men."

In fact Kao K'o-kung is placed in a class of his own,
his manner of painting was such a perfect example of the
wên jên hua ideal:

"I have often seen that during the former dynasty
the Fang-shan hermit (Kao K'o-kung) was placed to the
right (i.e. at the head) of the four masters. Every time
Chao Mêng-fu found a picture by him, he wrote an
appreciation on it extolling his superiority to the utmost.
But among modern critics there are those who do not
hold the same opinion; it is because they have not
seen Kao K'o-kung's real works. This year, in the sixth
month, I obtained at Wu-mên a large scroll by him.
It represents the diffused effects of vapours and clouds
with so much spirit and life that neither Huang Kung-
wang nor Wang Mêng could have reached it even in
their dreams."

We have already heard something of Tung Ch'i-ch'ang's appreciation of Huang Kung-wang's paintings which meant so much for his own development as a painter; he was hardly less impressed by Wang Mêng's great landscapes, which certainly were most characteristic examples of *wên jên hua*, and Ni Tsan he sometimes placed above all others and on a level with Mi Fei:

" Wang Mêng's painting had its origin in the harmony of Chao Mêng-fu's work, and he was thus very like his uncle. He surpassed the famous painters of T'ang and Sung, but considered Tung Yüan and Wang Wei as his masters. His manner of painting became very rich and beautiful, so that he often surpassed the rules of Chao Mêng-fu. If Wang Mêng had kept simply to the school of Chao, he would have been completely covered by him. I am telling this, because I am now painting in the style of Wang Mêng."

" Those who study the old masters and do not introduce some changes are as if closed in by a fence. If one imitates the models too closely one is often still further removed from them." The last two phrases are said in appreciation of Ni Tsan who, although he learned from the old masters, kept quite independent and created a style of his own. Tung Ch'i-ch'ang never tires of praising him: " Old Yü (Ni Tsan) of the former dynasty may be placed in the *i* (spontaneously free) class, which often has been considered by critics of former times as superior to the *shên* (divine) class.* During the ancient dynasties there were only Chang Chih-ho † and Lu Hung (?) who were worthy of this class: among the men of the Sung dynasty Mi Fei did the utmost in expressing much by little, the

---

* The question of the relative position of the *i pin* and the *shên pin* which occupied some of the old critics, previously quoted, is referred to by Tung Ch'i-ch'ang in the following words: " The painters consider the *shên* (divine) class as the highest, yet there are those who consider the *i* (spontaneous) class as superior to the divine class. They say that as the men lose the quality of *i*, they become *shên*. That may be a right opinion, but it is to be feared that those who wish to screen their faults hide in this class." Their splashy way of painting was sometimes simply an excuse for lack of correct drawing and spacing, a ' short cut ' used by painters of different schools and ages who did not possess the patience or power to completely master the means of expression.

† Chang Chih-ho was a highly eccentric painter of the 8th century. Lu Hung is a name not quoted in Chinese historical records.

others were simply licking things into shape (like potters and founders). Although there were many skilful men in the Yüan period, they took over the Sung manner making it thinner and looser. Wu Chên possessed great spirit and life. Huang Kung-wang was wonderful in mastering the rules. Wang Mêng followed the style of his predecessor (Chao Mêng-fu). All these three men worked with great freedom as the spirit moved them. Only Ni Tsan was old-fashioned, simple and natural, he was the only one after the mad Mi."

It may not be necessary to quote here more of Tung Ch'i-ch'ang's opinions about the Sung and Yüan masters in order to give an idea of his predilections. He was, strictly speaking, much less of a theoretician than a connoisseur and art lover with a keen eye for the characteristic features of the various masters. The theories he took over from Mo Shih-lung or earlier writers, but the critical opinions he formed by personal observations; they form consequently the most interesting part of his notes and are important not only for understanding the writer's æsthetic attitude but also for a closer knowledge of the painters. The artists of the Ming dynasty interest him very little except in so far as they transmitted the characteristics of the 'gentlemen painters.'

" Shên Chou copied all the famous masters of the past (Yüan) dynasty without exception. His copies are very like, some of them are even superior to the originals; only Ni Tsan's pictures were difficult for him to render. This was because his strong brush-work and deep thoughts were so different from the light and diffusing manner of Ni Tsan. But this present scroll of his is quite out of the common, beautiful and 'moisty.' It is very like old paintings and the work which satisfied himself most."

" Every time Shên Chou painted in the manner of Ni Tsan his teacher Chao T'ung-lu exclaimed: 'You are wrong again, you are wrong again.' Ni Tsan's most wonderful qualities cannot be learned. Shên Chou's force was stronger than his harmony. The two masters differ and are separated by 'a grain of dust'."

Ch'iu Ying is praised for his faithful copies after the academicians; he was the only Ming painter who could transmit " not only the workmanship but also the beauty " of Li Chao-tao's and Chao Po-chü's paintings. He worked with such concentration that " he did not hear the drums or trumpets or the noise of the crowd, and he did not even look at the ladies beyond the wall." Tung Ch'i-ch'ang could not help admiring him in spite of the fact that he belonged to the Northern rather than to the Southern school. " His manner of working was very difficult. I am now 50 years old, and I now realize that this kind of painting cannot be learned by exercise."

Wên Pi is also mentioned several times with approbation. " His paintings were quite like Chao Mêng-fu's only somewhat more detailed, it is, however, better to make something of one's own than to be absolutely like others."

But some of the other well-known masters like Tai Chin and T'ang Yin are conspicuous by their absence from Tung Ch'i-ch'ang's notes. The explanation may be that he found them too much tied up in the academic tradition to be worthy of his attention. Their way of study and copying was not in conformity with Mo Shih-lung's and Tung Ch'i-ch'ang's theories. Yet, there were other critics who thought otherwise, as for instance, Tu Lung (a writer and poet who passed his *chin shih* degree in 1577). He insists on the most faithful and thorough rendering of ancient models : *

" To make copies or tracings of old pictures in colour is very difficult. If one uses great effort in doing imitations, one may obtain likeness, but the colour will not be right. It is impossible to do better than the Sung painters; their copies after pictures of the T'ang and the Five Dynasties period seem to be made by the same hand as the originals. A great number of such treasures are preserved in the Palace Collection. When people nowadays make copies, they simply seek for the shadow and the sound. Most of the modern artists follow their own ideas, and the works of their hands are loose and simple even when

---

* From *K'ao Pan Yü Shih* quoted in *Shu Hua P'u*. vol. 16, l. 13.

PLATE XVI

FISHERMEN ON THE RIVER
Tai Chin (1388-1462, Ming dynasty)

PLATE XVII

女几山前路横松聲偏鮮合水聲試從

靜裏閒倾耳便覺沖然道氣生

治下唐寅畫呈

孝父母大人先生

LISTENING TO THE WIND IN THE PINES
T'ang Yin (1470-1523, Ming dynasty)

the execution is extremely careful. There is no inspiration of Heaven : the picture may be wonderful, yet it is stiff.

" Tai Wên-chin of the present dynasty copied famous works by painters of the Sung period, he grasped their secrets and came really very close to the truth. He imitated Huang Tzŭ-chiu and Wang Shu-ming and surpassed them both. Shên Shih-t'ien is a great talent, though not much known. When he copied or imitated the old masters, he grasped the real thing with his brush except in the case of Ni Tsan, whom he could not reach and whose brush-work was superior to his. The critics say : ' Chao Tzŭ-ang approached the Sung painters and surpassed them in his figure paintings. Shên Shih-t'ien approached the Yüan painters, but in his landscapes he was their superior.' Nowadays Mo Lou-ch'üan lives in Wu, and it is said that he is one of the best copyists of the time."

The questions relating to the proper way of copying old pictures assumed a still greater importance with the Ming critics and painters than it had had in earlier periods, it is broached by most of these men both theoretically and practically. Sometimes they speak of *mo* (tracing), sometimes of *lin* (faithful reproduction), but more commonly the two words are used together (*lin mo*) ; in addition to these, the critics also speak of *fan*, imitation or a freer rendering of the originals. Such paintings could, indeed, be of great individual merit, in some cases even superior to the originals. And there were many different degrees among the various kinds of copies ; they marked not only the students' way of learning but also their deference to some old master or school of painting which had served as their guide or inspiration. This may be realized from the following words by T'ang Chih-ch'i (partly borrowed from Mo Shih-ling) who also was an ardent supporter of the Southern school : *

" The painters have transmitted the old models by drawing ever since the time of Hsieh Ho. This method was a ' short cut ' for the painters, because such copying

---

* T'ang Chih-ch'i, *tzŭ* Fu-wu, and Yüan-shêng, born c. 1565. Author of *Hui Shih Wei Yen*, parts of which are reprinted in *Shu Hua P'u*, vol. 14, pp. 28-30, and vol. 16, p. 11. Only the first chapter in this publication is by the author, the rest is made up of quotations from earlier writers.

and tracing is very easy, while it is very difficult to transmit the soul and life (of a picture). But real copying consists in following the idea and not the lines, as in the case of Chü-jan, Mi Fei, Huang Kung-wang and Ni Tsan, who all studied Tung Yüan; although there was only one Tung Yüan, each of them was different from the others. But when, an ordinary man makes copies his endeavour is to follow the original with every brush-stroke; how could he then become famous?"

In addition to this may be quoted a pronouncement by a man called Lien An who evidently held practically the same views as T'ang Chih-ch'i and Tung Ch'i-ch'ang. He introduces his remarks by repeating Su Tung-p'o's well-known words as to the 'constant form and constant principle,' to these he adds the following characterization of painting and condemnation of superficial copying : *

"Painting is an art; those who specialized in it became men of great fame. They all started from representing outward likeness but arrived at expressing the meaning, feelings, and innate character of things. The inspiration in their works is so far-reaching that it cannot be realized except by superior men and great scholars who can see beyond the dust of the common world. Mêng-tzŭ said : ' The great workman can teach people how to use compasses and squares, but he cannot impart skill to them. Chuang-tzŭ in telling about the wheelwright makes him say : ' I cannot teach it to my son, nor can my son learn it from me.' Such is the kind (character) of it. It is something the heart must grasp and the hand respond to, though the heart and the hand are not conscious of it, still less can it be explained in words. Nor can it be learnt by listening (to explanations) or by imitating the works of the hand. To imitate the drawing of the old masters is like attaching oneself to the dust and dirt, or like taking husks and chaff instead of the grain. It is not the true thing."

---

* From *Chin Ch'uan Yü Hsieh Chi*, quoted in *Shu Hua P'u*, vol. 16, p. 9.

THE MING PERIOD

ÆSTHETIC PRINCIPLES AND TECHNICAL METHODS.

THE discussions of the Ming critics were not limited to the questions of schools, traditions of style and methods of study, copying, etc., but included also those general principles of appreciation which had occupied so many of the writers on art ever since the fifth century. Hsieh Ho's Six Principles formed still the backbone for the criticism of painting and they were commented upon with the same eagerness as during the T'ang, Sung and Yüan periods. The contributions of the Ming critics to these discussions were not particularly original, but some of them are nevertheless quite interesting and valuable, because they contain more explicit definitions of the fundamental ideas than we have found in the commentaries offered by their predecessors. They analyse these ideas in a way which is perhaps more akin to the Western mode of thought, even though their terminology is much the same as that of the earlier writers. Some shorter pronouncements on *ch'i yün shêng tung* may be quoted as an introduction to the translations of two or three more comprehensive treatises, in which this central problem also is discussed.

The following remarks by T'ang Chih-ch'i show that some vagueness still adhered to the popular interpretation of this fundamental principle :

"*Ch'i-yün shêng-tung* * are not the same as the effects of vapour and moistness (or brilliancy). When the people of the world point to vapour and moistness and call such

---

* The quotation is from *Hui Shih Wei Yen* as reprinted in *Shu Hua P'u*, vol. 14, l. 30. The word *yün* is here rendered by the character 運 meaning to revolve or revolutions, not the character 韻 which usually stands for *yün* in the above combination and which means harmony or resonance. In the combination with *ch'i* the difference in the meaning of the two characters is not very great, both imply a manifestation, i.e. revolvings or resonance, of the spirit. The above translation of *ch'i yün* may therefore be used also in this case.

effects life-movement (*shêng tung*), they are quite mistaken. It is a serious error. The breath of the spirit (*ch'i*) may be in the brush, in the ink, or in the colour, one may say that it is in the virility (*shih*), in the strength or in the moving power, which all reflect the revolutions (resonance) of the spirit, but life-movement must not be substituted for spirit-resonance. Life is incessantly producing life; it is deep, far-reaching and inexhaustible, always moving and never stiff, but throbbing according to the desires of men. This may all be understood in silence but cannot be explained in words. It is like Liu Pao's * picture of the 'Clouds and the Milky Way,' which made those who saw it feel warm, or his picture of the 'North Wind,' which made those who saw it feel cold, or as the picture of a cat which could drive away mice, and the picture of Kuanyin crossing the sea, which calmed the wind, or as the dotting in of the eyes in the picture of the Dragon, which made it fly away. Such paintings may be said to have had it (i.e. *ch'i yün shêng tung*). Whereas the effects of vapour and moistness may be produced by dotting without visible brush-marks or wrinkles. The two things should not be mixed up."

Tu Lung, the poet and writer of the Wan Li period, already mentioned,† expresses some thoughts about painting which are rather akin to those of the 'gentlemen painters' and poets of the Sung period. His warning is directed particularly against a too close dependence on objective models and a too finicky execution:

"When an inspiring idea preceds the brush-work, the finished picture will beccme soulful, dignified and well balanced; it is not the result of cleverness and skill but something naturally wonderful. Modern painters work out their ideas in detail with great pains; they get the likeness of the objects but not the inspiration of Heaven.

---

* Liu Pao, a famous painter of the second century. Cf. Giles, *Introduction*, p. 8.

† The quotation is from *Hua Shih Hui Yao* as reprinted in *Shu Hua P'u*, vol. 16. A work by the same author called *Hua Chien* is reprinted in *Mei Shu Ts'ung Shu*. Tu Lung served as prefect of Ying-shang and of Ch'ing-p'u, and travelled widely along the lakes and rivers.

" In painting flowers Chao Chang aimed at likeness with nature, while Hsü Hsi did not aim at likeness. But one who is not a great connoisseur of painting will not be able to classify the painter's works by their likeness or lack of likeness with nature. The quality resulting from not aiming at likeness may be found in the writings of Ssŭ-ma Ch'ien and the poems of Tu Fu."

Tu Lung's close connection with the critics of Sung may also be observed in the following paragraph, called " Study of Painting," which might almost have been written by Kuo Hsi:

" When a man is able to express his ideas in painting he places himself at a bright window before a clean table in order to draw some scenery or some objects. If he has contemplated some beautiful views, pictures of the scenery will quite naturally be born in his mind. If he has contemplated rare flowers or cut branches, he will recall the gentle and enchanting appearance of the flowers and the windings and joints of the branches and twigs ; how the flowers open smilingly to the sun, how the branches bend under the wind, how they are enveloped by mist and spoiled by the rain, and how they begin to fade and droop. Then, as he prepares the brush, he will quite unconsciously do something wonderful that harmonizes with the inspiration of Heaven and becomes a thing of joy. But if he does not do it with the sparkling life which is a gift of Heaven and simply draws the outward likeness of the objects on some ordinary paper, the result will be of a common class. The great scholars and gentlemen of former times like Li Kung-lin, Fan K'uan, Li Ch'êng, Su Shih, Mi, father and son, and their like all belonged to the divine class. To become an accomplished connoisseur one must first study one or two famous masters, then only can one grasp the deepest meaning of painting."

Quite similar ideas are expressed by Li Jih-hua (1565-1635), a prominent painter and writer of same learned type as Tung Ch'i-ch'ang, and he develops them further by discussing the painter's preparation and manner of study, his technical methods, the handling of the brush and the ink in a way which rather reminds us of Kuo

Jo-hsü's famous treatise. Li Jih-hua was evidently one of the leading connoisseurs of the age. The following extracts contain some of his essential ideas : *

" The monk Chüeh-yin of the Yüan period said : ' I used to give vent to my gladness in painting orchids (*lan*) and to my anger in painting bamboos.' Now, it may be said that the leaves of the orchids are as if blown about or lifted up and the pistils of their flowers are budding and expanding with the spirit of joy, while the branches of the bamboos are sticking out horizontally and vertically like knives and lances, as if they were beset with anger.

"In painting one must understand how to take and how to yield. To take, means to give the formal likeness by catching it with the brush. It may seem a matter of boldness, but it depends on the mysterious turnings of the brush and on the proper and elegant interruptions and continuations of the strokes. If the brush is moved quite straight (without turnings), it will lead to the fault of wooden stiffness. To yield, means that the idea is carried on (by suggestion) even though the brush-strokes are interrupted, as for instance when huge mountains are vaguely indicated or trees are drawn without separate branches. Everything is there, even though not executed.

"Chiang Po-shih said in talking about calligraphy : ' It is most important that the man should be of a high class.' Wên Chêng-lao (Wên Pi) wrote himself on a painting of a mountain by Mi : ' If the man is not of a high class, he uses the ink without any method.' From this one may realize that the least drop of ink which falls on the paper is no small matter.

" The painter must keep his mind open and free from all matters of the world. Then the effects of vapours and clouds and the beauty of the colours will come out spontaneously in accordance with the spirit of Heaven and

---

* Li Jih-hua wrote extensively not only on painting but also on poetry, philosophy, medicine and other subjects as witnessed by his *Liu Yen Chai Pi Chi*. Writings by the same author more specially devoted to painting are *Chu I an Hua Ying*, containing mostly poetic colophons composed for pictures by Yüan and Ming painters (collected by his son) and *Wei Shui Hsüan Jih Chi*, which contains his daily annotations about paintings and calligraphy from 1589 to 1616. The quotations in *Shu Hua P'u*, vol. 16, are taken from this book.

Earth, and the most wonderful things will take shape under the brush. But if thoughts of the world are buzzing in the mind and not completely washed out, he will—in spite of daily contemplation of hills and valleys and incessant copying of wonderful pictures—arrive at something which hardly can be distinguished from the laborious works of varnishers and masons.

"I often discussed the fact that students of painting must be skilled in writing in order to know how to use the brush. Those who study calligraphy must also, to begin with, keep in their minds old and modern examples. They cannot, however, thoroughly grasp such old and modern examples, if they are not sincere, open-minded and respectful ; nor will the roots and stems be firmly planted and the branches and leaves properly attached (if they are not in the right attitude of mind). Such words have also been pronounced by Su Shih, Mi Fei and Huang Kung-wang ; it has always been so, as one may find in their writings.

"The works of painting must be fine (detailed) and yet expansive ; they must be done with great pains in order to become wonderful. If the spirit of the painter is not keen and broad at the same time, he cannot succeed and make his point. That which is called spirit-resonance (*ch'i yün*) is inborn in the man, and it is in a state of emptiness and tranquility that most ideas are conceived. He may fill up his picture with fine details and develop skill and strength in every direction, but what interest have such things for superior people ?

"Wang Chieh-fu (Wang An-shih) was timid, hurried, stupid and mean. I thought that he could do nothing but write prose compositions, yet in a poem he says : 'I want to express desolation and chill, but I am not able to paint ; only by playing the *ch'in* can I give vent to my joy and sorrow.' For expressing his joy and sorrow he wanted the *ch'in* and did not try to cleanse (his feelings) with lutes or flutes, while for expressing chill and desolation he wanted to paint. He cannot be called a poor connoisseur.

"The prefect Ch'ên used to tell me how Huang Tzǔ-chiu spent whole days among the wild mountains and rugged cliffs seated in the thicket of trees or in bamboo groves, quite lost in his thoughts. Nobody could guess what he was doing. At other times he went to the estuary of the Mao river and sat in contemplation of the rapid current and the roaring waves; even when storms were raging and sea monsters wailed and cried, he remained undisturbed. Such was the profound and melancholy manner of Ta-chih (Huang Kung-wang), whose extraordinary spirit competed with the creative power of Nature.

"When one is rambling in the mountains one should always have paper and ink at hand, so as to be able to make rough sketches of the strange trees and queer stones that one may come across, just as the poet Li Ho, who collected provisions (of phrases) in a brocade bag.

"Painting is like vapours and clouds which rise into (the) space and gather around the cliffs, covering or disclosing vast expanses. The dark and the clear parts cannot be determined beforehand, but in order to make them harmonious one must not lose the effect of nature. The study of writing is like cleaning stones; when the sand on the surface and the foul mud have been completely removed, the fine points (subtleties) will be revealed quite naturally with their beauty and colour. In both arts one should from the beginning (then and there) establish the proper method and then take time for practise, exercising one's power of observation to the utmost. Thus the beginning is made.

"Whenever I looked at representations by Liang K'ai and others of Buddhas and Taoist sages, I found the figures minutely executed down to the smallest hair, while the trees, the rocks and the accessories were made in sketchy fashion without deliberation. By such a careful execution of the figures their strange and bold characteristics are accentuated. Wu Tao-tzŭ used his fine and finished brush-work for the heads, faces, elbows and wrists and painted the folds of the garments with swift and wavy lines, his intentions being the same as Liang K'ai's.

"The old painters worked in the same way as did the Buddha in explaining the law. He spoke by natural inspiration, without any effort, about past kalpas, their causes and effects, which manifest and dissolve in a mysterious fashion beyond human comprehension, though never contrary to truth and reason. Both Heaven and men listened to him with fear, and nobody had any criticism to offer. In painting one should not seek for the strange, nor be tied by the rules. The point of greatest importance is to carry in the mind what one is going to express. Then it will be right.

"The old painters made distinctions between the front and the back, the straight and the slanting in every tree and stone. Not a single brush-stroke was done thoughtlessly. In their paintings of forests in various layers, of paths with windings and turnings, of peaks and slopes, either single or doubled, they introduced cloud effects to close or to open up the views. The winding rivers and the sandbanks they represented both near and far. Their vaporous ink is diffused (pleasant) and unfathomably deep and rich. But if one looks at their pictures with close attention, one can see that every detail is clearly set forth, even the minutest thread is in order. Thus, the clearer (more firmly) the scenery and the ground are established, the freer flows the expression (effect) of life. Such pictures may contain a great many things without being crowded, or only a few things without being scattered and thin; they may be thick without being muddy and dirty, or thin without being empty and unreal. That is what may be called spiritual emptiness or the mystery of emptiness. Everything that here appears or disappears is really moved by the creative power of Nature, whereas pictures in which every leaf is carved out separately and every object is represented according to its outward form will show no difference from the exertions of varnishers and masons. What value have such paintings?

"Among scholars the art of literary composition and noble principles of conduct are most appreciated. But too many talents are worse than too few; they enslave the man and make him spoil his rank. Liu Chün-fu*

---

* Lin P'u, *tzŭ* Chün-fu (c. 965-1026), a poet and painter who retired from the world and lived the life of a recluse near the West Lake in Hang-chou. He threw away his poems (and pictures ?) as fast as they were done, declaring that he did not care for fame. Giles, *Biographical Dictionary*, 1258.

had a great sentiment for painting, but when he saw Wên Yü-k'o and Li Po-shih exhausting themselves the whole day in working for the people, he made the firm resolution not to work any more. I often said that Wang Mo-ch'i cut and polished his emotions in jade. If he had not been able to chant some poems, he would have been no better than a *p'i-pa* player * and his ink paintings would have simply been artisan's work."

Truly words which characterize the careful manner of Wang Wei (and his poetic inspiration) no less than the standpoint of the *wên jên hua* artists : Although the purity and originality of the inspiration was to them of the greatest importance, no less interest was attached to the manner and means by which this inspiration was transformed into a painting, i.e. ' the art of rendering much by little.'

Ku Ning-yüan (*hao* Ch'ing-hsia) who was a painter of the same age and class, expressed in his *Hua Yin* similar ideas in slightly different words : †

" When the inspiration does not rise and the wrist does not move freely, the feelings simply move ahead and nothing whatsoever is accomplished. But if one observes dry and decaying tree-stubs, stones, pools of water, distant woods and all sorts of ruined things, which are quite different from those fashioned by men, and seeks for their hidden meaning with deep feeling and clear eyes, the picture will become a thing alive (emanate living thoughts). It is like collecting phrases of poetry in a brocade bag.

" Among the Six Principles the first one is *ch'i yün shêng tung*. Where there is spirit-resonance, there is also life-movement. The spirit-resonance may be either within or without the scenery. It may be grasped in the seasonal aspects, in the cold or in the heat, in the clear sky or in the rain, in darkness or brightness ; it does not consist in piling up ink."

Ku Ning-yüan's remarks about the *ch'i yün* as being something that also may be found in the objective motif,

---

* *P'i-pa* is the common Chinese guitar or lute.

† *Hua Yin* by Ku Ning-yüan is reprinted in *Mei Shu Ts'ung Shu* and partly quoted in *Shu Hua P'u*, vol. 16.

in the scenery and the moods of nature are a departure in a new direction. This explanation of the essential principle may have been hinted at by some of the earlier critics, but most of them insist on its subjective nature, its dependence on the creative mind of man. By this fresh approach it becomes a more pantheistic quality, something more closely akin to the all-pervading Tao which, however, cannot be represented except by reflection from the individual mind. The essential nature of this great quality does not change in Ku Ning-yüan's interpretation, but its scope is widened and it becomes more comprehensible to Western students.

In the following paragraph Ku Ning-yüan offers some short but significant observations on the proper use of brush and ink and on the relative importance of such qualities as artistic skill and naive simplicity or spontaneity.

"If one uses dry and astringent ink as a groundwork in the picture and then goes on painting in dots in a stupid and thoughtless way, there will be neither ink nor brush (no technical quality), and if one makes the groundwork by piling up the ink in layers without washing and spreading it, the result will become as poor. One should first settle the tendons and the bones (i.e. the constructive lines of the composition) and then gradually add on flesh with a firm and bold movement of the wrist, yet with ease and lightness; then real ink-and-brush quality will result. Such is the general method, but the brightest masters and the most gifted scholars let the brush soak and the ink float, nevertheless even the beards and eyebrows in their pictures are quite distinct. They have no need of joining the bones and pasting on the skin.

"In painting one should strive for life (*shêng*) which is beyond mellow ripeness; after one has reached mellow ripeness, one can no longer give life. It is important to distinguish between excessive ripeness and proper ripeness; the latter can still produce life. Skill does not equal simplicity; after one has reached skill, one cannot return to simplicity. If one does not covet and strive for skill, fresh ideas will rise quite naturally. The result may be simple, but it involves skill, and this skill is simplicity. Only the painters of the Yüan period reached life and simplicity.

"When students first enter on their career they are tied by rules, while good men, modest women and children, who try to write, express quite naturally the inspiration of Heaven. They do it unostentatiously fearing that people should look at them and criticize them; yet, although everything may not be perfect, there is something in their works which famous men cannot give, i.e. life and simplicity. Life and simplicity are not the same as the first efforts of students, they constitute the essential spirit of painting, the wrapped up and pregnant inspiration which does not leak out. They may be described as the first division of chaos in regard to the origin of painting.

"The painters of the Yüan period used their brush spontaneously and expressed their ideas with simplicity. They were men of great virtue and succeeded in concealing their technicality. They were afraid of becoming famous through their painting and of not being able to avoid the entanglements of the world. Only Chao Mêng-fu stood out brilliantly and competed with the famous masters of the T'ang and Sung periods. He was very bold, but when he became a high official, he must nevertheless have found his great skill in art an embarrassment.

"But what is there to be found in life and simplicity? Life (in painting) means the exclusion of the spirit of coarseness; it is an accomplishment known as the brush of a scholar. Simplicity means not to be ostentatious; it is the same thing as that which is called the refinement of a really cultured man."

To the above may be added Ku Ning-yüan's remarks on "Dry and Moist Ink":

"If the ink is too dry, it has no *ch'i yün*, and if one absolutely strives for *ch'i yün*, the result will be an excessive diffuseness. If the ink is too moist, beauty and reason will be lost, but if one absolutely strives for those qualities, the result will be a finicky style (or carved painting: *k'o hua*). The mystery of all the Six Principles cannot be found before one knows how to handle the ink."

In spite of some differences, the æsthetic attitude of Li Jih-hua and Ku Ning-yüan are closely related. Painting was to both of them a creative activity by which the emotions of the heart or the ' hidden ideas ' of the natural motifs could be rendered in visible shapes. It must be done freely and spontaneously, otherwise the resonance of the vital spirit is not released, the picture will have no æsthetic significance. And whether this essential quality is inborn in the painter or inherent in the motif, it must be brought out by the proper handling of brush and ink. The genius or character of the man is reflected in the brush-strokes whether he writes or paints. He cannot be a painter of the highest class until he has mastered all the rules, yet he ' must not be tied by the rules, nor seek for the strange,' or to use, the words of Ku Ning-yüan : he must keep to ' simplicity and spontaneity,' qualities which are superior to every kind of skill ; they form the very heart and soul of painting. When these qualities are perfectly realized, they culminate in the brush of a scholar and the refinement of a truly cultured gentleman, ideals which had been reached by some of the poet painters of Sung and the landscapists of the Yüan period. To them painting was something sacred, almost like a religion, they were afraid of profaning it by exhibiting skill or accumulating personal fame.

A similar standpoint may also be observed in the writings of other critics of the same period, although they do not express it as completely as do Li Jih-hua and Ku Ning-yüan. They dwell on special points, as for instance skill versus simplicity, or the importance of the great Yüan masters as precursors of *wên jên hua*.

Ho Liang-chün* writes as follows : " Critics of painting have said : ' In painting one should particularly avoid insisting on outward shapes and elegant colouring ; one should not indulge in calculations and minute details or try to expose surpassing cleverness.' The people of the world, however, consider carefulness, exactness of

---

* Ho Liang-chün, *tzŭ* Yüan-lang, born c. 1510-20. Han-lin academician in the Chia Ching period. Wrote the *Ssŭ Yu Chai Hua Lun,* consisting partly of extracts from earlier writers, partly of his personal remarks. Quoted in *Shu Hua P'u,* vol. 16.

detail and cleverness as skill (in art), but those who have a deeper knowledge of painting do not agree with this; they think that the said qualities approach the three faults."

Ch'ên K'an dwells on the importance of Huang Kung-wang as an ideal: " The great genius of the Yüan period Huang Kung-wang taught that the thing which is to be most avoided in painting is sweetness. It is made up of luxuriant elegance and mellow ripeness. Everybody recognizes that which is vulgar, rotten and stiff, but people do not avoid sweetness; they rather take pleasure in heaping it up. Huang Kung-wang picked it out and wrote about it most wonderfully."

Tung Ch'i-ch'ang has also left some notes on *ch'i yün*, which characterize the writer no less than the subject. He speaks not only as a painter and art lover but also as a man of learning: Although *ch'i yün* is to him a mark of genius or a gift of Heaven, he thinks that something of it may be acquired by study or that it may at least be developed through intellectual culture. To be a great painter meant, after all, not only to have genius but to possess ' the brush of a scholar.'

" Among the Six Principles of Painting the first is *ch'i yün shêng tung*. The resonance of the spirit cannot be acquired by study but is inborn, a gift of Heaven, yet some of it may be learned. If one has studied ten thousand volumes, walked ten thousand *li*, and freed one's mind from all dust and dirt, beautiful landscapes will rise quite naturally in the mind, and the outlines produced by the work of the hand will transmit the spirit of the landscapes.

" Some critics of ancient times who discussed painting said: ' As soon as the brush touches the paper there appear forms which recede or stand out in relief.' This is very difficult to explain, but I have by now arrived at some comprehension of it. Although I could not reach the greatest masters of the various ages, yet in trying to imitate them, I obtained about one per cent of their art. It is enough; I may retire and go rambling among the hills and valleys.

"Li Ch'êng spared the ink as if it had been gold; Wang Hsia splashed the ink abundantly with water. Students of painting should always keep in their minds these four words: *hsi mo, p'o mo* (spare ink, splash ink); if they do it, they will understand more than half of the Six Principles and the Three Classes (of painting).

"Painting and calligraphy have both their special characteristics. Calligraphy can be produced but painting cannot (be produced) without thorough preparation; (on the other hand) preparation will necessarily beget calligraphy, while in painting it must lead beyond the limits of (technical) preparation."

The last very laconic pronouncement seems to imply that Tung Ch'i-ch'ang, after all, considered painting as a higher form of art than calligraphy, it was to him something that could not be accomplished simply by thorough preparation. He knew by his own long experience that it was possible to learn to paint in the manners of the various great masters but also, that all this technical accomplishment did not necessarily lead to the production of great works of art. Yet, he thought that he had acquired (by the eclectic method) about one per cent of the real thing, i.e. an artistic capital sufficient to live on, an estimate which may be true (comparatively speaking) not only in regard to Tung Ch'i-ch'ang himself but also in relation to the other adherents of the *wên jên hua*. None of them had much to add of his own (except technical skill) to the more or less restricted capital which they had appropriated from their predecessors.

The æsthetic attitude of these men was fairly homogenous; they all accepted Hsieh Ho's Six Principles as a kind of common starting point for the appreciation of painting, and it made little or no difference to them whether the motifs of the paintings were figures, landscapes, flowers, birds, animals or something else. The general principles of appreciation remained the same to them. But there were exceptions, critics who took a somewhat different view of these problems, and who did not think that Hsieh Ho's Principles were applicable to every kind of painting. Prominent among these was

Hsieh Chao-chih,* who seems to have been something of an engineer besides a literary writer and an art critic. In his " Discussion of Painting " he points out the limited value of the traditional principles ; they do not fit modern painting (the art of the late Ming period), which he finds far too summary and individualistically independent to be measured or appreciated according to the standards of Hsieh Ho. The following are some extracts from his *Wu Ts'a Tsu* (quoted in *Shu Hua P'u*, vol. 16) :

" The ancient critics said : ' The first thing in painting is spirit-resonance and life-movement, the second is structural use of the brush, the third is to conform with the objects so as to obtain their likeness, the fourth is to apply the colours according to each species, the fifth is plan and design, place and position, the sixth is to transmit models by drawing : How could these formulas contain the whole secret of painting ? They do not go beyond principles for painting human figures, flowers and birds. If one applies the rules of the ancients to the works of modern men, there is no correspondence : the handle does not fit the socket.

" When human talents find expression in painting, they have reached the highest limit. It may be said, that they snatch the labours of Heaven and Earth and reveal the secrets of Nature (the Creator). Shao-ling (Tu Fu) said : ' When this was reported by the gods, Heaven did weep,' which is true, indeed. The paintings of the ancients were very fine down to the smallest hair, yet done swiftly as with a flying brush and with utmost strength ; they could move the spirits and subdue the devils.

" Nowadays painters think that they can render the characteristic aspect of things by piling up ink and chopping with the brush (as with an axe), but they give only summary abridgements. It may be said, that they amuse themselves with brush and ink. If they really wished to arrive at perfection they could not do it without taking the old masters as their models. But these modern

---

* Hsieh Chao-chih, *tzŭ* Tsai-hang, passed his *chin shih* degree about 1600. He made an official career, served in the Kung-pu and rose to the dignity of a vice-minister. He was active in practical engineering work, wrote a treatise on the Pei-ho river, but also literary works such as the *Wu Ts'a Tsu*.

painters follow simply their own fancy and do not represent the figures in accordance with history. The pictures of flowers, birds and animals are done quite hastily and carelessly, the Buddhist images and the paintings of hell are quite arbitrary; not one in a hundred (is worth while). Briefly speaking, they like to avoid exerting their faculty of observation and in their representations of living things they are missing the essentials."

Hsieh Chao-chih was, no doubt, a man of classical culture and taste; his remarks on the difference between the works of the old masters and those by the men of the late Ming period are quite to the point, though his æsthetic prejudices make him represent the contemporary painters in a too unfavourable light. But such was the habit of the Chinese critics.

The taste and æsthetic ideals of the collectors and art critics of the Ming period are illustrated in a no less amusing than aphoristic fashion by Ch'ên Chi-ju in his *Shu Hua Chin T'ang*, where he enumerates series of good and bad conditions for the study, enjoyment and preservation of paintings. His observations are of particular interest from the collector's point of view, but the collectors were also the leading critics, and their principles for handling and preserving their treasures were, indeed, significant expressions for the æsthetic culture of the period. The right and favourable conditions for the study and preservation of pictures he calls " Virtuous Amusements," the opposite ones, " Wicked Demons." The former are defined as follows:

" A party of connoisseurs. A nice cottage. A clean table. A clear sky with a beautiful moon. A vase of flowers. The season of tea, of bamboo shoots and oranges. In the midst of landscape paintings. A host who is not bold and severe. Dusting and drying (the paintings) in the sun. Burning incense and cultivating fine manners. Examining old paintings. No cares of the world. A great monk in the snow (i.e. philosophical discussions). To be surrounded by rare stones, tripods and vases (*ting* and *i*). Awakening from sleep. Recovering from illness. Slowly unrolling and rolling the pictures."

The bad conditions or " Wicked Demons " are more numerous :

" The season of yellow prunes (humid season). Below a lamp. After drinking. When the ink-stone is filled with floating ink. To take by force, by cunning or deceitful borrowing. To collect and store up many seals. To write colophons in a confused way. To use pictures as cushions. A hurried visitor at one's side. A room where water is dripping in. Rainy season or a parching wind. To carry off pictures for study. To pick out and appraise pictures without order. To be disturbed by vulgar talk. The hands covered with grease and sweat. To dry pictures in the sun on a dirty ground. Poor mounting and repairing. To defile and spoil by copying. Eaten by bookworms. To undo the pictures violently. Sneezing rats. Servants standing about. To ask for the price. Marks of finger nails. To cut, to fold, or to wrinkle the pictures."

He gives furthermore some directions for the protection of pictures and enumerates certain paraphernalia which should belong to them :

" Rollers of tortoise shell, of red polished gold, of glass, of white jade, of rhinoceros horn or of choicest *kuan yao* porcelain. Embroidered ribbons. A secret pavilion for keeping the pictures. Precious labels. Name tablets of five-coloured jade. Old brocade covers. Seals by emperors and dukes. Rare and richly coloured bags. Colophons by famous scholars. To have belonged to a literary courtesan. A sandalwood box inlaid with gold, mother of pearl and lapis lazuli."

The calamities which may befall a picture are the following :

" To fall into the hands of a peasant. To be pawned. To be given to haughty people. To be cut up for making coats and stockings. To be left to an unworthy son. To be stolen by thieves. To be exchanged against wine and food. Calamities of water and fire. To be buried in a tomb."

PLATE XVIII

MISTY HILLS, IN THE MANNER OF MI YU-JEN
Ch'en Shun (1483-1544, Ming dynasty)

PLATE XIX

PEACH-BLOSSOM SPRING
Tao-chi (1641-ca. 1717, Ch'ing dynasty)

THE CH'ING PERIOD

NEW INDIVIDUAL DEPARTURES

THE generation which witnessed the fall of the great Ming dynasty and the advent of the glorious Ch'ing produced not only a number of very able painters but also some writers of remarkable originality. We will here limit us to two of them who have discussed the painter's art in treatises which are quite unlike those of the preceding generation. The one was Shên Hao, the other the monk Tao-chi (Shih-t'ao).

Their years of birth and death are not recorded and we know very little about their personal history, because they were not government officials nor men in prominent social positions. Quite the contrary; they seem to have remained relatively unnoticed by their contemporaries, practising their art and noting down their thoughts merely for their own pleasure. They were in this respect more akin to the great masters of the Yüan period than to the learned painters of the Ming dynasty, whose thoughts have been recorded in the previous chapters, and their ideas about painting were rather different from those which inspired the *wên jên hua*. They may, relatively speaking, be classified as individualists, though it goes without saying, that no Chinese writers or painters could stand quite independent of the age-old traditions.

Shên Hao from Wu-hsien, *tzǔ* Lang-ch'ien, claimed to be of the same family as the famous Shên Chou and appropriated therefore later in life the latter's well-known *hao*: Shih-t'ien. He passed in early years the *chu shêng* examination, but devoted himself subsequently to the study of Buddhism and lived for some years in retirement as monk. This kind of life does not seem to have satisfied his natural disposition. If we may believe one of his biographers (Ch'ien Shang-hao in *Mai Ch'ou Chi*) he preferred the company of carefree idlers and beautiful women. He said : ' the same passion pervades Heaven and man ; I regret that I was born in the world of men. What chance have I to mount the phœnix ? I sing in vain my shepherd song for the Peach Blossom girls.'

His free mode of living outside official circles contributed to make him little known and esteemed by his contemporaries in spite of his gifts as a poet, calligraphist and painter, but this does not seem to have lessened his self-esteem. It is most prevalent in all his writings. At least two of his works are devoted to the history of painting: *Hua Chü* and *Hua Ch'üan Têng*. The former has survived in many reprints and has made its author famous with posterity.

It is divided into thirteen short chapters and opens with a few quite irrelevant "Remarks about the Origin"; in the second chapter he relates the division of the Southern and the Northern school in accordance with the well-known scheme. The third chapter is written in opposition to "Fixed Rules" or conventional methods in painting. He praises pictures which are done with a few strokes of the brush without any calculation of details and comes to the conclusion, that the simpler they are, the better. "Ordinary painters make things complicated in order to hide the difficulties." The fourth chapter contains some quite short but strikingly poetic definitions of the appearance of mountains at the four seasons. The fifth chapter is devoted to "Brush and Ink" and contains certain technical terms and advices of interest, but the poems which the author introduces as further expositions of his ideas can hardly be said to serve the purpose. They are consequently left out in our translation. The sixth chapter deals mainly with "Composition" and shows rather close dependence on Kuo Hsi's essay on landscape painting from which several ideas are borrowed. Most characteristic of the author's own position is again the emphasis that he lays on spontaneity in painting: "When one is about to start one should do it as Ts'ao did when he was going to fight : one should make a semblance of not wishing to fight, yet put one's whole mind into it in order to conquer."

The seventh chapter contains only a few remarks about the relative importance of ink and colours, the eighth some critical observations on how old and modern painters have spotted the moss on the mountains, which evidently was considered an important feature in landscape painting. In the ninth chapter he explains how the titles for pictures should be chosen and how they should be written in order to complete the compositions; here it is also pointed out that such motives as fishing, wood-cutting, ploughing and pasturing can be properly re-presented only by men who, like the sage of old, have lived in the wilderness. The tenth chapter is a completion of the preceding one; the dedicatory inscriptions are further discussed; they must cling gracefully to the painted compositions; there is a proper place for them in every picture, and "if one misses this place, the composition will be spoiled." In the eleventh chapter, "Copying and Tracing," this much propounded question is tersely dismissed with the remark, that copies should not be reproductions of pictures in front of the painter but ren-derings of their ideas, "they must be accomplished in the soul." The formal similarity is secondary; the expression of primary importance also in copies; different artists may render the same original in quite different ways and yet all be right. The old masters did not limit themselves to copying; they studied from nature in order to grasp the most intimate aspects of certain landscapes.

The twelfth chapter is a still stronger opposition to the traditional methods of imitating the predecessors and an affirmation of the necessity to follow one's own natural disposition. The painter who in his dreams entered into the divine or the inner nature of things was able to do the most wonderful pictures: "He got hold of the real creative power, because he harmonized with the mountains and streams, with the great earth and with every living thing and saw (or projected) his own genius in all these things. He worked freely, as the clouds drift over the empty sky and the reflections of flying wild geese float on dark waters."—In the last chapter, which is called "Appreciation and Criticism," the author once more draws the line between the works of 'gentlemen painters' and professional artists and likewise between two different types of art lovers, i.e., those who appreciate painting in their heart and those who are interested in its commercial value. The real thing in art was never reached by professionals, who followed traditional methods of study and copying, drawing and composition, and who thought of the profit they might earn by their work ; it is beyond their ken, because it can be reached only unconsciously by those who have no other intention than to express their own genius or to give vent to the joy and sadness of their hearts. But only for those "who appreciate a picture with clear eyes will the soul of the work become manifest, while people who ask the price of it can find no spiritual response in the work."

This, of course, was the classic position of the 'gentleman painter' in all ages, but it had been most definitely applied in the Sung period, and it was among the men of this period that Shên Hao found his ideals. He despised without exception his own contemporaries and immediate predecessors and as he, at the same time, never tires of extolling his own paintings as examples of a superior art, he rather reveals his lack of unprejudiced judgment, a weakness which, however, does not lessen the value of his general æsthetic pronouncements. Taken as a whole, the essay may be designated as an abridged summary of the theory of painting expressed in a highly individual fashion and often in very terse terms difficult to render in a foreign language. The following translation includes the whole thing with the exception of the poems.

Hua Chü. Talks on Painting. (edit. *Chao Tai Ts'ung Shu*)

REMARKS ABOUT THE ORIGIN.

" The world knows only Fêng Mo as the originator of painting, but does not know that it really started with Lady K'o-shou (the sister of the Emperor Shun). A friend of mine said : ' It is to be regretted that this divine art took its origin from a woman.' But I pointed out that Ko saved her brother Shun from the wrath of Sou (his blind father) and Hsiang (his younger brother). She possessed the power of creation and was capable of becoming the originator of painting."

DIVISION INTO SCHOOLS

" Ch'an Buddhism and painting both divided at the same time into a Southern and a Northern school. The moving spirit was different in these two schools. The Southern school began with Wang Wei whose manner was pure and refined ; he expressed the spirit-resonance in a subdued and quiet fashion and opened the way for the *wên jên* such as Ching Hao, Kuan T'ung, Pi Hung, Chang Tsao, Tung Yüan, Chü-jan, the two Mi, Huang Kung-wang, Wang Mêng, Chao Mêng-fu, Wu Chên and Ni Tsan until Shên Chou and Wên Pi of Ming, and a great many others. The Northern school was Li Ssŭ-hsün, whose style was clever and vigorous. He moved the brush with strength and firmness, and formed a school which was continued by Chao Kan, Chao Po-chü, Po-su, Ma Yüan and Hsia Kuei until Tai Wên-chin, Wu Wei, Chang P'ing-shan, etc. But gradually the school fell into ' marvels ' and the succession became covered with dust."

FIXED RULES

" Tu Fu said : ' The ideas of a poet are noble and simple.' Modern painters strive intentionally for simplicity by imitating Ni Tsan, but it must be reached unintentionally if one is to be like Ni Tsan ; otherwise it is impossible.

" Chao Ta-nien painted wide and open views. He held a dominating position in the spontaneous (*i*) school. He cut out fields and river-banks, representing them with their natural freshness and beauty in accordance with the tradition of Wang Wei. But some old critics have said : ' If he had been a more learned man, he would have been still more wonderful and old-fashioned.' Then one could not paint without being learned.

" I composed a ten-stroke picture (*shih pi t'u*) and showed it to some comrades of mine who like extraordinary things in order to shape and cleanse their eyes. Fallen trees and broken river-banks should have an air which leads beyond the air of beauty in accordance with the saying of the Buddhist sutra : ' Thunder and lightning are hidden in the pure and cold clouds.'

" Ten-stroke painting means to do the wrinkles on stones, the furrows on trees and the boundary lines of high buildings and pavilions in an unconventional way. There are old pictures in which the orchids are painted with a double brush without any calculation of the flowers, and there are other pictures in which Kuanyin is painted with a triple brush without any design of the ears, the eyes, the nose or the mouth.

" The soul must be put into the work, the drawing must have structure, and the whole thing must give harmonious enjoyment. A man of the T'ang period said : ' Far and wide goes one stroke of the brush ; in every herb and every tree there is a divine spirit.'—It is as if there were a living thing in the picture and in the thing were sound ; but this can be explained only to the intelligent. But alas ! the pictures produced after the Chia Ching and Lung Ch'ing epochs (1567-72) have neither soul nor structure and still less of harmonious resonance.

" To pile up layers and peaks of mountains is like composing long popular songs. The pictures of far-away mountains and scattered hills should be like stanzas of five or seven words ; the simpler they are, the deeper and more lasting. Ordinary people make things complicated in a stupid fashion in order to hide the difficulties.

" The essence of Tung Yüan's soul was in Yün-chien (Sung-chiang), Chao Mêng-fu's inspiration was in Chin-ch'ang (Soochow). Afterwards these two schools became separated, but the opposition was not between Tung and Chao, it was caused by the malpractices of their followers. These malpractices were carried to the extreme, and then there came some painters who straightened the crooked, but they formed again habits which were combined with the malpractices. The whole movement proceeded thus further and further, and the more the painters were removed from the old masters, the more independent they became. Why did they not climb step by step trying to form a school and an original style, not that of Tung Yüan, nor of Chao Mêng-fu, nor of Sung-chiang, nor of Soochow, not imitation, nor the straightening of the crooked? I am walking quite alone, but my steps raise an echo, and I have confidence in myself."

DISTINCTIONS OF LANDSCAPES

"The mountains of spring seem to be joyful. The mountains of summer seem to express emulation. The mountains of autumn seem to be suffering. The mountains of winter seem to be meditating."

BRUSH AND INK

"It is very difficult to harmonize the brush with the ink. When the outlines have been made and one puts on the wrinkles, their clearness or muddiness depend on the brush, while their appearance and disappearance (relief) depend on the ink.

"Mi Fei used Wang Hsia's *p'o mo* 潑墨 (splash ink), he combined it with *p'o mo* 破墨 (broken-up ink), *chi mo* 積墨 (piled-up ink) and *chiao mo* 焦墨 (burnt-black ink). Consequently he obtained effects of vapour and airiness. I read the biography of T'ien Sui-tzǔ,* and from this I understood the *fei mo* 飛墨 (flying ink) (i.e. using insufficient ink and leaving white spots). After I had made the outlines and put on the wrinkles I dried the back of the picture (over a stove) in order to make the *ch'i yün* appear deep and rich in a way which could not be found out easily."

Here follows a poem on landscape painting which ends with the words: "One drop of ink contains a world, an infinity of time, all manifest to the heart (as said in

---

*Lu Kuei-mêng, a poet of the T'ang dynasty whose chief delight was to travel about in a small boat with fishing tackle and tea utensils (Giles, 1420).

Buddhist scriptures). I discussed with Han-shan Fan-fu the point of the brush and the handle of the brush, whether it should be held obliquely or straight. One day when I saw a specimen of calligraphy by a man of the Chin dynasty I grasped the method of painting " (which is further expressed in a poem).

COMPOSITION

"Modern paintings are lacking in hills and valleys (i.e. depth of thought); they confine themselves to the habit of introducing some changes in the foreground and the background.

"Huang Kung-wang said: 'In the paintings one must leave some space for the sky and the ground.' It is a common method. In my pictures the clouds and the mist reach down to the bottom, dangerous peaks rise up unexpectedly, and there is only a single figure who (as said in the poem) 'shakes his garments on a lofty height.' As my visitor feels surprised, I tell him: 'This high peak is the master, the small cliffs around it are like his grandsons, they do not need to be so evident. The gorges and the feet of the mountains, the tree stumps and the roots may be hidden or not completely brought out by the brush.' My visitor said: 'When the old masters painted plum-trees or bamboos they represented only a single warped branch reaching over the wall. If they had represented the complete tree with all its branches, their paintings would have been uninteresting. Do you think they were right?' I said: 'Certainly.'

"The compositions by professional painters are dense and crowded; they have no empty space, and their emotional resonance is reduced to a minimum. But when the stirred clouds and drooping mist envelop the mountain peaks and cover the trees, there is the moving power of life. Mi Fei said: 'I have seen many of Wang Wei's paintings; they are all done in the minute manner (*k'o hua*) and should not be taken as models, only his cloudy mountains are done as ink-plays (*mo hsi*). The point of these words may not be quite correct, yet they have some sense.

"The paintings of the old masters contain parts which are alive and parts which are dull, parts which are incomplete and parts which are crowded, parts which are delicate and parts which are strong.

"Kuo Hsi said: 'Far-away mountains have no wrinkles, far-away waters have no ripples, far-away figures have no eyes.' I say: 'Far-away mountains are even without curves, far-away waters recede, do not approach, far-away figures must be alone, not in crowds.'

"In a picture there may be parts which are of little importance beside others which should be particularly strong and effective.

"When I conceive a plan in the mind and the brush does not respond to it, the ideas may not be right, but as soon as I touch the paper, there is nothing wrong. The parting and meeting of creative forces, the going and coming of the spirit is neither in me nor in the picture. When one is about to start painting, one should do it as Ts'ao did when he was going to fight, i.e. one should make a semblance of not wishing to fight, yet put one's whole mind into it in order to conquer.

"One must first find out the proper relation between the master and the servants (i.e. the principal and the secondary motifs) in the composition, which mountain should be the master and how it is supported by the trees, and which tree should be the master and how it is supported by the mountain; then one should play with the brush and the ink. If one uses rotten charcoal and works hesitatingly, the soul of the picture will become feeble, its vital spirit cramped, and the more one toils, the worse it becomes."

To Brush with Colours

"Wang Wei said: 'Fluent ink is supreme.' Quite right; only one must not start the moment the brush is grasped mixing the fluent ink with colours. The harmony of the ink must be enough until the design is complete, then there is no objection to brushing with colours."

Spotting the Moss

" It is a common method to use spotted moss on the mountains and stones and along the winding waters and springs. Wang Mêng's dry moss and Wu Chên's accumulated moss are two kinds which grow from the same seed. Students of to-day try to imitate these manners of doing the moss, but they do it rather stupidly. Among the old painters were many who never used moss, because they were afraid of hiding the subtlety of the mountain veins and the beauty of the wrinkles. The works of modern painters are not worth looking at ; they make absolutely a mess of spots. They cannot avoid adding on the ridiculous scab of old witches."

To Write Titles on Paintings

This chapter opens with a quotation from Kuo Hsi ; then the author discusses how the titles or names should be written, whether before or after the picture. It is better to use an old title than to compose a new, and if one finds no old title which explains the work, it is better to give it no name. The writing and the painting should explain each other mutually.

" When the great men of olden times could not find expression for their wishes, they occupied themselves with fishing and wood-cutting ; they went into retirement and often entrusted themselves to the brush. Their works expressed harmony, i.e. poetry without a sound. Thus passing their time in playing with the brush they composed landscapes out of things that filled their minds and their eyes. When modern painters represent fishing, wood-cutting, ploughing and pasturing they do it without penetrating into the meaning of these occupations, and their works become worthless. The anglers and wood-cutters are hunchbacked or stooping, they work with great pains without the least pleasure. Yet, these painters are satisfied with themselves, but intelligent observers cannot help laughing at them."

DEDICATORY INSCRIPTIONS

" Before the Yüan period inscriptions were not much used. Sometimes the inscriptions were hidden in the crevices of the stones ; one was afraid of making the writing evident and of injuring the picture by it. Later on the writing and the painting were made together ; the former clung gracefully to the latter and completed it.

" Ni Tsan's style of writing was vigorous and spontaneous. Sometimes he wrote a colophon at the end of a poem and sometimes he wrote a poem after the colophon, thus completing the meaning of the work. He is a good model.

" Wên Pi wrote his inscriptions very clearly and neatly. Shên Chou in his old age wrote the inscriptions in a bold fashion encroaching upon the picture and spoiling some wonderful parts. Ch'ên Shun (Po-yang) and others imitated him.

" In every picture there is a proper place for a dedicatory inscription ; if one misses this place the composition will be spoiled."

COPYING AND TRACING

" The copying of old masters should not be done by keeping the original in front of one ; the copy must be accomplished in the soul. One must concentrate on the idea (of the work) without the least deflection (a grain of dust). Whether it becomes like or not like the original is something that does not depend on any deliberation.

" Sun (Ch'ien-li) and Yü (Sh'ih-nan)* both inherited Wang Hsi-chih's style of writing, yet they were different. Li (K'ung-t'ung) and Ho (Ta-fu)† both imitated Tu Fu's poetry, yet each one was different from the other. Other men got their eyes opened by looking at sword-dancers‡ or acrobats walking on earthern jars. They took such

---

* Two famous calligraphists of pre-T'ang times.

† Two poets of the Ming dynasty.

‡ Cf. the story about Wu Tao-tzŭ looking at the sword dance of General Wu.

exhibits for guidance, but would not have been able to profit by it if they had not been of superior intelligence.

"Tung Yüan made sketches of the real Chiang-nan landscapes. Huang Kung-wang retired to the mountains and there he painted the Yü Shan, rendering exactly its wrinkles and colours. He used to carry brushes and ink-slab in a bag, and when he saw some strangely shaped clouds or trees, he copied them instantly. Kuo Hsi painted the mountains after the fashion of startled and rising clouds; he was called the clever thief (as he stole the shapes from the clouds). One should know how eagerly the old masters took sketches (*kao pên*) from nature and preserved them in their heart. Those who have sharp eyes (or a clear perception) will find this out for themselves and will know how to follow the methods of idlers and vagabonds."

To Comply with Natural Dispositions

"When the intelligent man conceives an idea he follows it up with the brush, soaking the ink and sweeping over the paper, and thus there appear picked flowers and beaten bamboos.

"Ku Han-chung wrote a colophon on a picture by Ni Tsan in which he said: 'He started by following Tung Yüan.' Afterwards Ni Tsan himself wrote on his picture of 'The Lion Grove': 'In this picture I have followed the ideas of Ching Hao and Kuang T'ung, which Wang Mêng could not conceive even in his dreams.' According to these writings, Ni Tsan could not avoid depending on his predecessors, yet in his old age he followed his own ideas; rubbed and brushed and was like an old lion walking alone without a single companion. One day he painted in the lamplight some bamboos and trees, grasping their proud beauty. When he rose the next morning and unrolled the picture he found that it did not quite give the likeness of bamboos, whereupon he remarked smilingly: 'This is not a representation of outward likeness; it is not easy to do such a thing.'

" There was once a painter who worked in the day-
time, but in his dreams he entered into the picture and
next morning he did it over again. The dreams opened
to him the way into the divine — and thus it happened
that a fly settled on the edge of the painted screen, the
sound of water rose over his bed, fishes splashed in the
water, and dragons pierced the walls of the house. All
corresponded to the working of his own genius. He
got hold of the real creative power, because he conceived the mountains and streams, the great earth and
every living thing according to their characteristics.
He rolled and unrolled, grasped and discarded (i.e.
worked freely) as the clouds scatter over the empty sky,
or as reflections of flying wild geese float on the dark
water."

APPRECIATION AND CRITICISM

" Those who copy only one school cannot discuss
painting ; those who like only one school cannot discuss
appreciation of painting. One of the old critics (i.e.
Kuo Hsi) said : ' Looking at pictures is like the pleasures
of woods and waters : if one looks with proud and haughty
eyes, they seem quite trivial. Those who ask the price
of paintings and those who appreciate them in the heart
cannot be placed in the same class.' Therefore I say :
' If one appreciates a picture with clear eyes, the soul
of it will dominate, but if one asks about its value in gold,
one finds no spiritual response in it.

" When people nowadays see pictures which are simple,
pure, noble and spontaneous, they call them ' gentleman
paintings ' and say that the painters did not reach the real
thing. The real thing they find in the methods of the
professional painters, not knowing that Wang Wei, Li
Ch'êng, Fan K'uan, Mi, father and son, Su Shih, Ch'ao
Pu-chih, Li Po-shih and others were all ' gentlemen
painters.' Was it these men or the professional painters
who did not reach the real thing ?

" People of the world appreciate paintings done by
men of the world, intelligent men appreciate paintings

done by intelligent men ; their mutual habits bring them close to each other. To deliberate for one day is not enough, to deliberate for a whole year is more than enough. If the right men are not there, the right pictures will not be produced."

*   *   *

More original than Shên Hao, both as writer and painter, was the monk Tao-chi, better known by his *tzŭ* Shih-t'ao and also under other appellations such as Shih-kung Shan-jên or K'u-kua ho-shang, "the Monk of the Bitter Cucumber." He may also be counted to the 'transition period,' as he was born under the Ming, though mainly active during the early years of the Ch'ing dynasty. His position as a painter is well established ; as a writer he is less known, though from the art-historian's point of view hardly less interesting.

His main essay on painting, the *Hua Yü Lu* is one of the most extraordinary contributions to the discussions of the theory and practice of painting, but couched in terms which, in part at least, offers evasive problems of interpretation. The terminology is largely borrowed from Taoist sources and it is applied with an abundant use of antitheses, repetitions and cosmological metaphors of a very abstruse kind. A full translation of the whole essay, which is divided into 18 chapters, would hardly be enjoyable to Western readers, nor is it necessary for our purpose, because the fundamental ideas, which determine the author's outlook on painting, may be found in practically every chapter, though variously applied. The seven chapters of which we offer translations contain all the essential elements of Shih-t'ao's æsthetic ideology.

His sources of inspiration must have been not only Taoistic writings but also the Classics and most particularly *I Ching*, the " Book of Changes," from which he has taken over some of the cosmological ideas. Painting is to him a microcosmic activity, a miniature parallel to the creative activity of the macrocosmic forces, which express themselves in the movement of the heavenly bodies and in all the living organisms of nature. But not every kind of painting; most of the products which pass under this name are simply laborious efforts with brush and ink, or results of learning and skill produced according to some more or less artificial method. These are not works of natural genius, nor examples of the primordial all-inclusive creative art, which Shih-t'ao calls *i hua*, an expression apparently formed on the model of such terms as *i yüan, t'ai i,* etc., which all refer to the primordial orign of cosmic creation. The general purport of the expression seems quite evident, but we get no closer explanation or definition of its meaning, except such statements as " all methods have their origin in it, and it is the root of numberless representations." It is a road open to the gods but hidden to men ; the author has discovered it by following his heart instead of adhering to traditional methods. As to its further meaning or application it must become a matter of individual experience, because it is not a method that may be intellectually defined. Those who can completely enter into the reason of landscapes and figures and give the substance of everything will understand this method—a path evidently leading in the same direction as the ideals of the Ch'an painters. But though the parallel is undeniable, it should be remembered, that the latter had a background of spiritual or mystical knowledge which can hardly be traced in Shih-t'ao's writings. They are more playfully intellectual, more detached from the realities of life, and full of far-fetched cosmological speculations.

In some respects he approaches quite modern artistic ideals. His individualism is carried to the utmost limit. He has no use for the old masters and considers his own genius as the only guide worth following. " The method which consists in following no method is the perfect method." No matter what the paintings look like : if they only express the essence of life and the painter's creative mind, they are examples of the all-inclusive creative art (*i hua*). Genius is the primary thing, knowledge is secondary ; if one does not know how to expand the gifts allotted by Heaven, one will never do anything worth while. In the hands of the inspired painter even the technical means, such as brush and ink, become transformed into some mysterious forces, which act like the generative influences of nature by which all things are reproduced. Like so many other critics and painters he extolls the life-imparting power of brush and ink; but it must be acquired by early training, otherwise one cannot move the brush freely nor impart and transmit the spiritual force. On this point he could, no doubt, have found the agreement of practically all Chinese painters, whatever school or style they followed, but when he describes the painter's psychological attitude, he is no longer in accord with the *wên jên* or other famous painters of the time : " Men who are dominated by things reap trouble in their hearts . . . . . they are carving their pictures and wear themselves out." The real painter must be completely detached from all worldly cares ; he must concentrate on the inner meaning of things ; his whole soul must be in the work, only then can it become inscrutable. A peculiar combination of Chinese traditionalism and extreme individualism permeates Shih-t'ao's essay from the first to the last chapter.

Hua Yü Lu. NOTES ON PAINTING. (Edit. *Chao Tai Ts'ung Shu*).

I. *I Hua.* ALL-INCLUSIVE CREATIVE PAINTING.*

" The most ancient had no method ; their state of natural simplicity had not been shattered. When this state of natural simplicity was broken up, a method was established.† In what did the method consist ? It was the *i hua*. In this all-inclusive creative painting all

---

* Our translation of *i hua* by the above explanatory words is merely tentative. Its correspondence to the Taoist expressions *t'ai i*, *i yüan*, etc., is evident, but it should also be remembered, that Confucius uses the expression *i i kuan chih*, translated by Legge : " all pervading unity."

† This statement reminds us of certain passages in Chuang-tzŭ, as for instance the following : " The knowledge of the ancients was perfect. How perfect ? At first they did not yet know that there were things. This is the most perfect knowledge ; nothing can be added. Next they knew that there were things, but did not yet make distinctions between them. Next they made distinctions between them, but did not yet pass judgment upon them. When judgment was passed, Tao was destroyed. With the destruction of Tao individual preferences came into being."

methods have their origin; it is the root of numberless modes of representation. It lies open to the gods but is hidden to men. The people of the world do not know the *i hua* method, but I have established it for myself. I have established it by creating a method from no method. It pervades (includes) all other methods.

"In painting one should follow the heart (mind). If one cannot completely enter into the reason and render all the details of beautiful landscapes and figures, the characteristics of birds, animals, grass and trees, or the designs of pavilions, buildings and terraces, the great principle of the all-inclusive creative painting cannot be grasped. If one is going to walk far and climb high, one must start by taking a small step. Thus one can completely gather, in the all-inclusive creative painting, the whole chaos, and numberless works of brush and ink will find their beginning and end in it. If men only fall in with it and grasp it, they can give by this *i hua* the gist of everything on a small scale. Their ideas will be clear and their brush will be bold, whereas poor pictures reveal a lack of spiritual force in the wrist. The movements of the wrist must be freely revolving, they must transmit the richness of the ink and dominate the open spaces; they must start out as if cutting, draw in like ripping, form circles and squares, straight lines and curves, make swellings and hollows, break and cut resolutely, move horizontally and transversly like water that penetrates deep, or like rising flames of fire, and they must do it all naturally without being in the least forced. If this is done without spirit, the manner is not penetrating, there is no reason in it, and the appearance is not complete. But if one does it without hesitation, with a stroke of the brush, landscapes, figures, birds, animals, grass, trees, pavilions, buildings and terraces will be represented with proper form and strength, life and character. One must give the emotional expression of the landscapes by making some parts in them wide open and other parts hidden or screened. People cannot discover how such paintings are done, but they are never contrary to the heart's desire. Thus ever since the state of natural simplicity was shattered and the method of the all-inclusive original painting (*i hua*) was established, innumerable things of nature have been made manifest by this method. Therefore it has been said :* 'My doctrine is that of an all pervading unity.' "

II. *Liao Fa*. PERFECTED METHOD.

"The compasses and squares produce perfect circles and squares.† The circulations of Heaven and Earth are the origin of compasses and squares. The world knows that there are compasses and squares, but it does not know the principle of the circulations of Heaven and Earth. Yet, it is Heaven and Earth which form the rules (methods) of men. The methods people commonly use are stupid. Some methods are derived from the natural disposition of the painters, some from what they have learned, but they do not contain either reason or meaning. The painters cannot command their methods but are, on the contrary, obstructed by them.

"Such obstructive methods have been practised from old to modern times, because the principle of the all-inclusive original painting (*i hua*) has not been understood. When the *i hua* is understood, there is no longer any veil before the eyes, and painting follows the heart. When painting follows the heart, the obstructing veils are removed, and all the innumerable things of Heaven and Earth can be represented. But nobody can do it without the use of brush and ink. The ink is a natural product, it may be rich or thin, dry or moist, but the brush-work is accomplished by man ; he makes the hooks and wrinkles and soaks and dries the colours.

"The ancients never did it without a method. If there is no method, then nothing has a proper limit. In the *i hua* there is nothing which has not its proper limits. There is no method, yet there are proper limits. It is a method without obstructions, or obstructions without a method : The method is born by painting and the obstructions disappear ; the method and the obstructions

---

* Confucius, *Analects*. Book IV, *Li Jên*.

† This expression is taken over from Mêng-tzŭ.

do not blend. The principle of the circulations of Heaven and Earth is reached, and the Tao of painting is made manifest. That is the perfection of *i hua*.

III. *Pien Hua*. TRANSFORMATIONS.

"The works of the old masters are instruments of knowledge. Transformations mean to understand (these instruments), but not to be as they. I never saw a painter who being like the old still could transform them, and I have often regretted the (conventional) manner of adhering to them, which causes no transformations. This depends on a limited understanding and on adhering simply to the outward likeness. When the superior man borrows from the old masters, he does it in order to open a new road. It has also been said: 'The perfect man has no method,' which does not mean that he is without method. The method which consists in not following any method (of the ancients) is the perfect method.

"Everything has its constant principle but has also its variations. The method should also include transformations. If one knows the constant principle, one can modify it by variations, and if one knows the method, one is also skilled in transformations.

"Painting is the great method to be in harmony with everything in the world. It gives the very essence of the aspects of mountains and rivers. Like the Great Creator it gives shapes to everything, be it old or new. It gives the circulations of the Yin and the Yang. It borrows brush and ink to draw innumerable things of Heaven and Earth and puts one into a happy frame of mind.

"Painters of to-day do not understand this. They say quite often: 'This painter's wrinkles and dots stand on their feet (are firmly fixed); they are not like those of another man whose landscapes will not survive to posterity.' Or: 'This painter is pure and fresh; he is of a high class and not like that other man whose great skill and cleverness serve simply to amuse people.'—One becomes thus the slave of a certain painter instead of using him for one's benefit. Even if one's work is quite like that of a certain painter, one simply eats the dregs of his soup. What is there in that for oneself?

"Someone said to me: 'Through this painter my knowledge has been extended, through the other it has been restrained. I am now going to follow a certain school, I shall climb certain steps, I shall imitate certain points, I shall follow certain models, I shall learn how to use colours, how to draw wrinkles and outlines, how to render the shapes; when I know all this, I shall become one of the old masters, and the old master will be myself.'

"He who talks this way knows only that there are old masters, but does not know himself. I am always myself and must naturally be present (in my work). The beards and eyebrows of the old masters cannot grow on my face. The lungs and bowels (thoughts and feelings) of the old masters cannot be transferred into my stomach (mind). I express my own lungs and bowels and show my own beard and eyebrows. If it happens that my work approaches that of some old painter, it is he who comes close to me, not I who am imitating him. I have got it by nature (genius), and there is no one among the old masters whom I cannot follow and transform."

IV. *Tsun Shou*.   RECEIVINGS FROM NATURE (APPRECIATION OF NATURAL GIFTS).

"Natural gifts and knowledge (are different things); first come natural gifts, then comes knowledge. Gifts which have been acquired by knowledge are no gifts. The greatest among old and modern masters availed themselves of knowledge, but projected (issued forth) their natural gifts. If one has no natural gifts but expresses simply what one has learned, it does not exceed the work of a minor talent. By such small gifts and little knowledge one cannot realize the power of all-inclusive creative painting (*i hua*); one cannot expand nor grow. The all-inclusive creative painting contains innumerable things.

"Painting receives (depends on) the ink, the ink depends on ('receives') the brush, the brush depends on the wrist, the wrist depends on the heart (mind), just as Heaven creates life and Earth makes it mature. That is really what is meant by natural gifts (receivings). But one must know how to esteem them. If one has gifts by nature but does not appreciate them, it is like throwing oneself away; if one has reached this kind of painting, but does not apply transformations one is tied up. Those who have the gift of painting must know to appreciate it and how to take care of it. They should use it with strength and not open any loop-holes for it, nor let it stop within. In the *I Ching* it is said : ' The heavenly bodies are regular in their courses, so should the superior man be (strong and indefatigable) in his practice of virtue.' In this saying the gifts of nature are rightly esteemed.

V. *Pi Mo*. BRUSH AND INK.

" Among the old painters there are some who have both brush and ink, others who have brush but no ink, others again who have ink but no brush. It is not the boundaries of the mountains and streams which are unequal, but the human talents which are disparate. The ink should be spread about as by the spirit, and the brush should be moved as by a god. If one has no early training, there will be no spirit in the ink ; if the brush is not alive, it cannot be divine. If one has acquired the spiritual quality by early training but cannot express the soul of life, then one has ink but no brush. If, on the other hand, one knows how to convey the soul of life but does not combine it with spirit acquired through early training, one has brush but no ink.

" Mountains and streams and the innumerable things of the world are sometimes turning backward, sometimes forward, sometimes inclining one way or other, sometimes brought together, sometimes scattered, sometimes near, sometimes far away; they may be within or without, empty or full, broken or continuous, forming series or appearing without order, luxuriant or like floating fairy mountains. These are all important manifestations of life. Thus mountains and streams and the innumerable things of the world all reveal their spirit to men. Therefore the power of imparting life can be grasped by early training ; but how can those who have not grasped it manage brush and ink and express the pregnant things and the bones, the open and the hidden, form and substance, shape and strength, bending and upright, squatting and jumping, things that dive into the sea or soar to the sky, collapsing ruins, vast spaces, hills and mounds, lofty peaks, strange cliffs and dangerous ravines with all their spiritual force and divine qualities ? "

VI. *Yün Wan.* TURNING THE WRIST.

VII. *Yin Yün.** THE GENERATIVE INFLUENCES OF HEAVEN AND EARTH.

" The union of brush and ink is like *yin yün*. This *yin yün* has no divisions ; it is like chaos. In order to open up chaos one must use the *i hua*. But how ? In painting mountains one must give them spirit, in painting water one must give it movement, in painting trees one must make them grow, in painting figures one must give them ease.

" When one has mastered the union of brush and ink, one can express the divisions of *yin yün*, open up chaos, transmit everything old and new and form a school of one's own. All this must be done with intelligence, one must not carve or chisel the paintings, not be stiff or weak, not make things muddy or confused, not neglect the partitions (of the compositions), nor leave out reason. The first thing to be established in the sea of ink is the divine essence ; then life must be brought in at the point of the brush. On a scroll which is no more than a foot long every hair and every bone can be rendered. One must bring light and clearness into chaos.—Even though the brush is not brush, the ink not ink, the painting not painting, I am in it myself : As I turn the ink it is no longer ink, as I grasp the brush it is no longer brush, and as I find an outlet for my pregnancy it is no longer pregnancy. By *i hua* (all-inclusive creative painting) all the innumerable things of the world may be divided, and these will again

---

* *Yin Yün* is a term used in Taoistic philosophy signifying the generative influence of Heaven and Earth by which all things in nature are constantly reproduced. Cf. Giles, *Dictionary* 13.826.

unite in regulating the whole. When by this transformation the *yin yün* has been achieved it is the consummation of ability."

The titles of the following seven chapters may be noted as they give some general idea about their contents which are, on the whole, less original than those communicated above : VIII. *Shan Ch'uan.* Landscapes. IX. *Ts'un Fa.* Methods for Wrinkles. X. *Ching Chieh.* Outlines. XI. *Hsi Ching.* Short Cuts. XII. *Lin Mu.* Forests and Trees. XIII. *Hai Tao.* The Sea and the Waves. XIV. *Ssŭ Shih.* The Four Seasons.

XV. *Yüan Ch'ên.* FAR FROM THE DUST OF THE WORLD.

"Men who are beclouded by things become attached to the dust of the world. Men who are dominated by things reap trouble in their hearts. With such trouble in their hearts they carve their pictures and wear themselves out. The dust of the world beclouds their brush and ink, and they become tied up. It is like walking into a blind alley. There is no advantage, only disadvantage in it, it gives no joy to the heart.

"As to me, I leave things to be concealed by things and let the dust mix with the dust. Thus my heart is free from trouble, and when there is no trouble, painting will ensue. Painting may be done by anybody, but 'all-inclusive creative painting' is not done by anyone. It is not done without penetrating thought, only when the thought reaches the origin (or meaning) of things, the heart is inspired, and the painter's work can then penetrate into the very essence of the smallest things ; it becomes inscrutable.—As it seems to me that the ancients have not taken note of this, I mention it in particular."

The last three chapters are devoted to the following subjects :

XVI. *T'o Su.* To Escape from the Common. XVII. *Chien Tzŭ.* To Combine with Calligraphy. XVIII. *Tzŭ Jên.* To Nourish Oneself (with Painting).

A further characterization of Shih-t'ao's ideas and his highly original personality may be left over for a later occasion, when his painted work also can be taken into consideration ; it is through this that he has won the admiration of modern critics and collectors. But it may well be admitted, that his essay also is one of the most significant expressions of the æsthetic revival which started at the end of the Ming period and reached its full development during the early years of the Ch'ing dynasty. It reflects a fresh attempt to reach down to the original sources of creative art, something of the same endeavour that we have observed in the writings of the ' gentlemen painters' and the Ch'an buddhists, though presented in terms which have lost something of the poetry of earlier interpretations.

THE CH'ING PERIOD

TRADITIONAL PRINCIPLES REASSERTED

THE writers quoted in the preceding chapter may from a chronological point of view be classified as of the Ch'ing period, but it would certainly not be correct to consider their essays as characteristic introductions to the theoretical writings of this period. Their strongly individualistic tendencies were not in harmony with the general drift of art-criticism during the Ch'ing dynasty. The leading painters and critics of this period had little use for eccentric originality or abstruse Taoistic philosophy; they were men of classical bent, more or less penetrated by Confucian principles, and they lost no occasion to express their opposition to every attempt to cut loose from the time-honoured traditions of the old masters. The reverence for the great models of T'ang, Sung and Yüan was never stronger than in the Ch'ing period, and it seems indeed to have been asserted with more emphasis in the theoretical field than in the creative activity of the painters. Yet, it must be admitted that the critics as well as the painters of this time were less doctrinal than their predecessors of the Ming dynasty, they were not so strongly biased against men of differing ideas as Tung Ch'i-ch'ang and his contemporaries; their outlook was, on the whole, broader and more eclectic.

The question of the division of the Southern and the Northern school, which absorbed so much interest in the Ming period, remained still a topic of discussion, but it lost most of its entrancement as the Northern school ceased to exist as an independent current and the Southern School broke up into a number of contending local factions. Some of the best painters saw no reason why they should keep strictly within the stylistic limitations of one single school; they found it more advantageous to combine freely elements from various sources creating thus modes of their own in which historical knowledge is contending with individual inspiration.

This is not the place to dwell on the abundant growth in the field of painting during the hey-days of the Ch'ing dynasty, but it may be pointed out, that this great affluence was to some extent paralleled by a corresponding increase in theoretical writings on the aims and methods of painting. These problems aroused interest in ever widening circles, there was a growing curiosity in the theory as well as in the practise of painting: a certain amount of knowledge about this art became a prominent feature in the outfit of the cultured people of the time. It should also be noted, that the painters' habit of accompanying their works with poetical or explanatory colophons developed more and more, and not a few of these colophons are of great interest from a historical as well as from an æsthetic point of view. On the other hand, it should be remembered that the more comprehensive writings on painting are now more than before devoted to technical questions and intended to serve as practical guidance for students of art.

It goes without saying that much of this material has a relatively small intrinsic importance, as it contains re-statements of the viewpoints and thoughts which are known from earlier writings, but it is historically interesting and would be worth a more complete presentation than we can devote to it in this connection. We are obliged to limit ourselves to some observations on the æsthetic attitude of the leading personalities, in so far as it appears from their writings, and to the translation of two of the most comprehensive treatises in which the aims and principles of painting are discussed.

The most authoritative interpreters of painting at the beginning of the Ch'ing period were the famous "Four Wangs," to whom may be added Yün Shou-p'ing in the field of flower painting. Their influence was, indeed, mainly based on their abundant creative activity and their position as teachers for crowds of younger men, but their ideas became also known through a certain amount of writing, partly by themselves and partly by other men who reported their words. A certain number of the colophons, which they composed for their own pictures or for those of their friends, have been preserved, and beside these we often find references to their sayings in the writings of contemporary critics. Only the last of them, Wang Yüan-ch'i, has left more extensive notes on painting relating to theoretical as well as to practical problems and based on ideas which he had assimilated in the workshop of his grandfather Wang Shih-min, the oldest of the four and the one who first gave expression to the æsthetic attitude that prevailed during the first half of the Ch'ing period.

Wang Shih-min's colophons* are largely written in praise of the brilliant artistic achievements of Wang Hui, his somewhat younger contemporary, who is extolled as a genius of the highest rank, one who " exhausted the essence of the great masters of the past and put it all into his own bag." The extraordinary admiration for Wang Hui, expressed by Wang Shih-min and Wang Chien and repeated by most of the later critics, seems to have been based on two main considerations : He stood above all the multifarious school divisions of the time, and he possessed the most thorough knowledge of the great masters of the Sung and Yüan dynasties thus being able to adopt their methods freely in his own creations. The following observations on the evolution on painting by Wang Shih-min give some idea about the historical orientation of these men :

" Although painting is only one of the fine arts, the ancients investigated it most thoroughly and thought

---

* There are two different collections of colophons by Wang Shih-min, the one called *Hsi Lu Hua Po* (containing 18 items) is included in the *Hua Hsüeh Hsin Yin*, the other, which is more extensive, is separately edited under the title : *Wang Fêng-ch'ang Shu Hua Ti Po*.

A few colophons by Wang Chien, collected under the title *Jan Hsiang Lu Hua Po*, are reprinted in the *Hua Hsüeh Hsin Yin*, and the same work contains also some of Wang Hui's colophons under the title *Ch'ing Hui Hua Po*. A larger edition of Wang Hui's colophons and miscellaneous poems was edited by his descendants under the title *Ch'ing Hui Tsêng Yen*.

Wang Yüan-ch'i's colophons collected under the title *Lu-tai T'i Hua Kao*, are included in the *Chao Tai Ts'ung Shu*, which also contains a reprint of his notes on painting, known as *Yü Ch'uang Man Pi*.

In addition to these writings may be noted an essay by Wang Yü, a cousin of Wang Yüan-ch'i, called *Tung Chuang Lun Hua* (reprinted in *Mei Shu Ts'ung Shu*) in which the ideas of the older Wangs are more or less repeated.

about it deeply. They knew how to harmonize their works with those of Nature (the Creator) and penetrated with their thoughts the boundless chaos. Their art has been transmitted for ages and has opened a path for later students.

" If one tries to trace the origin of the various schools of painting, one will find that each one of them started from a different master. Thus Li Ch'êng and Kuo Hsi of Sung had their roots in the art of Ching Hao and Kuan T'ung, respectively, whereas the four great masters of the Yüan period all were followers of Tung Yüan and Chü-jan.

" Nowadays the students of painting are as numerous as the trees of the forest and every one of them considers himself most excellent and boasts of being a great master ; yet most of them pursue simply the fashion of the time and few know how to benefit by studying the old. Even among those who know the old masters' works and try to imitate them there are many who nevertheless fall into bad habits as their brush does not follow their minds (hearts).

" In Soochow at the time of Shên Chou, Wên Pi and T'ang Yin, there were still many famous works by masters of T'ang, Sung and Yüan and great connoisseurs who discussed them freely. If we look closely at their way of painting, we can seen that every stone and every tree in their paintings is derived from some old master. The art of painting was then most flourishing. Later on other famous painters appeared, the one after the other, each one of them following some particular master (or model of old). Although the spiritual resonance gradually died out, still the rules and principles were kept up. But then there appeared some superficial men who did not know anything about the old manners and simply tried to expound their own ideas. They transmitted seeds of false habits, which were taken up by their contemporaries, and caused a complete abandonment of the rules and traditions of the preceding generation, a tendency which nowadays has become more and more prevalent. It makes one sad to think of it."

Wang Shih-min's criticism was evidently turned against painters who did not possess sufficient classical culture and who considered the stylistic traditions of the old masters as less important than their individual impulses (as did for instance Shên Hao). He repeats this in various colophons, and the opinion is also voiced, with minor individual variations, by Wang Chien and Wang Hui. The last one, who no doubt exercised the greatest influence through his paintings, exclaims in one of his colophons : " Alas, how the Tao of painting has been lost in our days.... This decline was caused by the many schools which branched off in recent times. Ku and Lu, Chang and Wu are indeed far from us.".... Then follows characterizations of the four Yüan masters, who " although they all came out of Tung Yüan, separated widely by their individual transformations (of his style) and thus became the teachers (or models) of numerous generations without causing any abuse. And then, in more recent times, as the styles and manners declined and the customs and habits fell low, the different schools branched off. From the time of Tai Chin and Wu Wei the Chê school became firmly established, and after Wên Pi and Shên Chou the Wu school flourished. Tung Ch'i-ch'ang rescued the Tao of painting from an age of decline and grasped the essentials of Tung Yüan's and Chü-jan's art. Later students called him quite wrongly the founder of the Yün-chien school. My elders from Lang-ya and T'ai-yüan (Wang Shih-min and Wang Chien) had their roots in the art of the Sung and Yüan periods and were equal to the old masters. Students from far and near imitated them, and thus the Lou-tung school was formed. Beside these there are a number of minor schools and side currents, and more painters who consider themselves great masters than can be counted on the fingers. They all continued false manners and bad habits and thus all good traditions were brought to an end."

The strong denouncement of the local schools and stylistic currents expressed by Wang Hui and some of the other leading critics was apparently caused by the fact, that these showed a tendency to stiffen into stereotyped habits and manners particularly through the affluence of secondary talents, who simply imitated their predecessors. Their idea of a " school of painting " (*p'ai*) implied definite modes or manners of composition and brush-work, certain formal conventions by which the students were tied and hampered rather than helped along in their evolution. More or less opposite to this was the tradition of 'the old masters'; it signified a succession of thought and inspiration rather than a transmission of definite stylistic formulas. Those who followed 'the old masters' could be quite different between themselves, from a stylistic point of view, and yet reflect the same ideals of classical culture and spiritual inspiration. Their art was creative and not imitative.

Most of the great artists of the time dwelt on these questions in their colophons, expressing some thoughts on the old masters' art versus that of contemporary painters, but one or two examples may here suffice. Thus for instance Yün Shou-p'ing wrote as follows : * The Sung masters used the minute manner (*k'o hua*), whereas the style of the Yüan painters was based on transformations (*pien hua*), but these had their origin in the minute manner, and the greatest wonder was the free blending of these two manners. Students who consider them as two separate things are quite confused ; they act as general Chêng and general Li† did in handling their troops, the one being very severe, the other quite lenient. Yet, general Li had no difficulty in applying severe measures, and general Chêng did not mind to accord freedom to his soldiers. The whole thing depends on the right kind of divine transformations."

The same painter also wrote : " The two words : *hsieh i* (the spontaneous manner of writing down an inspiring thought), are very subtle, and they have often led people astray. I do not know how to apply my mind in order to reach what the ancients did not know.

---

* Yün Shou-p'ing, better known under his *hao* Nan-t'ien (1633-1690), prominent as landscape and flower painter, wrote many interesting colophons, some of which have been collected under the title *Nan-t'ien Hua Po* in *Hua Hsüeh Hsin Yin*.

† The two famous generals who fought for supremacy at the beginning of the Han period.

I do not know how to apply the thoughts so as to produce this spontaneous manner of painting (*hsieh i*).

"Modern painters apply their mind only to brush and ink, whereas the ancients paid attention (applied their minds to) the absence of brush and ink (i.e. the empty spaces). If one is able to realize how the ancients applied their mind to the absence of brush and ink, one is not far from reaching the divine quality in painting."

The painter returns to the same essential point in other colophons as for instance when he writes : " The brush-work in the paintings of the ancients may sometimes appear quite solid and crammed, but there is nevertheless space for (moving) life, whereas in modern paintings even the corners are crammed. If there is solidity in places which are empty, then the whole composition seems alive ; and the more such places there are, the better for the whole picture."

Both these statements by Yün Shou-p'ing give some idea about the fundamental importance attached by the Chinese to the problem of spacing : how well they realized that the portions of the compositions which were left empty had at least the same expressional value as those which were filled with painted forms. The artistic significance of the *hsieh i* manner was, indeed, to no small extent dependent on the proper use of intervals.

The same problem is perhaps still better defined by Tan Chung-kuang, a contemporary landscape painter, in the following words : " If the composition is not well balanced, the painted parts of it will become like excrescences, but when the empty and the filled parts are mutually balanced, the unpainted portions all contribute to the wonderful effect. When one has got hold of this, one should follow the idea and carry out the plan (of composition) ; every corner will then be right. But if one has lost it, the thing cannot be put right through any exertions of the mind (heart) ; the whole picture will become a failure."

The psychology of the painter, his mental attitude and relation to his work is also interestingly discussed by Yün Shou-p'ing : " In painting one should act in the same way as when one is undressing, i.e. do the work as if nobody was around. Then the power of creation will be held in the hand and the breath of life will be spread all over the picture. One is not tied by the rules and manners of ancient artisans but walks quite independent. One can go in and out of the winds and the rains, one can roll and unroll the mountains, follow the hills and the valleys through all their intricacies just like the Creator. Unless one possesses the art of forming a style, one cannot attain the most wonderful. Such art may give rise to a spiritual style and mould the character of the man."

The point of view is practically the same as in so many utterances by the great painters of the Sung and Yüan periods : The great artist must stand detached, unconcerned with worldly conditions and unhampered by formal rules. He must be free to use it all according to his own genius. This is also confirmed in a colophon by Wu Li, another of the leading landscape painters, who actually repeated some words by Su Tung-p'o, when he wrote : " The most prominent among the ancient writers did not ask for praise or fame ; the greatest among the painters did not seek for honours or success, they said : ' I write in order to express my heart, I paint in order to comfort my mind. I may wear rough cloths and eat coarse food, but I would not ask support from others.' Neither kings, nor dukes or nobles could command these painters, they were unattainable by worldly honours. Nobody can understand the Tao of brush and ink unless he himself possesses Tao."

The same painter points out in another connection that the study of Tao is more difficult than the study of brush and ink. One must have a clear idea in the mind before one starts on the work, an often repeated statement forming so to say the pivot around which all this spontaneous ink painting (sometimes called *hsieh i*) was turning. It reached its finest effects by suggestion rather than by representation ; the essential point was the inner significance, not the formal likeness, which also is implied in the following saying by Wang Chien :

" In contemplating a beautiful landscape one often says : ' It looks like a picture,' and in looking at a picture

PLATE XX

WHITE CLOUDS ON THE HSIAO AND HSIANG
RIVERS; IN THE MANNER OF CHAO MENG-FU
Wang Chien (1578-1677, Ch'ing dynasty)

PLATE XXI

THE COMING OF AUTUMN
Hung-jen (Fl. ca. 1650-1663, Ch'ing dynasty)

one often exclaims : ' It is like the real thing.' From this one may realize that there is no difference between the effect of the real (true) and the rendering (the false). But only those who are able to grasp the mysterious will know how to give it ; if they do not, their works cannot reach a superior class, however skilfully they may be done. Therefore critics of painting made divisions between the divine and the wonderful class and between great masters and famous artists."

There are many sayings of a similar kind showing that the appreciation of painting was now as in former days based on something more essential than formal likeness with material objects or decorative effect. And these are supplemented by other sayings referring to the paramount importance of a proper handling of brush and ink. If the brush-work was not spontaneous, it would not reflect life, if the ink was not rich and variegated, the picture would look barren. Both Wang Shih-min and Wang Hui have said significant things about this point. The former wrote : " Painting does not depend on resemblance of forms. Some paintings are wonderful in brush-work but not in ink, others are wonderful in ink but not in brush-work. If one can grasp the mystery of both brush and ink, one becomes a good painter."

Wang Hui is still more explicit : " The brush-work of a picture should be coarse and fine, heavy and light, dry and moist ; then it is well done. If it is simply of one kind, the picture looks bare (naked)."

" In painting the light and the dark form so to say the two wings of the bird ; one cannot dispense with either of them. If one can give the (right) combination of light and dark, spiritual vitality will ensue. . . .

" Take the brush and ink of the Yüan masters, paint with them the hills and valleys of the Sung masters, and fuse into this the spirit resonance (*ch'i yün*) of the T'ang masters—that will give the great completion."

All these various points referring to the painter's psychology, his way of working and the means he employs, are also brought out in Wang Yüan-ch'i's " Scattered Notes at a Rainy Window," which were collected into a kind of short essay by some follower of his. They contain the most complete presentation of the æsthetic attitude of the leading painters of the 17th century beside a number of very interesting technical remarks expressed in original terms, which may have been coined in the studio of his grandfather, Wang Shih-min. He too emphasizes the importance of a spontaneous execution, which however is possible only if the idea has been conceived before the brush is grasped : " Such is the principal point in painting." Even the most elaborate design will be useless, if there is not an initial breath of life (i.e. *ch'i yün*). The whole essay may, in spite of its somewhat fragmentary character, be considered the most significant piece of æsthetic writing of the Ch'ing period. It spans the psychological as well as the technical field and reflects altogether a tone of imaginative creative activity, which makes it particularly interesting :

Yü Ch'uang Man Pi. SCATTERED NOTES AT A RAINY WINDOW. (Edit. *Mei Shu Ts'ung Shu*.)

" The ancients have discussed the Six Principles in detail, but I fear that later students have adhered to ready made opinions and not expressed the intentions of their own hearts (minds). They have been hesitating and guessing at their meaning, going backward and becoming depraved (or heterodox). Now, I am going to explain the general meaning of the principles of composition (plan and design, place and position), of the brush and ink and the colouring in accordance with the transmitted opinion of my grandfather Fêng-ch'ang (Wang Shih-min) and my own views in order to make known both the sweet and the bitter. Whatever I have grasped I like to note down as the brush moves.

" At the end of Ming there were some bad habits and schools of painting ; the Chê school was the worst among them. As to the great painters of the Wu and Yün-chien schools such as Wên Pi and Shên Chou and the chief of the school, Tung Ch'i-ch'ang, their works are all mixed up with fakes. One false thing transmits another thus gradually producing a current of corrupt practices.

Thus the bad habits of those schools (the Wu and the Yün-chien) were hardly different from the bad habits of the Chê school. Those who desire to learn ink painting must particularly avoid them.

" The idea must be conceived before the brush is grasped—such is the principal point in painting. When the painter takes up the brush he must be absolutely quiet, serene, peaceful and collected and shut out all vulgar emotions. He must sit down in silence before the white silk scroll, concentrate his soul and control his vital energy. He must look at the high and the low, examine right and left, inside and outside the scroll, the road to enter and the road to leave. When he has a complete view in his mind, then he should dip the brush and lick the tip.

" The first point to settle is the effect of life, then one must draw the framework (make the design) ; then spread out the dense and the scattered portions, then make distinctions between the thick and the thin parts, turn them and change them, trying to make them accord (tap and rub), so that east answers to west harmoniously. Thus the bed of the stream will be ready for the water when it arrives, and as it flows in freely and without hesitation, it brings the whole thing together quite naturally. If one has no definite views and the thoughts are rushing towards profit and fame, seeking simply to please the people, and if one spreads out the trees and stones, piling them up in disorder, twisting and fidgeting everything in the scroll without thought or taste, the brush-work will become vulgar. Present-day people do not understand the reason (or right principle) of painting, but grasp only the formal resemblance.

" When the brush is fat and the ink is thick, they call the picture rich and great, and when the brush is thin and the ink light, they call it noble and original ; when the colour is brilliant and the brush soft, they call it bright and graceful. They have no idea of how wrong they are. Generally the ancients made their compositions condensed (tight), but their brush-work was free and easy, whereas the compositions of modern painters are loose and their brush-work is tied up. If one pays proper attention to this, then sweetness and corruptness, vulgarity and plagiarism disappear by themselves without any effort.

" The ' dragon veins' (or magnetic currents),* the spacing intervals (opening and closing) and the rising and falling (rhythm) form parts of the old methods in painting, yet they have not been properly recorded. Wang Shih-ku explained these principles, and later students have followed them, but according to my opinion, the students cannot finally grasp these things without combining style (or theory) with practice.

" The ' dragon veins ' are the source of vitality and strength in painting. They may be slanting or straight, complete or fragmentary, broken up or continuous, hidden or exposed. They may be said to form the style. The spacing intervals follow from the top to the bottom, the principal and secondary ones in proper succession, sometimes they are brought closely together, sometimes open and vast. The turning peaks, the winding roads, the closing up clouds, the dividing water-currents, all have their origin in them. The rising and falling movement should continue from near to far, so that the foreground and the background become clearly divided. These moving shapes may rise high and lofty or be drawn out evenly. The leaning forms must correspond mutually ; the top, the body and the feet of the mountains must be perfectly weighed and balanced. These elements (*k'ai ho* and *ch'i fu*) constitute what is called practice. If one understands the ' dragon veins' but does not make distinctions between the open (*k'ai*) and the closed (*ho*), and the rising (*ch'i*) and falling (*fu*), the picture becomes tied up and has no strength. If one understands the rising and the falling, the open and the closed, but does not base these elements on the ' dragon veins,' it may be said that one considers the child but neglects the mother. The forcing and twisting of the 'dragon veins' produces faults ; the contracting or superficial expanding of the open and the closed portions also produces faults. If the

---

* *Lung mo*, see Giles, *Dictionary*, 8011 ; here evidently signifying the life-carrying lines or arteries of the composition.

rising and falling rhythm is dull and heavy, or drooping and defective, it also produces faults. But, on the other hand, if the painting has spacing intervals (*k'ai ho*), every portion of it partakes of them, and if the whole painting has a rising and falling movement, each part has it also, and it becomes still more wonderful by the connection and correspondence of the parts within it ; the excessive is restrained and the wanted is supplied.

"Make the 'dragon veins' slanting or straight, complete or in fragments, hidden or visible, broken or continuous, but all bristling with life, then you will make a real picture. If one understands how to do all this, then the minor portions will combine to make the larger sections perfect, and one will arrive at the most wonderful results.

" The painters must pay particular attention to the effect of life and to the outlines. It is not necessary to seek for beautiful scenery or to hold fast to the ancient models. If one is able to give the spacing intervals (*k'ai ho*) and the rising and falling (*ch'i fu*) movement, and if furthermore the outlines and the effect of life are harmoniously rendered, then the 'dragon veins' are turning and bending with proper rhythm. Wonderful landscapes appear as in nature and in accordance with the old methods. For painting trees and forests special methods exist.

" The copying of pictures does not equal the examination of pictures. When one comes across a true work by an old master, one should study it very closely and look for its main idea. One must find out how it is composed, how the things move out and in, how they are slanting or straight, how they are placed, how the brush is used and how the ink is accumulated. There are certainly parts in it which are superior to one's own art ; after some time one will quite naturally be in close harmony with it.

" The old painters of the Northern and Southern Sung periods were all divided according to families (schools), but in each school there were some who used the ' dragon veins' and some who used the spacing intervals and the rising and falling rhythm. The effect of life was particularly strong in their works ; some of them are worthy of being studied with the greatest attention, as for instance Tung Yüan and Chü-jan, whose style was absolutely complete and whose original vitality was so strong and unrestrained, that it seemed incomprehensible to the people. Then at the end of the Yüan dynasty appeared the four masters, who followed in their wake, i.e. Shan-ch'iao (Wang Mêng), who used ' dragon veins' abundantly, drawing them like winding snakes, Chung-kuei (Wu Chên) who painted them as straight lines ; each did it in a different way and one must search for their points of connection. Huang Tzŭ-chiu neither took off nor added on anything ; in using he did not use and in not using he used (the ' dragon veins'). If one compares him with the two masters mentioned above, one may observe how different they were. Ni Yün-lin was not stained by a grain of dust (worldly desires) : There was great sympathy in his ease and quietness ; refinement and beauty in his abridged manner. He went beyond the common rules and manners of brush-work. These four masters belonged to the first and supremely free class.

" Formerly my grandfather Fêng-chang (Wang Shih-min), who had learned particularly from Ni Yün-lin and Huang Kung-wang, explained their art in deep words, and I note it down here respectfully as a guidance for connoisseurs.

" In painting you should avoid smoothness, softness, hardness, heaviness and coagulation (too great solidity). Furthermore, avoid haste and confusion, avoid brilliant clearness and glossiness, avoid crowding and mixing things in disorder. You should not intentionally apply a good brush nor intentionally avoid a tough brush, but work leisurely without pressure (or haste). You should start from the light points and proceed to the thick and rich parts, be superior to the sweet and common, suppress the delicate and the weak, and if the work becomes too stiff and heavy, break it up. But from the moment the brush touches the paper, either intentionally or without intention, you must go on turning and cutting with the brush even the edges and curves of the roof* (i.e. complete the picture) without becoming the servant of the brush.

"The use of the brush and the use of the ink complete each other mutually. The five manners of using the ink have not two meanings. To sum up : *Ch'i-yün shêng-tung* is, properly speaking, in this (the brush-and-ink work). To paint with colours is also like working with brush and ink. The aim of it is to give lustre to an insufficient brush-and-ink work, and it may serve to bring out the wonderful parts of this. But present-day artists do not understand this. In their pictures the colours are simply colours and the brush and ink are simply brush and ink, which do not convey the characteristics of the landscapes or enter into the tissue of the silk. One sees simply a blaze of red and green colours which are enough to make one disgusted and satiated. If one does not aim particularly at colouring but rather strives for vitality (*ch'i*), trying to stir it and to bring it out in the light and the shade, in the foreground and the background, the colouring will be strengthened by the vitality. It will not float about, nor be coagulated, but complete the design in a natural way. One cannot accomplish these things in a hasty way ; every element, the light and the shade, the clear and the obscure, the morning brightness and the evening dusk, the shape of the hills and the colour of the trees must be continuously practised in a leisurely mood. But whether the colouring is light or laid on thickly—according to the requirements of the different parts—the meaning of it must be grasped by the heart ; there are no complete rules by which it can be fixed.

"It is of the greatest importance in painting that reason, vitality and attractiveness should be combined. If these three qualities are not present, the picture does not become of the most wonderful, the divine and supremely free class. Therefore one must look for the rare in the common, for the needle in the floss of silk, for that which

---

* *Ku-lêng*, see Giles, *Dictionary*, 6221, an expression used for Peking, but according to *Tzŭ Yüan*, it signifies the edges and curves of the palace roof, here evidently used in a figurative sense.

is produced by an interaction of the empty and the full. Those painters who simply complied with the rules and expressed no ideas beyond such formulas, have ever since olden times been considered worthless fellows. When the student of painting has started on his career, he should strive for gradual daily progress. He must convey between the lines and in the ink that which the skilled cannot give but the unskilled give; then only can he obtain the secrets of the Sung and Yüan masters. And he should never be too satisfied with himself."

*   *   *

Beside these "Notes" by Wang Yüan-chi there are a number of essays by contemporary or slightly younger men, who largely drew their inspiration from the Four Wangs. Most of them are however of a more technical kind, i.e., devoted to the painter's craft rather than to the general principles of his creative activity. This is true for instance of Tan Chung-kuang's *Hua Chüan* and T'ang-tai's *Hui Shih Fa Wei*, which are devoted to methods of landscape painting. The latter is evidently moulded on the pattern of Han Cho's well-known treatise, *Shan Shui Ch'un Ch'üan Chi*, though still more detailed.

Less specialized and more concerned with questions of historical and æsthetic interest is Wang Yü, *tzŭ* Tung-chuang, a younger member of the Wang clan, whose notes are known as *Tung-chuan Lun Hua*.* He wrote as follows:

"I often heard my master say: 'The original points in painting are not to be found in the composition, but in *ch'i yün*; it is not in the outward forms, but in the absence of forms.' I grasped the meaning of his deep words, and (I transmit them so that) later students may assimilate them. The study of painting serves to nourish the character and the emotions; it calms the troubled bosom, it alleviates bitter suffering, it sets free the restless heart, and it welcomes a quiet spirit. The ancients said: 'Landscape painters always lived to a great age, because

---

* Wang Yü's essay, which is written in close adherence to his master, Wang Yüan-ch'i's ideas, is included in the first section of *Mei Shu Ts'ung Shu*.

the mist and clouds by which their eyes were nourished produced life. . . .'

" Everybody knows that right principles (reason, *li*) and life (vitality, *ch'i*) are necessary in painting, yet they are much neglected. The important point is, that the heart and character of the man should be developed; then can he express high principles and a pure vital breath. Great ideas will issue from his breast and stupendous effects will be produced by the turning of his wrist. He will become a man of great fame.

" Before the painter starts with the brush, his thoughts should be high and far-reaching; when he is working his vital pulse must be quiet and his soul tranquil, no matter whether he uses the *kung pi* (elaborate) manner or the *hsieh i* (spontaneous) manner.

" It is of the greatest importance for students of painting to be humble at heart and not boastful or proud when they have reached some skill. When they see works by other painters they should not magnify trifling faults. When they meet those who are superior to themselves, they should diligently seek for their advice. When they meet those who are not their equals, they should scrutinize their own hearts. If they know about some famous paintings, they should try to see them, or possibly to borrow them in order to study them. They should assimilate (breathe) the spiritual resonance of the paintings thus increasing their knowledge. They should stroll about observing famous mountains; in this way they will grasp the pictures of nature, which have the power of touching the heart. Hills and valleys will then naturally merge in their hearts, and beautiful things will be produced by the turning of their wrists. Then they will become great painters.

" Although painting is only one of the fine arts, it contains Tao. You should seek for it in the true works of the ancients, observing their compositions, their structural designs, and their spiritual beauty (flavour). Students who can do this thoroughly will obtain the points and finally reach to the very origin of art. But if they cannot do it, they will simply accumulate heaps and mounds of paper and brush-work and never perceive Tao for a single day. . . .

" In a picture life and structure (*ch'i*, *ku*) should be simple and noble, the resonance of the spirit spontaneous and refined, the brush-work should leave no scars, the ink should be variagated, the arrangement (composition) should have transformations, the colouring should be brilliant. If one understands these six points, one will realize the meaning of all the sayings of the ancients ; it is all there. But if one does not sit quietly in meditation, trying to grasp the meaning in silence, how can one completely understand these ideas and transfer them into a picture (by the turning of the wrist)?

" Before one starts on a painting the inspiration must be nourished either by looking at clouds and springs, or by contemplating flowers and birds, or by strolling about humming songs, or by burning incense, or by sipping tea. . . One must wait until something has been grasped in the bosom and the desire for expression is overwhelming. When the inspiration rises, spread the paper and move the brush, but stop as soon as it is exhausted ; only when it rises again, you should continue and complete the work. If you do it in this way, the work will become alive with the moving power of Heaven and far superior to the things of the dusty world.

" After the T'ang, Sung, Yüan and Ming periods there have been many styles which may be easily grasped, but the knowledge of these can only serve to bind one. Do not stick obstinately to the ideas of the old masters, but try to use their manners intelligently, then you will reach the maturity which is beyond maturity. If you can do it without a special effort, your work will contain life quite unexpectedly. He who is not tied by any of the old schools, creates a school of his own. . . .

" There is a kind of painting which at first sight looks quite rough and confused and not in accordance with rules, but when one observes it more closely, one finds in it resonance of the spirit and life-movement, which produce limitless effects. This is so because it is produced according to the supreme rule, through a surpassing natural inspiration and as a result of diligent study (which enables the painter to introduce transformations). It may be said, that it grows like the lotus out of the clear water without any ornamentations. Superficial students cannot dream of doing it. . . . .

" The wonderful points in painting are not to be found in luxuriant beauty, but in refined strength ; they are not in the exactness of the execution but in its spontaneous ease. Luxuriant (ornamental) beauty and fine execution can be produced by effort (practice), whereas spontaneous ease and refined strength depend on the resonance of the spirit and the structural design, which cannot be forced."

The above extracts from Wang Yü's treatise may serve to illustrate the attitude of these painters which, indeed, was not very unlike that of the great masters of the Sung and Yüan periods. Much of what he says might just as well have been written by Kuo Jo-hsü or Hsia Wên-yen, the essential ideas were the same now as then, but the historical background was different. The realization and application of these ideas required now a larger amount of historical knowledge than in the Sung period ; it had to be done through the intermediary of the old masters. The best among the leading painters of the Ch'ing period were potentially hardly inferior to their predecessors of former times, but their excessive veneration for the " art of the ancients " made it practically impossible for them to leave the beaten track and contribute something new to the development of painting.

*   *   *

The completest summary of the æsthetic principles prevalent in the Ch'ing period is to be found in a treatise of Chang Kêng,* who evidently held a more important place as a writer than as a painter. He is best known as author of *Kuo Ch'ao Hua Chêng Lu*, a work containing

---

* The author's real name was Chang Tao, but he changed it later to Chang Kêng. He was born in 1693 and received a literary degree in 1735. Among his various *tzŭ* the best known is P'u-shan, and among his *hao* the best known is Kuan-tien I-shih (Strange scholar of the Melon field). As a painter he was an adherent of the Southern school, but he seems also to have been acquainted with Western art.

biographies and critical remarks on the Ch'ing painters prior to the Ch'ien Lung period. But beside this he composed a theoretical essay, known as *Hua Lun*, in which he briefly epitomized the evolution since the Ming period and discussed the principal æsthetic and technical requirements of the art of painting. He speaks about the brush and the ink, the 'gentleman spirit,' the *ch'i yün*, the psychological attitude of the painters, i.e. their character, the proper methods of study, their relation to the great masters of former times and the classification of there works, elaborating these various points in accordance with the classical tradition. He may not have anything new of essential importance to add, but he expresses the time-honoured ideas in a concise and clear way. His treatise may thus be said to form a fitting conclusion to our review of the Chinese writings on painting :

Hua Lun. INTRODUCTION

"The division of painting into a Southern and a Northern school started in the T'ang period, but the division in schools was not in accordance with localities. At the end of the Ming dynasty the name of the Chê school was introduced. This school started with Tai Chin and ended with Lan Ying. It had four faults, it was hard, stiff, bare and clumsy. The school of Sung-chiang started in the present dynasty ; it followed Tung Ch'i-ch'ang and Chao Tso (Wên-tu) ; the paintings were done in a vaporous and diffused manner and became gradually delicate, soft, sweet and weak. In the Nanking (Chin-ling) school there were two divisions, one resembling the Chê and another resembling the Sung-chiang school. The Hsin-an school attracted many people, since Hung-jên (Chien-shih) excelled in the manner of Ni Yün-lin. If it has not the fault of knotting (tying), it has the fault of scattering brush-work. That is the third school. Lo Mu (Fan-niu) rose eminently in Ning-tu (Kiangsi) and transferred his art to the provincial capital (Nan-ch'ang) ; his fame reached all the dukes, ministers and schools, the students all took him as their master and this is now called the Kiangsi school. Its faults are too much ease and polished smoothness. The manner of the Fukien school is thick and dirty. The manner of painters from the North are heavy and clumsy. These various schools were all famous at their start, but in the course of their transmission they deteriorated through successive imitation.

"These are the general lines since the beginning of this dynasty. Those who can avoid enclosing themselves in such habits (of imitation) and follow in the steps of the ancients, and who take counsel from the wise ones among their predecessors become the models of later men. Wang Yüan-ch'i (Lu-t'ai) is the only one who did it to some extent. As to Wang Hui (Shih-ku), he is certainly very talented, but he did not avoid entirely the habits of painters who are bound by a school.

THE BRUSH

"Ch'ien Hsiang-shu* said in discussing literature: 'The brush must be bold, that is to say rich and simple' (old-fashioned). These words express thoroughly (deeply) the secret of literary writing. According to my opinion the same holds true of painting. Wang Lu-t'ai (Yüan-ch'i) himself wrote on his picture of 'Autumn Mountains under a Clear Sky': 'It is not within the old method nor in my hand (style), yet not outside the old method nor foreign to my hand. The point of the brush is like a diamond pestle and entirely free from all habits.' What Hsiang-shu called boldness means exactly the same as the diamond pestle. Wên Chi-t'ang † said: 'Every time my teacher grasped the brush, his wrist and arm were all strength.' If one considers these words by the three gentlemen, one may realize how the brush should be used. In examining true specimens of the old masters I found that although the brush-strokes and the outlines of stones and mountains were made with a fine and subtle brush and a light and soft touch, their vital energy was deep and rich beyond words. The handling of the brush was not simply a matter of boldness; the divine transformations of the old

---

* Ch'ien Chên-ch'ün (1686-1744), one of "the Five Men of Letters" of the Ch'ien Lung epoch, popular as a writer and poet (Giles, 358).

† Wên I, tzŭ K'o-hsiang, hao Chi-t'ang, first half of the 18th century, painter, famous particularly for his technical knowledge.

masters were not restrained by material objects. But for beginners boldness is most essential as a first step.

THE INK

" Whether the ink is thick or thin, dry or moist, it must not have the taste of worldly things (cooked food) if the finest effects shall be reached. Wang Lu-t'ai said : ' It is possible to learn the brush-work of Tung Ch'i-ch'ang, but his ink is so fresh and variagated, so pure, bright and attractive that it moves people irresistibly ; how could such a thing be produced by human power ? I have often read Tung Ch'i-ch'ang's own inscription on a picture in which he says : ' I amuse myself with brush and ink and in recent times people have distinguished ' the art of Tung,' but they do not understand my particular method of using the ink, which is master Tung's true face (most essential point). But he also says on a scroll of grass writing : ' People know only the spirit of ink in painting ; they do not know the spirit of ink in writing.' It is evident that Tung Ch'i-ch'ang had confidence in himself and in his way of using the ink. Consequently it is not necessary to seek the models for handling the ink among the ancients ; by grasping the ideas of Tung, one may surpass the old.

GENERAL CHARACTERISTICS.

" Some of the ancients said : ' The important point in painting is the ' gentleman (scholarly) spirit.' These words indicate a proper classification. But when modern people talk about the ' gentleman spirit ' they mean by it simply dry brush and spare ink. When they find that the colour (ink) is laid on heavily, they despise the picture and call it artisan's work. Such critics are merely pretending connoisseurs. Many ancient artists such as Wang Wei, the Great and the Little General Li, Wang Hsia Wen Yü-k'o, Chao Ling-jang and Chao Mêng-fu excelled in blue and green colouring. Can they be called artisans ? Their high or low standing does not depend on the painted works but on the ideas. Those who understand such ideas cannot be called artisans, even though they may use blue and green colouring and gold dust and not be among the academicians, while those who do not understand such ideas are of a common class even though they follow Ni Tsan or imitate Huang Kung-wang. What is meant by ideas? It is to seek with the spirit of a scholar for the meaning of the words of the ancients.

Ch'i yün. RESONANCE OF LIFE.

" Ch'i yün may be expressed by the ink, by the brush-work, by an idea (intention) or by the absence of intention (ideas). The absence of intention is superior to the intentional expression; then follow the expression by the brush-work, and the expression by the ink, which is inferior.

" How is it expressed by ink? By drawing the out-lines and completing the picture with dots of ink which produce a vaporous effect. How is it expressed by the brush-work? By rubbing with a dry brush so that the strength penetrates, and an effect of luminosity floats up (is spread about) in a natural way. What is the expression by intention? It is to move the brush and use the ink (according to the principle) : ' as I want it, so I get it '; every feature, the scattered and the dense, the many and the few, the thick and the thin, the dry and the moist, is exact. What is the expression without intention? It is to concentrate the soul, to fix the thoughts, to direct the regard, to turn the wrist; at the start one has no intention of doing it, but suddenly it is like that. It is said to be enough but really it is not enough; it may be called not enough, but nothing can be added to it. It (ch'i yün) is something beyond the feeling of the brush and the effect of the ink, because it is the moving power of Heaven, which is suddenly disclosed. But only those who are quiet can understand it, while for those who are somewhat dull it becomes confused with the intentions and disappears in the ink and the brush-work.

NATURAL DISPOSITION.

" Yang Tzŭ-yün* said : ' Writing is mind-painting : as this is formed into shapes, the vices and virtues

---

* Yang Hsiung (53 B.C.-A.D. 18), a well-known philosopher and writer who served in high offices published commentaries on the classics, philological works and poems. Cf., Giles, 2379.

of men may be distinguished. Painting has the same origin as writing which is mind-painting. Could those who use the brush do it without reflecting ? ' In looking at the paintings by the old masters, I did not feel certain ; but when I studied their lives, I realized that it must be so, and that the words of Yang Tzŭ-yün were quite correct.

" Let us discuss this point in reference to the painters of the Yüan period : Ta-ch'ih (Huang Kung-wang) was of a placid and lofty disposition and free from every trammel ; consequently his manner of painting was tranquil and light, but also dashing and soaking. He was the most generous among all these painters. Mei-hua Tao-jên (Wu Chên) was a great solitary, pure and proud, consequently his paintings were bold, lofty and beauti- fully refined.   Ni Yün-lin was entirely free from the common, consequently his paintings give impressions of loneliness, far distances, and stern emotions ; he left out everything ornamental. Wang Shu-ming (Wang Mêng) did not abstain from seeking for honours and the praise of the world (attaching himself to the heat) ; consequently his pictures seem rather flimsy.   Chao Mêng-fu did not hold to the great principles (of fidelity) ; consequently his writings and paintings are graceful and pleasant, but have something of the vulgar spirit.   Hsü Yu-wên was honest, pure and very refined, while Lu T'ien- yu and Fang Fang-hu* stepped outside of the objective world ; consequently they were free from the dust of the world and not enclosed within the limits of common paths.   In the *Li Chi* it is said : ' That which is done by virtue is superior and that which is done by art inferior.' True, indeed.

SKILLED WORKMANSHIP.

" Though painting is a handicraft, it is based on study and succeeds by skilful work.   The study (in painting) is devoted to the various methods of representing mountains, stones, water and trees.   One should start by seeking to establish what the mountains, stones, water and

---

* Hsü Pên, Lu Kuang and Fang Ts'ung-i, three minor painters of the Yüan period.

trees ought to be and not venture to throw out scattered thoughts in an incoherent fashion or to make strange things in accordance with the impulses of the heart, but carefully follow the rules of the ancients without losing the smallest detail. After some time one will understand why one must be in accordance with nature, and after some more time one will realize why things are as they are. When this has been realized, one is able to introduce transformations (individual variations). And then, when the transformations have been mastered, although there are still mountains, stones, streams and trees, the connoisseurs will say in looking at it : ' This is art, it has entered into Tao.' The success is complete. But modern students claim, as soon as they have grasped the brush, that they have reached the extraordinary. I do not understand this kind of talk.

STARTING IN A SCHOOL OF PAINTING.

" People are different in regard to their natural dispositions, some are clever and some are stupid, but the way they start and the way they live is the same. What is there in the lives of the stupid that is not right ? It is the tendency of forming bad habits and of not being simple. Therefore those who enter a school cannot practise too great caution ; if they once lose their foothold, the bad habits penetrate into the marrow of their bones. They may realize it afterwards and try to get rid of the habits, but that is very difficult indeed. Every particular locality has its traditions. Students who are from a certain place grow into that place ; what they see and hear does not surpass the traditions of that locality. They may not have occasion to see true works by the old masters, and if they see one or two such works, they are not willing to appreciate them respectfully and to assimilate them, nor are they capable of reflecting quietly and of learning the secrets of the ancients. Thus they work hard the whole of their lives, but in the end they have accomplished nothing. Because how can a man who is not practising study and deep thinking, and who does not assimilate the ideas (of the ancients) and strive to gather benefit from them,

eradicate vulgar habits ?   As to those who make a living
by painting, they simply try to seduce the eyes of common
people in order to earn much gold.   What is the use of
talking to them about habits ?

Ch'ü-tzŭ. To Seek Support.

"The methods should be taken from the ancients, but
the real support must be sought for in things which are
bristling with life. If one keeps obstinately to the
methods of the ancients, one finally finds no road away
from them. The wonderful qualities in the paintings
of the ancients depend simply on clear reason and conformity with (the spirit of) life. One should try to observe
the things created by Heaven such as mountains, streams,
plants and trees as well as things made by men such as
houses, huts, bridges and ferries ; each one of them has its
own reason and vital spirit (life). If they did not have
these qualities, they would no longer be things alive.
Thus as one looks around one finds great many (motifs of)
beautiful pictures, but it is necessary to grasp their meaning
and represent them in accordance with the brush-work
of the ancients. Hua-t'ing (Tung Ch'i-ch'ang) said :
'When during walks in the mountains one comes across
old trees one should observe them on their four sides,
because there is one side of the tree which can be represented
in painting, while the others do not enter.' This explains
the above.

"Furthermore, even those who are not superior to
me as painters sometimes reveal quite unexpectedly real
genius, which may serve to improve my art (knowledge).
How could I remain indifferent towards them ?

"There are also some false old pictures, but in these
neither brush-work nor *ch'i yün* are the same as in the
works of the ancients; only the compositions are similar.
One must leave out the weak points and take hold of
the qualities. By such a method one will not neglect
either the big or the small, but day by day increase one's
knowledge (by hearing and seeing) and gradually reach
the very source (of art). "

APPENDIX I

Ku Hua P'in Lu by Hsieh Ho (Reprints in *Chin Tai Pi Shu*, *Wang Shih Hua Yüan*, etc.)

All pictures should be classified according to their merits and faults. There are no pictures which do not exercise some influence, be it of an elevating or debasing kind. The silent records of ancient times are unrolled before us when we open a picture. Although the Six Principles existed (since early times), there were few who could master them all, yet from ancient to modern times there have been painters skilled in one (or the other).

Which are these Six Principles?

The first is: Spirit Resonance (or Vibration of Vitality) and Life Movement. The second is: Bone Manner (Structural) Use of the Brush. The third is: Conform with the Objects (to obtain) Likeness. The fourth is: Apply the Colours according to the Characteristics. The fifth is: Plan and Design, Place and Position (i.e. Composition). The sixth is: To Transmit Models by Drawing.

Only Lu T'an-wei and Wei Hsieh applied completely all (these principles). There have always been good and bad paintings; art as such is art, whether old or modern. I have now carefully arranged some painters of old and modern times and classified them according to the above principles, but I have cut out all introductory remarks and entered in no discussion of the origin of painting. According to tradition, it took its origin from divine beings, but these have never been seen or heard.

I CLASS. 5 men.

Lu T'an-wei from Wu. Epoch of Sung Ming Ti.

He gave the utmost of reason and character; his works surpassed all explanations in words. He included all his predecessors and gave birth to all later men. He is the only one from ancient to modern times who stands supreme; one cannot sing his praise too highly. He was truly priceless and superior, absolutely exceptional and beyond definitions. It is only by injustice that he is placed in the first class.

Ts'ao Pu-hsing from Wu-hsing. Epoch of Sun Ch'üan.

Of Ts'ao Pu-hsing's works almost nothing is left; only one of his dragon paintings is in the Imperial Collection. If one examines his style, one cannot say that his fame was empty.

Wei Hsieh.   Epoch of Chin dynasty.

When in the history of ancient painting one arrives at Wei Hsieh, one finds that he is the first who gives fine details and combines almost all the Six Principles.   Although he was not perfect in drawing, he obtained strength and vitality.   He surpassed all the great masters of ancient times and his brush-work was exceedingly good.

Chang Mo and Hsün Hsü.

Their style and temperament were divinely wonderful.   They grasped the spiritual essence of things.   They freed themselves from the bone-manner (drawing in detail) and were no longer bound by the shapes of things.   Their works were not remarkable for refinement and purity, but they contained something beyond the shapes and were satiated and rich.   They may indeed be called subtle and wonderful.

II CLASS.   3 men.

Ku Tsun-chih, Lu Sui and Yüan Ch'ien (characterized in the usual terms relating to form and vitality, new ideas and old traditions).

III CLASS.   9 men.

Yao T'an-tu, Ku K'ai-chih, Mao Hui-yüan, Hsia Chan, Tai K'uei, Chiang Sêng-pao, Wu Chien, Chang Tsê, Lu Kao.
(Of these men only Ku K'ai-chih and Tai K'uei have remained famous in Chinese history).

Ku K'ai-chih from Wu-hsi.   Epoch of Chin dynasty.

His style was fine and subtle, his brush without a flaw, yet his workmanship was inferior to his ideas, and (in his case) fame surpassed reality.

Tai K'uei.

The emotional resonance of his works was of a continuous kind and their expression was brought out with great skill.   He excelled in painting fairies and immortals.   All the painters imitated him.   He was the foremost after Wei Hsieh and Hsün Hsü until Tzŭ Yung who continued his art.

IV CLASS.   5 men.

Ch'ü Tao-min and Chang Chi-pai, Ku Pao-hsien, Wang Wei and Shih Tao-shuo.

V CLASS.   3 men.

Liu Hsü, Chin Ming Ti, Liu Shao-tzu.

VI CLASS.   2 men.

Tsung Ping, Ting Kuang.

APPENDIX II

Hsü Hua P'in by Yao Tsui. (Reprint in *Chin Tai Pi Shu*)

The greatest marvels of painting are not easily explained in words. Its primary elements have been transmitted from antiquity, but the style has changed in accordance with the conditions of later times. The numberless images conceived in the mind of the painters were transmitted to future ages at the point of the brush. Fairies and spiritual beings were made manifest on high towers, and sages and immortals were represented in great compositions on the walls of the schools. In the Yün Ko (the Cloud Pavilion of Han Wu Ti) there were paintings which inspired reverence, and in the courts of the palaces there were pictures of tribute bearers from far-off countries. But all these ancient records of painting can hardly be discussed.

However, there are still pictures to-day by men who are gone and dead long ago, but only those who have acquired great learning can distinguish the coarse ones from the fine, avoid the traps and grasp their meaning. But as things grow worse and then mend, and as men pass through periods of flourishing and decay, some reach great fame in early age, some only when they have passed into middle age, and it would be a mistake to compare the genius of the former with the gifts of the latter.

As to the art of Ku K'ai-chih, it has gained the highest fame in history. He was strong and independent and never had his equal in regard to spiritual expression. No ordinary man could reach him. It was as if he outshone the sun and the moon. How could such a man trouble himself with petty details? Hsün Hsü, Wei Hsieh, Ts'ao Pu-hsing and Chang Mo were quite worthless in comparison with him. There was nobody who did not treat him with great respect. Hsieh Ho's words that, his fame surpassed his merit, are really depressing, and it is most regrettable that he placed Ku in an inferior class. It was caused by the erratic feelings (of Hsieh Ho) rather than by the qualities or faults (of Ku K'ai-chih's paintings). The saying, that he who sings well will have few in harmony with himself, is true not only in regard to ballad singers, and one may weep blood over false reports not only concerning the uncut gem.* It seems to me that Hsieh Ho by his endeavour at classification has destroyed right principles and ruined them for ever.

---

* Pien Ho of the Ch'u state, 8th century B.C., offered an uncut gem to the sovereigns and had his two feet cut off, because the gem was believed to be false. The third sovereign had it tested, and it was then found to be genuine. It passed into the possession of the Chao state.

I can present only a corner of the subject but it is almost like the three precious things.*

When the painters mix the ink and soak the brush their endeavour is to work out cautiously the shape of things, but there is also a response which is not of the shapes. They kindle the fire by turning the ink, and they keep on with their work without rest. Their eyes are dazed by bright colours on the silk, but the ideas are not accomplished. Forms which are vulgar and trivial may however be improved by some slight accents (changes in the light and the heavy parts), and expressions of joy and sadness may be brought out by altering minute details the smallest hair. Moreover, in recent times the manners and the modes of dress used to change three times in a month; they were hardly completed before they were uncouth and old. It is certainly not easy for painters who strive for perfection. How can a man who never crossed the stream say that he has passed over the sea? When he has seen some turtles and fishes, he says that he has discovered crocodiles and dragons. It is of no use to speak about painting to people of this kind.

Ch'ên Ssŭ Wang† said: 'The art of literary composition was started by scholars; the art of painting by men of skill.' They formed two different currents in accordance with their characteristics, and it is difficult to succeed in combining the two. To follow the traces of the squares (i.e. to write characters) is easy, but this requires no knowledge of curving movements (as in painting) which is difficult. Estimating the wind that blows through the Hsiang Valley does not enable one to fathom the watercourses of the Lü-liang Mountain; though one makes a good beginning (splits with the blade),‡ the end (final thing) may remain obscure. It is useless to long for the response of the world (the falling dust), if one does not know the song completely. By consulting the most ancient records (those offered by the river dragon to Huang Ti) one can find that painting existed before writing, and in the *Lien Shan* (i.e. *I Ching*) one can find that the words (i.e. the written characters) had their origin in images. Nowadays everybody considers the bird trace characters (the earliest legendary writing)§ as inferior to the dragon writing. Decline and rise followed in succession, because when Ch'ui had cut his finger there was no skill left.¶

---

* The expressions are borrowed from the *Analects*, Book XVI, chapters 4-5.

† Ts'ao Chih (192-232), third son of Ts'ao Ts'ao, famous for his skill in literary writing and poetry. Cf. Giles, *Biographical Dict.* 1994.

‡ Reference to a saying by Tu Yü, 3rd century A.D. comparing the successful opening of a campaign with the splitting of two or three joints of a bamboo. Cf Giles, *Dict.* 5597.

§ The bird trace characters are further discussed by Chang Yen-yüan in the first chapter of *Li Tai Ming Hua Chi.*

¶ Ch'ui was an artisan who could draw circles with his hand better than with compasses; his fingers seemed to accommodate themselves so naturally to the thing he was working at that it was unnecessary to fix his attention. His mental faculties remained *one*. Cf. Giles, *Chuang-tzŭ*, p.242.

To walk off * or to sit down in meditation when one should be working for the country, is a shame ; and as I am a widower mourning my companion, I can no longer raise a family. If one despises to stay at inferior places one may burn the brushes, but if one is indifferent to official appointments, one may follow one's own pleasure.

In stating my humble opinions I am not going to distribute either slander or praise, but there may be some honourable people who are desirous of knowledge.† This book contains the things which Hsieh Ho left out ; it consists of only two chapters, but the most important things are recorded in them. Old and modern calligraphy has been discussed by many writers, but painting has been explained by very few ; consequently I took up this subject. Since the number of men mentioned here is quite restrained, I have not introduced any classification ; their merits and faults may be realized from the ideas expressed.

---

* The expression : *chang ts'ê* 杖策, take the staff, refers probably to a passage in Chuang-tzŭ : T'ai Wang Shan Fu 太王亶父 tried in vain to turn off the enemies from Pin 邠, "thereupon he took his staff and went off." Giles, *Chuang-tzŭ*, p.372.

† The expression is : in ten families, etc., borrowed from the *Analects*, Book V, ch.28 : "In ten families there may be found one honourable and sincere as I am."

APPENDIX III

Chang Yen-yüan, *Li Tai Ming Hua Chi*. Sect. I. Chap. I.
Origin and Development of Painting.

Painting promotes culture and strengthens the principles of right conduct; it penetrates completely all the aspects of the universal spirit (exhausts the divine transformations). It fathoms the subtle and the abstruse serving thus the same purpose as the Six Classics, and it revolves with the four seasons. It originated from Nature and not from any decrees or works of men.

When the sage-kings of antiquity received the orders of Heaven and responded to the call, the characters on the tortoise appeared and gave them spiritual power and the picture on the dragon, which also offered precious qualities.* From the time of Yu Chao and Sui Jên these happy omens always appeared (at the beginning of every reign). The records about them shone brilliantly; they were transmitted on slabs of jade and tablets of gold.

In the time of Pao Hsi (Fu Hsi) they were discovered in the Jung river, and records and paintings began to appear. In the time of Hsüan Yüan (Huang Ti) they were found in the Wên and the Lo rivers, and Shih Huang (the inventor of painting) and Ts'ang Chieh (inventor of writing) gave them their shapes. The K'uei star with pointed rays is the lord of literature on earth, and as Ts'ang Chieh, who had four eyes, looked up (into heaven), he saw images dropping down (from the star), and these he combined with footprints of birds and tortoises. In this way the forms of the characters were fixed. The Creator could no more hide his secrets, therefore he sent down a rain of millet; the spirits and devils could no longer hide their shapes and therefore they cried in the night.† At that time painting and writing were the same thing and showed no difference. Pictorial signs were now first invented, but they were still quite summary (incomplete). As there was no means of transmitting ideas, writing was invented, and as there was no way of showing the shapes, painting was introduced, all in accordance with the purpose of Heaven and Earth and ancient Sages.

By a study of the characters one will find that there are six manners of writing: 1. *Ku wên*, 2. *Chi wên*, 3. *Chuan shu* (Seal characters), 4. *Ts'o* (or *Li*) *shu*, 5. *Miu chuan* (ornamental seal), 6. *Niao shu*,

---

* This statement may also be referred to the inscribed tortoise shells used in the Shang period for divination and excavated at An-yang in Honan.

† Refers to a famous passage in Huai Nan-tzǔ.

used on signal banners and as initials; they are like birds' heads, i.e. a kind of painting.

Yen Kuang-lu* said that painted designs have three aims, first to serve as pictograms for *pa kua* (divination), second, to promote the knowledge of characters ; third, to serve as pictorial representations.

According to *Chou Li*, the sons of the noble men were taught six kinds of writing ; the third of these were pictograms which had the same purpose (meaning) as paintings. It may consequently be said that, although writing and painting have different names, they are the same thing.

When we arrive at the Yü period (the reign of the Emperor Shun 2317-2208 B.C.) paintings were fully developed. Then, gradually, variegated tones were applied, and the pictures became still more like the objects. Ritual and music also flourished brilliantly, promoting culture. Consequently the emperors could yield to virtue ; there was peace in the world and prosperity of literature and poetry.

Kuang Ya (of the Wei-period) says : ' Painting is to produce likenesses'. *Erh Ya* (of the Chou period) says : ' Painting is to represent forms'. *Shuo Wên* (of the Han period) says : ' Painting is to draw boundaries, that is to say, representation of paddy-fields with their boundaries became a cause of painting'. *Shih Min* (of the Han period) says : ' Painting is to represent objects by laying on colours'.

From the engravings on the tripods and bells we may know the monsters and devils, the good and the evil spirits. The inscribed banners and the seals served to make clear the rules and the measures and thus to perfect the regulations of the country. As the Ching Miao was highly venerated, the *tsun* and the *i* (sacrificial vessels) were displayed in it ; as measurements were taken of the ground, maps of it were made.

Loyal and filial men were all represented on the Yün t'ai (Cloud terrace). Brave and meritorious men were entered in the Lin k'o (Chi-lin pavilion). The contemplation of good men became a reason to avoid evil, and to look at the evil men was enough to make people turn to the sages of the past. The painted records of the old manners and miens became models for exercising virtue. The representations of the successes and failures transmitted the events of the past.

The written records tell about the acts of men, but they cannot convey their appearances. The poems and ballads sing about their virtues, but they cannot represent their images. By the art of painting the two (sides) may be combined. Therefore Lu Shih-hêng† said : " The exercise of painting may be compared to the recitation of ballads and songs extolling the beauty of great actions. Nothing

---

* Yen, the Director of the Imperial Banqueting Court, i.e. Yen Yen-chih (384-456), famous not only as a poet and writer but also as an exceedingly wild and outspoken character. Cf. Giles, 2481.

† Lu Chi (261-303) a famous warrior and poet. Cf. Giles 1402.

is better than words for praising things, and nothing is better than pictures for recording shapes." These words are quite correct.

Ts'ao Chih (192-232)* says : " When one sees pictures of the three kings and the five emperors, one cannot but look at them with respect and veneration, and when one sees pictures of the San Chi (the last rulers of the three dynasties, Hsia, Shan and Chou), one cannot but feel sad. When one sees pictures of rebels and unfilial sons, one cannot but grind the teeth. When one sees pictures representing men of high principles and wonderful sages, one cannot but forget one's meals. When one sees pictures of faithful subjects who died at the call of duty, one cannot but feel exalted. When one sees pictures of exiled citizens and expelled sons one cannot help sighing. When one sees pictures of vicious men and jealous women, one cannot but look askance. When one sees pictures of obedient empresses and good secondary wives, one cannot but feel the deepest admiration. By this we may realize that paintings serve as moral examples or mirrors of conduct."

When at the time of the decline of the Hsia dynasty emperor Chieh became cruel and disorderly, the historiograph (T'ai-shih) Chung took hold of the painted documents and saved them to Shang. When the Yin dynasty was declining Emperor Chou became vicious and cruel, the minister (Nei-shih) Chih transferred the painted documents to Chou. Prince Tan of Yen offered (a scroll) to Ch'in Shih-Huang who was without suspicion. As Hsiao Ho was the first to take hold of the charts and documents (in the Ch'in capital), Pei-kung became the ruler.†

Paintings (painted charts and documents) are, indeed, national treasures. They serve to establish law and order. Therefore in the time of Han Ming Ti (A.D. 29-76) paintings in colour were highly appreciated in the palace. In the country of Shu there was a school with paintings serving to exhort loyalty. Empress Ma (of Han Ming Ti) was a lady, who wanted to honour her consort like T'ang Yao (Emperor Yao, died 2258 B.C.). Although Shih Lo was a barbarian (273-332, assumed in 319 title king of Chao) he wanted to look at the virtuous and filial men of old.

To gamble and play chess is certainly not the same thing as to occupy the mind with philosophy and noble thoughts. I always disdained the stupid words of Wang Ch'ung‡ who said : " When people look at paintings, they see in them men of ancient times, but looking at such men of old is like contemplating dead people ; one

---

* One of the Seven Geniuses of the Chien-an period, famous poet and official. Cf. Giles, 1994.

† Hsiao Ho was the famous friend of Liu Pang (247-195 B.C.) the first Han emperor. He captured the Ch'in capital and got thus hold of the imperial documents and military charts which enabled his master Liu Pang (*han* Pei-kung) to seize the rule of the country.

‡ Wang Ch'ung (A.D. 27-97), philosopher and writer, served as an official under Emperor Chang Ti, wrote the famous work *Lun Hêng* in which he freely criticizes Confucian philosophy. Cf. Giles, *Biogr. Dict.* 7166.

sees their faces, but this does not equal perceiving their words and actions. The teachings of the ancient sages are transmitted in all their brilliancy on bamboo tablets and silk scrolls, and how could these be equalled by paintings on the wall ? "

It seems to me that such talk is like throwing ridicule on Tao and abusing the Confucian scholars, or like putting food into the ear, or playing the reed-organ to an ox. What is the difference ?

Li Tai Ming Hua Chi. Sect. I. Chap. IV.

Discussion of the Six Principles of Painting.

Hsieh Ho of old said : In painting there are Six Principles (manners). The first is called : Spirit-resonance, life-movement ; the second is called : Bone-manner (structural) use of the brush ; the third is called : Conform with the objects in giving their shapes ; the fourth is called : According to the species apply the colours ; the fifth is called : Plan and design, place and position ; the sixth is called : Transmit models by drawing.

Few painters since olden times have combined all (these principles). I, Yen-yüan, will now discuss them. Some of the ancient painters knew how to transmit the likeness of shapes without regard to structure and spirit (vitality), but the art of painting should be sought for beyond the outward likeness. This is, however, difficult to explain to common people. Paintings of the present time may possess outward likeness but the resonance of the spirit does not become manifest in them. If the spirit-resonance is sought for, the outward likeness will be obtained at the same time.

The most ancient pictures represent their ideas in a simple way but they are beautiful and true. Among those early painters were Ku K'ai-chih, Lu T'an-wei and others. The pictures of the middle ancient period are done in a more minute manner and full of fine details ; they are exceedingly graceful. Chan Tzǔ-ch'ien, Chêng Fa-shih and others were of this time.* Pictures of more recent date are luminously brilliant and reveal a research for completeness. The works of modern painters are quite confused without any meaning as if they were made by ordinary artisans.

The representation of objects requires likeness of the shapes but the shapes must all have structure (bone) and life (spirit). Structure, life (spirit) and outward likeness all originate in the directing idea and are expressed by the use of the brush. Therefore, those who are skilful in painting are also good in calligraphy.

As in ancient times the palace ladies had very thin fingers and narrow waists, and the horses had pointed muzzles and slender bodies, and the old pavilions rose on very high terraces, and the clothes of the people were wide and trailing, consequently the pictures of ancient

---

* Two famous painters of the Sui period.

times have not only a different appearance (from ours) but their ideas are strange and the shapes (of their objects) are quite out of the common.

As for terraces and pavilions, trees and stones, carriages and utensils, they do not need to be represented with life-movement, they can also be properly rendered without spirit-resonance, they simply require to be correctly represented from the front and the back.

Ku K'ai-chih said that human figures are most difficult to paint ; next follow landscapes and then dogs and horses ; the terraces, pavilions and immobile things may be handled more freely. This remark is quite true. As for ghosts and human figures possessing life and movement, they must show the operation of the spirit to be perfect. If they do not have this spirit-resonance, it is in vain that they exhibit fine shapes, and if the brush-work is not vigorous, their fine colours are in vain. They cannot be called wonderful. Therefore Han-tzǔ said : " Dogs and horses are difficult (to paint) ghosts are easier ; dogs and horses have been seen by everybody, but ghosts are quite effusive and strange." Which is a true remark.

As for planning and design, place and position (i.e. the composition), they form the summing up of everything in painting.

The pictures by Ku K'ai-chih and Lu T'an-wei and their followers are, however, very rare, and it is difficult to discuss them in detail, but if we look at Wu Tao-hsüan's pictures, it can be said that they contain all the Six Principles ; he expressed them altogether in innumerable shapes. A god guided his hand ; and he exhausted completely the creative power of Nature. Thus the spirit-resonance became so strong and heroic, that it almost could not be confined to the silk. The brush-work was very bold in the dashingly painted wall-pictures, but his finished pictures were executed with utmost care. They were most divine and extraordinary.

As for transmitting models by drawing which is the least important (of the Six Principles), the painters of present times are fairly good in drawing the outward aspects and in obtaining likeness, but they have no spirit-resonance. Their pictures may be prepared with colours but they are wanting in brush-work. How can such things be called painting ? Alas, for men of to-day ; they do not reach this art !

Ku Tsun-chih* of the Sung dynasty built a high tower where he worked ; and every time when he entered this tower, he took away the staircase, so that his home people could not reach him. If the weather was clear, he started to paint (dipped the brush in the mouth), but if the weather was cloudy, he did not move the brush.

The painters of to-day mix their brushes and their ink with dust and dirt and their colours with mud, producing simply dirty silk. How can that be called painting ? Since ancient times there have

---

* Ku Tsun-chih of the Sung dynasty (420-478) is mentioned by Hsieh Ho in the second class.

been no good painters who were not high officials, noblemen, great scholars or lofty characters, who exercised some influence on their time and whose fame has survived through ages.   Truly, no worthless and vulgar loafers could do what they did !

Li Tai Ming Hua Chi, Sect. II.   Chap. II.
Discussion of the Brush-work of Ku, Lu, Chang and Wu.

Someone asked me how was the brushwork of Ku, Lu, Chang and Wu ?   And I answered : " Ku K'ai-chih's brush-stroke was tight and strong, connecting and continuous, moving as in a circle exceedingly swift, accomplishing the design with freedom and ease. It was like a gust of wind or a flash of lightning.   The ideas existed before he took up the brush ; when the picture was finished it contained them all, and thus it was filled with a divine spirit.

Formerly Chang Chih* learned the running style (grass characters) from Ts'ui Yüan and Tu Tu.† Then he modified it to the style of the present-day grass-writing, which is done with a continuous stroke without a break in the life-arteries or separation between the columns. Wang Tzŭ-ching (Wang Hsien-chih) was the only one who realized the real secret of it ; therefore he always made the first word of a column connect with the (last of the) previous column.   This was commonly called one-stroke writing.

Afterwards Lu T'an-wei used the one-stroke method in painting, doing his work with one continuous stroke of the brush without a break.   Hence we know that the same brush manner may be used in writing and painting.   Lu T'an-wei's brush stroke was fine and sharp, yet smooth and graceful.   It was quite new and strange and unsurpassed in its subtlety.   His fame was great in the Sung dynasty and there was at that time nobody equal to him.

Chang Sêng-yu used dots and short strokes in a sketchy fashion. He followed Mme Wei's‡ *Pi Chên T'u* (a model map of writing) ; every point and every stroke had its meaning and character ;   they were like hooked spears and sharp swords very serried and dense. From this again we can see that the use of the brush is the same in writing and painting.

Wu Tao-hsüan of the present dynasty, stands alone (above everybody) of ancient and modern times.   Of his predecessors not even Ku K'ai-chih and Lu T'an-wei may be called his equals, and among his followers is nobody (i.e. of equal importance).   He learned his brush-method from Chang Hsü, and from this we may again realize that the use of the brush is the same in writing and painting.   As

* Great calligraphist of the Han period, known as the " Perfect Grassist " Cf. Giles, *Biographical Dictionary*, N° 32.

† Famous calligraphists of the former Han dynasty.

‡ Wei Shao, d.140, wife of Li Chü, famous calligraphist.

Chang was said to be mad on calligraphy, so Wu may be called the Sage of Painting When Heaven creates a great spirit, he is made brave and divine without limit.

While the common people fix all their attention on the outlines, I (i.e. the great painter) look for the splitting and spreading of the dots and strokes, and while they observe most reverently the likeness of the shapes, I avoid such vulgar and common points. In painting curves, lines straight as a lance, standing pillars and connecting beams Wu did not use ruler and foot-measure. He painted the curly beard and the foot-long tufts at the temples (of his figures), so that every hair was waving and fluttering and the muscles protruding with strength. There was, indeed, such an excess (of life) that he must have been in the possession of a great secret. People could not understand how it was possible for him to start a picture, some eight feet tall, either with an arm or with a foot, and then make it into a magnificent and imposing thing, with the blood circulating in the flesh. He surpassed Chang Sêng-yu.

Someone asked me : " How is it possible that Wu did not use ruler and foot-measure and yet could draw (perfect) curves and arcs, lines straight as a lance, standing pillars and connecting beams ?" To which I answered : " He concentrated his spirit and harmonized it with the working of Nature (or the Creator) rendering those things through the power of his brush. His ideas were, as has been said, fixed before he took up the brush ; when the picture was finished, it expressed them all."

Everything truly wonderful has been done in this way, not only painting. Thus worked the cook, who knew how to avoid the whetstone* and the stone-mason from Ying,† who knew how to use the adze. To imitate the knitted eyebrows (of Hsi Shih)‡ is vain trouble for offering the heart, and he who chops (the meat) instead of (cutting with skill) will wound his hands. If the ideas of a man are confused, he will become the slave of exterior conditions.

Who could paint a circle with the left hand and a square with the right ? He who does it with the help of a ruler and foot-measure produces a dead picture, while he who does it through the concentration of his spirit creates a real picture. Dead pictures covering a wall are simply like dirty plaster. In real pictures every brush-stroke reveals life. He who deliberates and moves the brush intent upon making a picture, misses to a still greater extent the art of paint-

---

* Prince Hui's cook who kept his chopper for nineteen years as though fresh from the whetstone, because he knew how to work in accordance with Tao or the laws of nature. Cf. Giles, *Chuang-tzŭ*, p.34, (2nd ed.), 1926.

† A man from Ying, who had his nose covered with a hard scab, no thicker than a fly's wing, sent for a stone-mason who chipped it off without hurting the nose. Cf. Giles, *Chuang-tzŭ*, p.321.

‡ The famous beauty Hsi Shih knitted her brows. An ugly woman tried to imitate her ; the result was that everybody fled from her. That woman saw the beauty of the knitted brows, but she did not see wherein the beauty of the knitted brows lay. Cf. Giles, *Chuang-tzŭ*, p.182.

ing, while he who cogitates and moves the brush without any intention of making a picture, reaches the art of painting. His hands will not get stiff, his heart not congeal and without knowing, he accomplishes it. Even for the curves and arcs, the straight lines, the standing pillars and connecting beams in his pictures there is no need of ruler and foot-measure.

Someone asked me : " How is it that subtle and deep thoughts may be expressed in pictures which are not finished in a thorough and intimate fashion ? " To which I answered : " Ku K'ai-chih's and Lu T'an-wei's spirit cannot be seen simply in the outlines, it is there, because their pictures are executed in a complete and intimate fashion. The marvels of Chang Sêng-yu and Wu Tao-tzŭ were in one or two strokes by which their pictures were completed or in the splitting and spreading of the dots and strokes ; their pictures seemed unfinished or broken up. Yet, though the brush-work was quite incomplete, their thoughts were completely expressed. It should be remembered, that there are two kinds of painting, the *shu* and the *mi* (the sketchy and the finished manner), then we may discuss painting."

My interrogator bowed and went away.

Li Tai Ming Hua Chi.   Sect. II.   Chapt. III.

Discussion of the Painters' Use of Facsimiles.

By the Yin and Yang innumerable forms are fashioned and produced, order is brought into chaos by their mysterious influence, while the indescribable spirit alone is revolving. As the plants and trees diffuse their glory, the red and the green appear, the snow-clouds begin to whirl and strew their white powder, then the mountains and the sky stand out in deep blue, finally the *fêng* bird appears with all the five colours. Therefore, when by revolving the ink one brings in the five colours, it is called to grasp the idea, but if the idea is fixed on the colours, the forms of the objects will become deficient. In painting one must particularly dread the colouring of the forms, calculate it very carefully and do it most delicately, yet without display of the secret of skill. Incompleteness should not be the cause of regret ; one should rather regret completeness. If completeness already has been understood (realized), what need is there for it (to work it out further) ? Such paintings are not incomplete. But if one has no knowledge of completeness, then the thing will certainly be incomplete. If one misses the self-existent (self-evident), the picture falls into the divine class ; if one misses the divine, the picture falls into the wonderful class ; if one misses the wonderful, the picture falls into the class of finely executed things, which have the weakness of being too cautious and minute.

The self-existing pictures are the uppermost in the highest class. The divine pictures stand in the middle of the highest class, the wonderful are the lowest in the highest class. The finely executed pictures are the highest in the middle class, the careful and minute pictures belong to the middle section of the middle class. The five classes established above comprise the Six Principles, and crowds of wonderful things may be here brought together. But within them one may distinguish hundreds of different degrees ; who is able to exhaust them all ? Those who do not have a surpassing spirit, great knowledge, contentment and a kind heart, how could they discuss and understand painting ? The workman who wished to do his work well, must first sharpen his tools.*

The Shantung silk (*chi wan*), the Wu silk, the white silk (*pin ssŭ*), the fog-like silk (*wu hsiao*) are fine and brilliant, close and delicate and wonderfully woven. The red colour from the water-well in Wu-ling (Hunan), the sand colour from Mo-ts'o (Ssŭchuan), the sky blue of Yüeh-chin (Ssŭchuan), the dark blue from Wei (Honan), the malachite blue from Wu-ch'ang (Hupei), the beautiful white lead from Shu (Ssŭchuan), the pewter colour from Shih-hsing (Kuantung), etc., all these colours must be chopped, ground, filtered and washed, and they may be used deep or shallow, heavy or light, fine or rough. There is also the yellow from Lin-i and from K'un-lun and the ant-red from Nan-hai (Kuantung). Stag-horn glue from Yün (Yünnan ?), fish glue from Wu (Kiangsu), ox glue from Tung-o (Shantung) should be mixed with the colours. The usual varnish is a vegetable liquid, but when the colours are heavy a decoction of melted ore should be used. The old pictures have no " head blue " or " big green " (rough blue and green), their pigments are prepared most carefully and mixed with century old glue, which makes them last for thousands of years. A brush made of the fibers of mountain bamboos will draw as sharply as the sword cuts.

There was a painter with skilled hands who said : " I can paint the life of the clouds." According to my opinion, the ancients did not reach the wonderful in their cloud paintings. If one moistens the silk and then strews light powder over it (which is blown about) it is called to blow the clouds. It produces a very natural effect and may be considered wonderful, but as one can see no brush-work in it, it cannot be called painting. The 'splash-ink' (*p'o mo*) method which also is used by landscape painters can neither be called painting. It is not worth imitating.

In Chiang-nan (Kiangsu and Anhui) the ground is moist with no dust and the people with artistic talents are numerous. The records of the three Wu (districts in Kiangsu) are full of famous men. Wang Hsi-chih and Ku K'ai-chih were the greatest masters of calligraphy and painting since olden times. Huai Nan-tzŭ said : " The

---

* *Analects.* Book XV. chap. 9.

people of Sung are skilled in painting, the people of Wu in melting colours." Isn't that right?

Amateurs should prepare hundred scrolls of *hsüan* paper by rubbing them with wax to be used for making copies. In former times excellent facsimiles were made; seven or eight among ten of them preserved the spirit of the colours and the brush-work. The facsimiles in the imperial collection were called 'palace copies.' During the present dynasty there was within the palace precincts a secret pavilion, where the Han-lin scholars assembled and copies were made all the time. As long as the peaceful times lasted this method was practised continuously, but after the period of trouble (An Lu-shan's rebellion 756-58) it was gradually abandoned. Consequently good facsimiles are now very rare and precious; very few of them contain the real brush traces or can be taken as proofs of the originals.

Among the crowds of paintings which I have seen only Ku K'ai-chih's painting of an old sage contains the mysterious fitness. One does not get tired by looking at it a whole day. By concentrating the spirit and far-reaching meditation one realizes the self-existent; both the (painted) thing and oneself are forgotten, the realization is separated from the form. ' The body becomes like dry wood and the mind like dead ashes.'* He reached the mysterious fitness, which is called the Tao of painting. Ku was the first to make a picture of Wei Mo Ch'i. He looked pure and emaciated with a thin and suffering face as he was seated leaning on a table in complete silence. Lu T'an-wei and Chang Sêng-yu both imitated this picture of Ku, but they could not reach him.

---

* From *Chuang-tzŭ*, Chap. II.

APPENDIX IV

Pi Fa Chi (Notes on Brush-work) by Ching Hao. (Reprint in *Wang Shih Hua Yüan*, Vol. I).

Among the T'ai-hang Mountains are deep valleys and large country fields which I used to cultivate when I lived there. One day I climbed the Shên-chêng ridge, which offers a view all around, and on my way back I came to an entrance between two steep cliffs. The moss was dripping with water, strange stones were strewn about, and the mist of good omen was hovering in the air. I entered quickly and found that the place was grown with old pine-trees ; the tree in the middle was the largest. The bark of it was overgrown by green lichen and covered by scales. It rose to the sky like a coiling dragon, trying to reach the clouds and dominated the whole forest. The spirit of it was vigorous and its beauty was rich. The smaller trees stood humbly bending down ; the roots of some were reaching out of the ground, others were coiling across the water current, others again were suspended on cliffs hanging over the brooks which wound among the moss and the crumbling stones. The sight seemed to me most marvellous ; I looked around with deepest admiration.

The following day I returned to the same place bringing my brushes along and made some pictures of the trees trying to render their real nature. Then in the spring of the following year, as I was walking among the Stone Drum Cliffs, I met an old man who asked me what I had been doing. When I told him about it, he said to me : " Do you know the method of painting ? " To which I answered : " You seem to be an old uncouth rustic ; how could you know anything about brush-work ? " But the old man said : " How can you know what I carry in my bosom ? " Then I listened and felt ashamed and astonished, as he spoke to me as follows : " Young people like to study in order to accomplish something ; they should know that there are six essentials in painting. The first is called spirit, the second is called harmony (or, resonance), the third is called thoughts (plans), the fourth is called motif (scenery), the fifth is the brush, and the sixth is the ink." I remarked : " Painting is to make beautiful things, and the important point is to obtain their true likeness ; is it not ? " He answered : " It is not. Painting is to paint, to estimate the shapes of things and really obtain them, to estimate the beauty of things and reach it, to estimate the reality (significance) of things and grasp it. One should not take outward beauty for reality ; he who does not understand this mystery, will not obtain the truth, even though his pictures may contain like-ness." I asked : " What is likeness and what is truth ? " The old man said : " Likeness can be obtained by shapes without spirit ; but when truth is reached, spirit and substance are both fully expressed. He who tries to express spirit through ornamental beauty will make dead things." I thanked him and said : " From this I realize that the study of calligraphy and painting is an occupation for virtuous men ; I am only a farmer and have not understood it ; I have been playing with the brush, but not accomplished anything ; I feel quite ashamed to receive your kind explanations of the essentials in art which were unknown to me."

The old man said : " Lusts and passions are the thieves of life. Virtuous men occupy themselves with music, calligraphy and painting and do not indulge in inordinate lusts. Since you have virtue, I hope that you will continue your studies without hesitation ; I will explain to you the essentials in painting.

" Spirit makes the heart (mind) follow the movements of the brush and seize without hesitation the shape of things. Harmony consists in establishing correct and perfect forms which are not conventional. Thought makes you deduct and detach the essential and concentrate on the forms of things. Scenery is (established by) observing the laws of the seasons, by looking for the wonderful (or mysterious), and finding the true. Brush-work means to follow the rules, but to be at the same time free and flexible in movement, so that everything seems to fly and move. Ink-tones (should be) high and low, thick and diluted, according to the depth and shallow-ness of various kinds of things ; the colouring (by these) so self-evident, that it does not seem to be laid on with the brush."

He said furthermore : " There are divine (*shên*), wonderful (or, mysterious : *miao*) , clever (*ch'i*) and skilful (*ch'iao*) painters. The divine makes no effort but achieves the forms spontaneously by following the transformations of Nature. The wonderful penetrates with his thoughts the nature of everything in heaven and earth, and thus the things flow out of his brush in accordance with the truth of the motif. The clever (or astounding) painter draws vast outlines which are not in accordance with the truth of the motif ; the things he makes are strange and queer and quite out of reason. This is the result of brush-work without thought. The skilful painter carves out and pieces together scraps of beauty, which but seem in accordance with the great principles ; he forces the drawing and works in a highly exaggerated fashion. It may be said that reality is not enough for him, as he makes such a display of floridity.

The brush-work has four aspects, called muscles, flesh, bones and spirit. The short and cut-off strokes are called muscles ; the strokes which are rising and falling and make up the reality are called flesh ; those which are firm and straight from the beginning to the end, are called bones, while the lines which are undefeatable (never break down) may be called the vital spirit. From this it may be realized, that ink is a great matter; if one loses the body of ink (i.e. if the tone is too slight), the spirit is defeated, the muscles are dead and there is no flesh. When the lines are broken off, there are no muscles, only a careless semblance and no bones.

The faults in painting are of two kinds; those dependent on shapes and those independent of shapes. Flowers and trees which do not conform in season, figures which are larger than the buildings, trees which are higher than the mountains, bridges which do not rest on their banks, are measurable faults of form. Such faults do not alter a picture. Faults which are independent of the shapes are caused by the absence of spirit and harmony (resonance), which makes the forms quite queer. Then, in spite of all efforts with the brush and the ink, everything in the picture is dead. Such clumsy paintings cannot be corrected.

As you like to paint landscapes with their clouds and trees it is necessary for you to understand the origin of every particular form. Every tree grows according to its natural disposition. The pine-trees may grow tortuous, but they do not fall in with the deceitful; they stand sometimes dense, sometimes scattered, and they are neither green nor blue. They are upright from the very beginning, the sprouts of their hearts are not of a low kind, their manly strength makes them solitary and high. Their branches grow low down, but they bend in an opposite direction and do not drop to the ground; they seem to divide the forest in successive horizontal layers. ' The virtue of the superior man is like the wind.'* When they are painted like soaring old dragons or coiling young dragons with the branches and leaves in confusion, they do not have the spirit-resonance of pine-trees. The *thuja orientalis* (arbor vitæ) often grows twisted and coiled, its leafage is abundant but it has no flowers; its joints are regular and its veins follow the sun. The leaves are like knotted thread and the branches like hemp cloth. Sometimes they are painted like serpents or like floss of silk, or they may be turning without any reason in a wrong way. There are furthermore catalpas, varnish-trees, oaks, elms, willows, mulberry-trees and *sophora japonica (huai shu)*, and everyone of them is different in regard to form and natural characteristics. They are like diverging thoughts which must be brought into harmony.

The formal aspects of the mountains must be combined with the effect of a living spirit. Thus the pointed forms are the peaks, the level ones are called heads, the rounded form the hills, while the connected ones are called ranges. There are caverns or gorges, steep walls and precipices; between and below the precipices are the grottoes. Hollow-ways which lead into the mountains are called gulleys, but if they do not pass through, they are called ravines.†

---

* From the *Analects*.

† Some of these Chinese expressions as well as their English equivalents are simply pleonastics.

The water in the ravines forms streamlets, but the water which comes out of the mountain makes the torrents. The peaks which rise above the rest should be free-standing, but the ridges and hills below continuous. The forest springs may be hidden or visible depending on whether the trees grow dense and whether they are near or far.

Those who paint landscapes without these forms (i.e. without properly using such elements of composition) make mistakes. In some pictures the water seems to be running in disorder, the lines are like snapped threads and there are no rising and falling waves. Such pictures are failures. The mist, the clouds and the vapours should be light or heavy in accordance with the seasonal aspects. If there is a wind, no forms should be steady. One must leave out the minor details and select the important points. Mistakes are unavoidable until one has learnt this, but no longer after one has grasped this method of working.

I asked: " Who were the most perfect among the learned painters of old ? " To which the old man answered : " Hsieh Ho classified Lu T'an-wei as the foremost ; but nowadays it is difficult to find original works of his. The pictures left by Chang Sêng-yu are weak in regard to rational principles. (Hsieh Ho said) : Apply colour according to species. In the past there have been men who could do it by harmonizing water and ink into luminous effects. In the T'ang period Chang Tsao painted trees and stones with an abundance of spirit-resonance ; his brush and ink amassed all details ; his thoughts were lofty and he attached no importance to the five colours. Nobody among ancient and modern men has surpassed him. Ch'ü T'ing, the monk of the White Clouds,* possessed the secret of spirit and form ; he grasped the very origin of things and painted with extraordinary ease ; the depth of his work was immeasurable. Wang Yu-ch'êng's (Wang Wei) brush and ink were subtle and refined ; his spirit-resonance was high and pure ; he drew forms with great skill and expressed deep and true thoughts. General Li's principles were deep, his thoughts far-reaching, his brush-strokes very fine ; his works exhibit great skill and ornamental beauty, but they are weak in regard to the handling of ink. The hermit Hsiang Jung† painted trees and stones in a coarse fashion with sharp edges and corners. He used only black Taoist ink, and his brush manner had no bones (structure). He painted in a free and easy fashion without losing the true spirit and form of things, nor the beauty of their appearance. Wu Tao-tzŭ's brush-work excelled in form, structure and spirit just as very high trees which are too lofty for ordinary pictures, but it is a pity, that he had no ink. Ch'ên Jo-yü,‡ and the

---

* Chü T'ing, who became the Taoist monk Li Tsun-shih, was particularly known for his paintings of pine-trees ; active in the reign of Emperor Hsüan Tsung.

† He was known as the Hermit of the T'ien-t'ai Mountain and excelled in the *p'o mo* style of Wang Mo.

‡ A Taoist painter from Shu, active towards the end of the T'ang period.

monk Tao-fên and their like rose hardly above the common style ; their manner of handling the brush and the ink had nothing extraordinary, though they were quite able in drawing shapes and contours.

" Now I have revealed to you the method (the path), though it cannot be done completely in words."

Then I showed him the pictures I had made of strange pine-trees. The old man said : " They are painted with a fleshy brush without proper method ; the muscles and bones are not completely brought out ; all these pine-trees are not of much use.—Since I now have taught you the method of painting, I give you some scrolls of paper and ask you to paint before me." The old man said furthermore : " It is your hand but my mind ; my way is to examine their words and understand their conduct. Could you now recite something to me ? "

I thanked him and said : " Since you now have reformed me (as an artist) thus accomplishing the aim of the virtuous and the wise, I cannot disregard it, whether it is for weal or woe it will influence me ; I must go on as you have told me and respect your orders. Then I sang the praise of the old pine-tree (i.e. by means of a poem in which its manly beauty and superior character are emphasized).

The old man sighed and said after a long silence : " I wish that you could forget all about brush and ink when you are painting. Then you might obtain the real truth of the scenery. I am living in the Stone Drum Mountain and therefore I call myself Shih K'u Yen-tzǔ."—My answer was : " I would like to follow you and to serve you." The old man said : " That is not necessary."—Then he took leave and disappeared suddenly. When I looked for him another day I could no more find him. But I have been practising his method, thus transmitting it, and I have now prepared it for publication, so that it may serve as a path for other painters.

INDEX OF CHINESE NAMES, TERMS AND BOOKS